The *Vegetarian* Gourmet

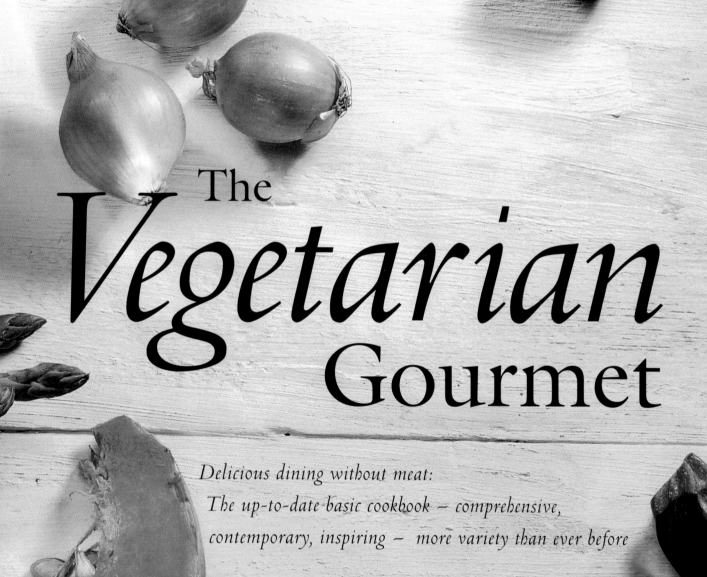

The Vegetarian Gourmet

Delicious dining without meat:
The up-to-date basic cookbook – comprehensive,
contemporary, inspiring – more variety than ever before

Recipes by Dagmar von Cramm
Photos by Barbara Bonisolli
Translation by Marga & Thomas Hannon

Table of Contents

Vegetarian Kitchen Fundamentals

The Recipes

For Reference

Vegetarian
Kitchen Fundamentals

Gone are the days when a "real" dinner consisted of a roast, steak or chops—and vegetables were just a garnish. Today more and more gourmets enjoy dining without meat, using a wide variety of vegetables, grains, seeds, nuts, cheeses, herbs and spices. This growing trend has been precipitated by recent meat scandals, an increased awareness of the methods used in intensive meat production and a raised environmental consciousness. But let's not dwell on the negative. Vegetarianism is "in" simply because it tastes good and feels right.

Enjoying Vegetarian Food

The term vegetarian was coined as early as classical Greek and Roman times. The Latin *vegetus* means animated and vigorous, i.e., a diet that provided vitality and strength—and contradicted existing preferences. Pythagoras viewed a meatless diet as a prerequisite for harmonious and peaceful living, thereby making vegetarianism an ideology.

Until recently, vegetarians were often considered intellectuals who were somehow out of touch with their bodies. Today, however, vegetarianism is much better understood. More and more people are discovering the taste and nutritional benefits of eating a vegetarian diet. Though a wide range of vegetarian styles now exists, the segment of the population which is strictly vegetarian remains small, between 1% and 4%, according to various polls. At the same time, more people consider themselves occasional vegetarians, that is, they do without meat every now and then.

International Culinary Influences

A lighter, vegetable-based Mediterranean cuisine is credited with giving vegetarianism its major boost in North America and western Europe. Not only did it supply a multitude of new recipes, but it also introduced a variety of fresh vegetables such as eggplants, peppers, zucchini, Chinese greens, Swiss chard and artichokes.

In recent years, the influence of many international cuisines has enhanced the original vegetarian repertoire, especially its use of herbs and spices. East Indian cuisine revealed a flood of fresh spices like turmeric, cumin and tamarind, previously known simply as "curry powder." The popular Italian herb, basil, is now making way for new herbs such as lemon grass and cilantro, or fresh coriander, which are used extensively in Asian cooking. Traditional Chinese and Japanese cooking also use more fish and soy products and less meat and dairy products. Adapting cooking styles specific to the wok has also opened up exciting new possibilities for vegetarian feasting. Finally, Central and South America supply amaranth and quinoa, the "ancient" grains of the Incas, as well as a variety of pulses like black beans.

Culinary trends from ethnic specialties to *nouvelle cuisine* have left their mark on the vegetarian diet and continue to influence the flavor and nutrition of the foods we eat. The whole foods diet which emphasizes unprocessed ingredients and natural cooking methods has brought about a renaissance in cooking with grains. Long-forgotten recipes from great-grandmother's kitchen are being rediscovered and are redefining vegetarian health foods. Now, natural cooking methods not only enhance flavor and preserve valuable nutrients, but provide crisp textures which are pleasing to the palate (page 14–15).

A diet that excludes meat will help you really taste the flavor of food and discover a whole range of essences, fermented concentrates and traditional seasoning sauces to add interest to cooking. Try preservative-free soy sauce and ketchup as well as Worcestershire sauce, Angostura, Tabasco and Sambal.

The Effects of a Vegetarian Diet on the Body

Two major studies proved that vegetarians not only live longer but are also healthier: a study of vegetarians in Giessen from 1989 and the long-term study of the Cancer Research Institute in Heidelberg from 1991. Their most important findings were:
- Vegetarians have noticeably lower cholesterol levels than the average non-vegetarian.
- Blood pressure is lower on average and so vegetarians are less likely to suffer from heart attacks.
- Vegetarians are rarely obese because they consume fewer concentrated energy supplies and more fiber than "omnivores." Their weight lies more within the ideal range.
- Vegetarians have a lower incidence of cancer.
- Vegetarians have fewer problems with colon diseases.
- Vegetarians suffer less from gout and gall bladder diseases.
- Their kidneys are healthier due to a reduced stress load.
- Blood tests revealed no lack of specific nutrients.

All Vegetarians Are Not Alike

Aside from the many "occasional" vegetarians, there are groups who observe the following vegetarian standards:

- Vegans follow the strictest rules, declining any type of food derived from animals, including dairy products, eggs and sometimes even honey. Here, it can become a nutritional challenge to get an adequate supply of calcium, iron and the important vitamin B_{12} (page 228–229). Recipes catering to this group have been identified as "non-dairy" and "egg-free" in this book.

- Lacto-vegetarians take a somewhat more relaxed stand. They don't eat eggs, but do enjoy the whole range of dairy products. From both culinary and health perspectives, lacto-vegetarians have an advantage.

- The lacto-ovo-vegetarians eat the same as the lacto-vegetarians but include eggs in their diet. There are no further nutritional benefits, but this group does enjoy a few culinary alternatives.

Nutrient Density Works Miracles

"Nutrient density" is a key phrase that describes the amount of valuable nutritional elements per calorie in a given food. Fruit and vegetables have the highest nutrient density; with relatively few calories they contain an abundance of vitamins, minerals and fiber. Grains also have a relatively high nutrient density. Foods high in fat, particularly sausages and meat, are much lower on the scale.

Vegetarian Cooking: The Right Combination is Essential

North American food guides do not set recommended daily allowances for meatless diets. The German Society for Nutrition (DGE) recommends the following distribution of basic nutrients for daily calories:
- 13% protein
- 30% fat
- 57% carbohydrate (not more than 10% of it as sugar)

The reality of most people's diets is quite different. We eat too much fat, protein and sugar, and we drink too much alcohol.
- There is often a concern that the vegetarian diet provides too little protein. This is just not the case. Plant foods like grains, nuts, potatoes, seeds, mushrooms and pulses contain ample amounts of protein. These foods are best supplemented with animal protein from dairy products or eggs. The DGE recommends a balanced combination of animal and plant proteins. This results in an ideal combination of the protein building blocks—the biological energy force.
- Plant-based foods contain adequate fat levels. The parts of the plant which contain the embryo (nuts, grain sprouts, seeds) are high in fat. Avocados and olives are also rich in fat. More importantly, they contain high levels of vitamin E and polyunsaturated fats. When eaten in moderation they actually clean out the arteries and prevent arteriosclerosis. Unprocessed, they do not create an excess of fat.

Nutrients Per Food Group

Nutrient density indicates the number of essential nutrients contained in a single calorie. Each of these nutrients is present in sufficient quantity to be of use to the body. Please note that not all vegetables, for example, have the same number of nutrients per calorie. These figures, then, represent an average nutrient-per-calorie count in each food group.

Food Group	Number of Nutrients per calorie
Vegetables	22
Potatoes	11
Fruit, lettuce	11
Milk, cheese	10
Bread, rice, pasta	8
Spreadable fats, oil	3
Chocolate, cookies	0

- When it comes to carbohydrates, vegetarian cooking comes out ahead. Carbohydrates are the main component of all plant foods. But sugar is also 100% carbohydrate and originates exclusively from a plant. While unrefined sugar retains many minerals, refined (white) sugar is devoid of nutrients. Therefore, a high carbohydrate count alone is no guarantee of a healthy food.

Meat is Not Essential, but...

Maintaining your regular diet and just leaving out the meat does not make for a satisfactory vegetarian diet. You can easily avoid meat by substituting desserts, chocolates and ice cream—but you will hardly have a healthy diet. Being vegetarian means becoming more conscious of what you eat. You will only get the necessary nutrients if your diet is balanced and adequate. For the average eater, vegetarian cooking is not a limitation, but rather an improvement. You don't have to avoid meat completely. However, reduced meat consumption will have positive influences on your health and body shape. There are financial rewards too—a vegetarian lifestyle is usually cheaper.

The Ecological Argument

...should not be ignored: 12 calories of feed are needed to produce just a single calorie of chicken meat. We would do better to consume those calories more directly as corn and soy. Forty percent of worldwide grain harvests, 65% of oil seeds and 50% of the world's fisheries go toward feeding livestock for meat production. If we ate more plant-based foods we could eliminate global food shortages. Those who choose vegetarianism for ethical reasons today are no different from those who did so in the thirties when the vegetarian movement was triggered by a respect for life.

Beautiful, Healthy and Fit with Vegetarian Food

Trends now favor a healthy diet—everybody wants to be "fit for life." Eating specific food groups at certain times is much discussed. The secret of these diets? All the rules and regulations lead to eating increased amounts of fruit and vegetables—high-protein foods such as meat and fish become secondary. And that is exactly what good vegetarian cooking is all about. Its impact on wellness, health and body shape are obvious:

• A diet high in vegetables, fruit and whole grains stimulates digestion.

Cooking for Weight Loss

The first thing to do when adapting recipes for a weight-loss program is to reduce fat intake. Fat, however, is the medium that carries flavor, so you should compensate for its absence by using generous amounts of herbs and spices.

• Replace the oil in a vinaigrette with some flavorful instant stock and creamy mustard. Replace high-fat milk products in creamy dressings with yogurt.

• Use a non-stick frying pan and you can reduce the amount of added fat to just 1/2 teaspoon.

• Whenever possible, replace boiling by steaming and frying by barbecuing.

• Try cooking in a foil "wrap" instead of stewing.

• Sauté vegetables in soup stock instead of oil.

• Replace nuts and seeds with herbs. Use flax seeds instead of sesame seeds.

• There are many varieties of low-fat cheeses available. Simply buy cheese and dairy products with a lower fat content.

• Mixed salads become lower in fat when you keep the same amount of dressing but add more lettuce.

Undesirable substances don't have a chance to develop in the digestive system, and harmful elements are expelled from the body.

• The naturally high potassium content in fruit and vegetables supports kidney function; potassium has a diuretic effect and strengthens tissue.

• Antioxidant vitamins (C, E, and A in the form of beta-carotene), especially present in fruit, protect cell membranes and ease the aging process.

• When drinking normal amounts of fluid, the high water content of fruit, salads and vegetables provides additional liquid.

• Salads, raw foods and vegetables are low in calories, but bulky, and provide a feeling of being full.

• Different accessory nutrients, vitamins, minerals and fiber have a positive effect on the body. They increase circulation, protect cells, improve the immune system and fight infection. These valuable nutrients simply provide extra vitality. You can read more about this on pages 227 to 229.

Being Slim: Is It Just a Matter of Calories?

Surely not. Naturally, constant overeating produces unwanted fat deposits, but genetic disposition, lifestyle and the way in which calories are consumed also play a role. Low body weight does not necessarily mean a person is slim—proportions are important, too. Those on a permanent diet sometimes don't lose any more weight despite low caloric intakes—their metabolism does not co-operate. Psychological problems, eating disorders, or resignation are potential threats. With constant dieting and calorie counting, eating becomes a struggle.

Why Do We Eat Too Much?

We no longer do the physical work that was demanded of our ancestors and so our bodies require proportionately less energy. At the same time, our diet has become more concentrated. Refined sugar, white flour, precooked meals, excess meat, fat and alcohol contain no fiber and are quickly absorbed by the body.

In the past, our diet was high in fiber, and it was unnatural—virtually impossible—to overeat. Unfortunately, our instincts have not caught up to these changes yet. Our stomachs are constantly being deceived by false feelings of hunger. For this reason it is important to know how much energy (calories) our individual lifestyle requires, and to consume those calories appropriately.

Why Diets Don't Work

When the body doesn't get enough energy, it starts to change. First it uses up natural fat and protein deposits stored in the tissues. Then it starts to economize: you have to eat less and less to continue losing weight. As soon as you return to your "normal" eating habits, your weight will increase dramatically. Your body is naturally replenishing its fat deposits.

Most diets are unbalanced. Diets that are low in carbohydrates or proteins only, or those that emphasize only one type of food result in a lack of vitamins, minerals and fiber. You may lose weight, but you will also lose strength and you will certainly not become more attractive. You will also be unable to maintain this diet for any prolonged period.

If you look to drugstore shelves for help, the disadvantages increase. Appetite suppressants create long-term dependency, and sometimes lead to severe malnutrition. Protein concentrates and "slimming" foods don't provide sufficient bulk, and weight gain is pre-programmed.

A Vegetarian Weight-Loss Program

When beginning a weight-loss program, a balanced, varied diet of 1,000 to 1,200 calories is recommended. This provides motivation and helps to "break down" some of the fat. Choose foods with a high nutrient density (see page 9) and eliminate concentrated high-calorie foods such as sugar, fat and alcohol.

However, to achieve and maintain your ideal personal weight, you will need to make long-term changes to your nutritional lifestyle. Our guide illustrates how to effortlessly save calories during meal preparation without sacrificing flavor. Balanced, healthy dieting should not attempt to achieve a super-model figure. Besides decreasing energy levels, this unnatural thinness would be neither healthy, nor beautiful.

Sports Help You Reduce

...unless you quench your thirst with beer or reward yourself with an extra snack after every exercise session. You don't need sports drinks, body-building foods or power bars either. Normal recreational exercise does not noticeably increase calorie requirements. However, exercise will improve your metabolism and strengthen your body. This is important, because the first effect of weight loss is that your body becomes weaker—and you don't want that. You should also drink a lot—preferably mineral water. Drinking water helps flush metabolic waste out of your body and replenishes the fluid lost through perspiration during exercise.

Eat Less, But More Often

You know it yourself: when you're really hungry you often eat more than necessary and end up feeling bloated and listless. You don't want to let yourself go to that extreme. Five or six small, healthy meals a day are better than the traditional three:

- A small, nutritious snack (muesli, shake, fruit, salad) can prevent a "low," and your body will not have to deal with a fluctuating blood sugar level.
- Your digestive system can work continuously.
- Your body can better absorb nutrients.
- You won't lose control over your appetite and snack on unhealthy foods.
- Small meals can be integrated into daily life just as easily as one big evening meal.

And how should you distribute these meals? Never skip breakfast. Whether you eat muesli, a slice of wholegrain bread with a flavorful topping or a banana "milkshake" is up to you. A second breakfast should supplement the first. Try wholegrain bread, dairy products, fruit or raw food.

A hot main meal is important because some foods, such as potatoes, can only be eaten cooked. The third main meal should feature raw food, accompanied by wholewheat bread with a little butter and cheese. Schedule the remaining snacks for the afternoon or evening.

Weekends with Great Results

Enjoy a weekend with a particular goal. Check the recipe lists that follow for tasty dishes, and lose a couple of pounds while enjoying yourself. After food-filled celebrations do you want to work toward your goal of better health and well-being? Our suggestions for a really healthy weekend will help. Try the Power Weekend plan if you are under stress or need an energy boost.

Weekend Recipe Lists

For a slimmer figure

Morning:
Kiwi Sour (189) and Fruit Salad with Crispy Quinoa (201), or Couscous-Berry Mix (200)

Midday:
Bouillon Potatoes (141) with mixed salad and Mediterranean Dressing (76), Steamed Vegetables with Parsley Sauce (123), or Vegetable Kabobs (130)

Evening:
Artichoke-Orange Cocktail (45), Orange-Endive Flower (59), or Marinated Zucchini (41)

For health

Morning:
Stuffed Pepper Slices (195) with 1 slice of wholegrain bread and Raspberry-Buttermilk Shake (190), or Sprout Pockets (198)

Midday:
Colorful Vegetables with Egg Dip (48), Broiled Mediterranean Vegetables (129), or Cabbage with Peppers (133)

Evening:
Wild Herb Salad with Nettle Gouda (55), Eggs in Sorrel Sauce (156), or Herb Soup with Baked Custard (86)

For energy and power

Morning:
Apple-Avocado Muesli (200), Carrot-Almond Milk (191), or wholegrain bread with butter

Midday:
Greek Potato Casserole (80), Saffron-Orange Risotto with Pea Pods (98), or Pizza Potatoes (140)

Evening:
Couscous Mix (57), Corn Salad with Cream Cheese (66), or Baked Rhubarb Pudding (183)

Cooking Solo

Vegetarian cooking meets the needs of many small households with its short cooking times and quantities of raw foods—this means quick and healthy enjoyment. Also, the basic ingredients of vegetarian cooking generally keep fresh longer than meat and fish.

Buying Tips for the Small Household

- Buy fruit, vegetables and dairy products in specialty stores. Such stores will often sell you smaller portions, such as only two eggs or a handful of salad greens.
- Buy grains, nuts and seeds from the self-serve bulk-foods section of the health food store. You'll be able to take as little as you need.
- Shop at local markets. You'll get the smallest sizes of cucumber, lettuce, cauliflower or squash.
- In addition, choose shallots instead of onions and the smallest grade of eggs for boiling and baking.
- Fresh is best, but packaged, frozen vegetables are also good because you can take out just as much as you need.
- The table at right shows how much one person should eat per meal.

Solo Serving Sizes
(In grams)

Food	Raw	Cooked
Soup as a meal	–	500
Soup as an appetizer	–	150–200
Vegetables as raw snack foods	75–100	–
Vegetables as a side dish	200–250	175–225
Vegetables as a main dish	400–500	100–500
Peeled potatoes as a side dish	150–200	125–175
Peeled potatoes as a main dish	350–400	400–500
Rice and pasta as a side dish	50–60	150–180
Rice and pasta as a main dish	80–90	240–270

Fresh Food for Single Cooks

- Buy herbs in sealed packages. Bunches of herbs will stay fresh longer in a tightly sealed container in the fridge.
- Grow sprouts at home. Read more about this on page 30.
- Look for fruit that won't spoil immediately after purchase. Apples keep well for at least a week, as do kiwis and pears. Ripen your fruit in a bowl on the counter (more about fruit buying and storage on page 16).
- Keep vegetables in the fridge. Peppers, cabbage, carrots and leeks will keep fresh for at least a week in closed plastic bags. Special vegetable storage bags (available at most health food stores) are highly recommended. They extend the freshness of most vegetables by several days.

Prepared Flavors

- A regular Romaine lettuce is usually too large for one person, so wash it, remove the leaves and dry them thoroughly (important!) with a kitchen towel. Store the leaves in a closed container in the fridge. In this way lettuce will keep fresh and crisp for one or two days.
- Prepare salad dressing for a week in advance (vinaigrette recipe page 22). Keep the dressing in a screw-top jar. Add fresh herbs and onion later.
- Cook your favorite meals in large quantities and freeze individual portions.

Muffins: A Big Hit

- Muffins are ideal for solo cooks. To make them, line a six-hole muffin tray with paper liners. Mix 1/2 cup (125 g) cornmeal, 1 pinch each of sugar and salt, 1 small egg, 3 tbsp quark (page 32), 1/3 cup (75 ml) milk and 3 tbsp oil to make a dough. Pour the batter into the muffin liners and bake at 375°F (180°C) for 55 minutes.

- Muffins are more flavorful with 2 tbsp chopped pumpkin seeds and 3 tbsp chopped chives or 2 tbsp grated Parmesan cheese, dried herbs, and 4 tbsp finely chopped black olives. Add 2 tbsp each of currants and almonds or blueberries to the dough for sweet varieties.

Feast for the Eye

Colorful fruits and vegetables are even more attractive when served decoratively. A few simple tools can create great effects when you are decorating salads and plates.

Cutters

Shaped cutters (for example, hearts or mushrooms) are used to give cheese or sliced vegetables an attractive, original look.

Decorating Knife

This knife is used for shaping citrus fruit or melons into "baskets." You can also section oranges or lemons with this sharp knife.

Egg Slicer

This tool slices not only eggs but also soft fruit and vegetables into equal pieces. Cooked peeled potatoes, avocados and bananas are particularly suitable.

Garnish Cutter

You can quickly create carrot flowers and cucumber wheels. The sharp tip also cuts regular wedges into the peel of lemons and oranges.

Melon Baller

You need the large melon baller in a vegetarian kitchen in order to make attractive fruit and vegetable balls.

Melons look particularly attractive when the balls are placed back into their hollowed out shells. Cut the melon into two parts with jagged edges using a decorating knife. Then hollow out the two halves with the baller and arrange the melon balls in the hollow shells with berries, chopped pistachios and a little liquid honey.

Garnishing Tool

This knife has a jagged blade for making wavy cuts in fruits, vegetables and decorative sticks of butter. Simple garnishing tools have straight, serrated blades.

Vegetable Corer

This sharp-pointed, semi-tubular knife is used to hollow out zucchinis and cucumbers.

Zester

The zester peels off the top layer of lemon or orange peel in very thin strips. It cuts firm vegetables like carrots or radishes into light curls.

Preparing Fresh Produce

You should have one slicer (preferably adjustable) and two different graters on hand.
- Graters have sharp teeth, which shred food. They range in size from the small-toothed citrus grater, which finely grates lemon peel or chocolate, to the cheese grater and the coarse vegetable grater.

Graters which stand upright are easy to use. A two-way grater allows grating in both directions.
- A grater with smaller teeth is sometimes known as a rasp. The smallest one is used for nutmeg, the largest for potatoes. You can also "rasp" apples, celery or carrots to the consistency of a purée.
- Slicers have one, or usually two parallel slicing blades. If they are adjustable, you can cut cabbage, onions, cucumbers and beets in slices of varying thickness. An extra attachment for julienne slicing is particularly useful. This produces small, fine vegetable strips.
- Chopping knives are an absolute must for preparing herbs. Knives with two parallel blades are the most efficient but use what feels most comfortable to you.
- Kitchen scissors cut delicate herbs like basil and tarragon very gently.
- Kitchen knives are a science of their own—the correct knife makes work much easier. Stock your kitchen with a small kitchen knife with a short, flexible, pointed blade for cleaning and preparing, a large knife with a broad, heavy blade for chopping and cutting, and a small paring knife with a curved blade for peeling and carving. A serrated knife for tomatoes and a slightly longer knife with a sturdy blade for peeling larger fruit and vegetables are also useful.

1. vegetable corer
2. melon baller

3. garnish cutter
4. zester

5. decorating knife
6. garnishing tool

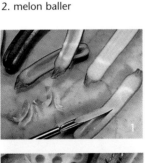

Gentle Cooking Made Easy

Vitamins, minerals and accessory nutrients (page 227) in grains and vegetables often react to heat, light, air and liquids. Any cutting, cooking and storing reduces the amount of available nutrients. Yet cooking also increases the digestibility of certain foods and enhances the availability of some nutrients. Nutrient loss can be minimized by using gentle cooking methods and by following some basic rules. Here are the most important gentle cooking techniques.

Simmering: The Ideal Method for Cooking Vegetables

Nutrients are affected by high heat, destroyed by oxygen and flushed out by liquids. Ideally, cooking is done with minimal liquid, over low heat and without much contact with air. This is called "simmering." Vegetables with a high water content can be simmered without adding much extra liquid. Sauté vegetables in oil first because the faster food reaches a temperature of 160ºF (70ºC), the more vitamins are retained. At this temperature damaging enzymes are created which reduce the vitamin content.

Steaming: The Low-Calorie Method

When steaming, vegetables do not cook in the water but above it. The rising steam provides necessary heat. Crunchiness, color, vitamins and minerals are retained to a high degree. It is almost like eating raw vegetables. This is the ideal cooking method for anyone who has to avoid fats. Steaming works best if you want crisp vegetables. A longer cooking time is needed to achieve a softer texture. A tight-fitting lid is essential. Steamers with fitted inserts are ideal. You can also place simple, flexible steaming inserts into regular pots.

Tips for Simmering and Steaming

Simmering

- Use pots with tight lids and heavy bottoms.
- Don't chop vegetables too finely before cooking.
- When sautéing, add just enough oil or butter to moisten the bottom of the pot.
- Add salt before sautéing; the vegetable juices will escape faster to prevent burning.
- Always keep the lid closed.
- It's better to cook fast than to leave food for too long over a low heat.
- Don't keep your vegetables warm, it's better to let them cool down and reheat them later, if necessary.

Steaming

- No oil needed.
- Periodically check the water level to prevent the water from completely burning off.
- Use restraint when adding seasonings and salt: steaming will preserve the food's natural flavor.
- Add aromatic herbs like laurel, thyme, rosemary, lavender, or aniseed to the liquid. These will impart lovely, delicate flavors to the steamed foods.
- Re-use the steaming liquid: it accumulates valuable flavors and nutrients through condensation.
- Steam vegetables when you want to retain the maximum amount of nutrients—especially when preparing vegetables for young children.

The Pressure Cooker: Cooking in a Flash

The principle is simple: when liquid is heated in a tightly closed pot steam is produced thus creating excess pressure. The boiling temperature is automatically raised, and the food cooks faster. This is particularly advantageous when cooking grains and pulses. Usually there is no need for soaking, and the cooking time is reduced considerably. Be careful when pressure cooking more delicate foods. If the proper cooking time is exceeded by several minutes the food not only becomes mushy, but it also loses a lot of vitamins. For this reason, quality pressure cookers have two settings. The lower, gentler setting should be used for fresh vegetables, and the higher setting for grains, pulses, beets and potatoes. You can also use the pressure cooker for steaming. There should always be about 1/2 cup (125 ml) of liquid in the pot—otherwise there will be no steam. Apart from preserving vitamins, the pressure cooker also saves cooking time and energy.

Tips for the Pressure Cooker and Wok

Pressure Cooker

- Cook delicate foods on a gentle setting and hardier foods on the higher setting.

- Bring cooking liquid to a boil, add food and only then close the pot.

- Check pressure indicator and do not reduce heat until cooking temperature has been reached.

- Follow cooking times accurately, then release steam according to the manufacturer's directions; otherwise contents will continue cooking.

- You will usually reduce your cooking time by 2/3. With larger quantities, however, cooking time is longer, because it takes longer to reach the right cooking temperature.

Wok

- Cut food immediately before stir frying—you may choose to add a bit of lemon juice to preserve vitamins.

- Add just a small amount (1 to 2 tbsp) of heat-tolerant oil to the wok.

- Soy sauce is ideal for flavoring, because it distributes itself better than salt.

- Food prepared in a wok should be eaten as soon as it is cooked.

- Quantities should not be too large, or liquid will form, and stir frying will become simmering.

Using a Wok

This cooking method is the opposite of what is usually considered to be gentle vegetable preparation. The food is cut into small pieces and temperatures are relatively high. Despite that, stir frying in the wok is one of the most gentle cooking methods. High temperatures and large contact areas quickly disable vitamin-killing enzymes. Constant stirring and the wok's unique shape make it possible to use only a small amount of oil. Combined with the small size of the food pieces, this technique results in extremely fast cooking. Special considerations are mentioned in the box to the left.

Cooking Without a Pot: A Practical Method

It started with aluminum foil, then there were roasting bags, and the latest trend in "wrapped" cooking is parchment paper. Cooking in a package means simmering, steaming, or stewing the food in its own juices. Cooking in a "package" not only preserves nutrients but also maintains the food's flavor and appearance. In addition, the dish may be given a decorative shape, and by adding herbs and other seasonings, interesting creations evolve. The valuable cooking liquid is saved as an excellent base for gravy. Lastly, this method avoids the production of harmful substances which are created by roasting.

What You Should Know About Potless Cooking

- Aluminum foil is available in various widths and thicknesses. It has both a shiny and a matte side. Always keep the shiny side toward the food and the matte side facing out. This way, the heat can penetrate more easily to the inside where it is retained by the reflection of the shiny side.

- Aluminum foil needs time to heat up, but it holds temperatures well. Food wrapped in foil continues to cook after being removed from the heat. The foil package is suitable for cooking in the oven, on the barbecue, in the frying pan and in water.

- There are also very thin, transparent roasting bags which can withstand temperatures up to 425°F (220°C). *Important*: Place roasting bags only on cold racks in a hot oven, and avoid contact with the hot oven walls. The bag should always be 12" (30 cm) longer than its contents, and the top surface should be pierced a few times to allow steam to escape. This will prevent the bag from inflating and bursting. Even when oven temperatures reach 425°F (220°C), the interior of the bag does not heat up to more than 300°F (150°C).

- Parchment paper has to be well greased with a solid fat (such as coconut butter) so that food doesn't soak through while cooking. This is a gentle way of cooking tender herbs and vegetables; you can even combine them with precooked noodles and cheese. And, because parchment paper "breathes" and will not overheat, this method produces wonderful aromas in the kitchen.

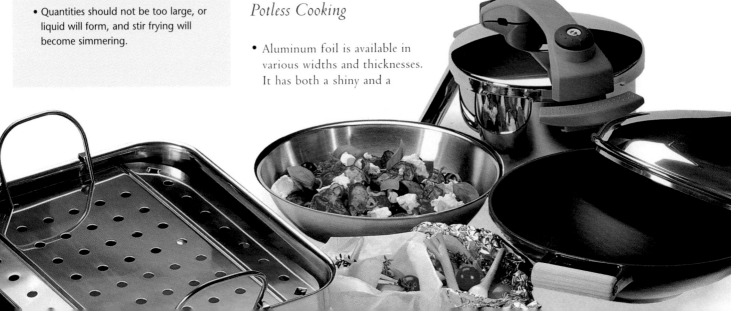

Shopping: As Fresh as Possible

The vegetarian cook must be aware that the vitamins in fruit, herbs and vegetables break down rapidly when stored for a period of time. Grains, seeds and nuts are much less sensitive. Always buy locally produced organic food from a market or farm stand, if possible. Otherwise, shop at health food stores and supermarkets where the vegetable department is kept cool and the assortment of produce is well maintained. Your chances are best for buying fresh foods where there is a high turnover of produce. Find out when stores receive their deliveries and shop on those days.

Information About Organically Grown Produce

Both Canada and the United States are working toward the development of federal standards for organic food production. The Canadian General Standards Board hopes to implement strict guidelines to unify the mandates of the many different Canadian Organic Associations currently in action. Talk to your local health food store to find out which body certifies producers in your area. Find out what their logo looks like and watch for it when shopping; organic produce is increasingly available in supermarkets too. Or, contact your local organic association for a list of farms from which you can buy directly.

Storage of Fresh Produce

Even if produce is fresh when it comes into your kitchen, storing it at room temperature dramatically lowers its vitamin content because warmth, oxygen from the air, and light, all attack valuable nutrients. Stored at room temperature for two days, cauliflower loses about 25% of its vitamin C content, while it loses only 8% in the fridge. With peas, the vitamin C content decreases by 36% at room temperature and by only 10% in the fridge.

Storage Tips

- Most vegetables belong in the fridge.
- Remove the greens from radishes, carrots and kohlrabi after purchase. The leaves use up energy from the root, so the part you want to consume quickly wilts and becomes tasteless.
- Do not keep herbs in water as you would flowers. They deteriorate quickly and wilt. Keep them in the fridge in a tightly closed plastic container. This slows deterioration and maintains the freshness of the leaves.
- Studies by the Federal Research Institute for Nutrition in Karlsruhe, Germany revealed that fully ripe and cold-resistant fruit and vegetables are best stored in plastic bags in the fridge at a temperature of 34°F (1°C). Freezer bags are fine, but special "freshness" bags are much more effective. The pantry or root cellar is the best place for these cold-sensitive vegetables: eggplants, avocados, peppers, okras, green beans, potatoes, zucchini, cucumbers, tomatoes and squash. You should store cold-sensitive fruit like pineapples, bananas, cherimoyas, pomegranates, guavas, mangoes, papayas, passion fruit, citrus fruit and melons at a temperature of 40°–54°F (4°–5°C). A cool cellar or basement is ideal for these fruits, as is the vegetable compartment of the fridge. Give cold-sensitive fruits 1–2 hours to "warm up" to room temperature; only then will they develop their full flavor.

Cooking with Stored Supplies

Dark, Dry and Cool

Grains, seeds, nuts, pulses and spices play an important part in vegetarian cooking. Store these staples in a cupboard—or, if possible, in a pantry or cool basement. If you store them in the kitchen, choose the coolest spot, certainly not next to the oven.

Fight Spoilage

Even dry foods can spoil, particularly those rich in fats like nuts, seeds and whole grains which can quickly become rancid. Corn and millet taste bitter when old, so don't store them for too long.

Deter Pests

Kitchens which store large varieties of grain can also fall prey to the harmless but annoying weevil. Weevils eat their way through bags and sacks. Once food has been attacked, kill the pests by placing the food in the freezer for 10 days or in the oven at 140°–175°F (60°–80°C). Once the pests are dead, throw out the food. Pesticides are always toxic and should not be used in the kitchen.

- Collect jars with screw tops, and transfer all supplies to jars immediately after purchase. Attach labels with dates. Metal and plastic containers also deter pests. Some health food stores carry

weevil traps which catch the male weevil without poisoning your food.
- Check your supplies regularly.
- Cool, dry and well-ventilated storage areas are best—pests like it damp, warm and stuffy.

Supplies to Keep on Hand

Dairy/eggs/fats:
- a mild and a strong cheese
- milk
- whipping cream
- crème fraîche, or sour cream
- quark
- yogurt
- butter
- eggs
- cold-pressed, extra-virgin olive oil

Vegetables:
- potatoes
- carrots
- leeks
- broccoli
- peppers
- onions
- garlic
- lemons
- apples

Dry Supplies:
- flour
- cornmeal
- oat flakes
- pasta
- rice
- bread crumbs
- red lentils
- muesli
- dried fruit (raisins, plums and apricots)
- dried yeast
- baking powder
- a variety of nuts and seeds

In Jars or Cans:
- tomato paste
- canned tomatoes
- dark sour cherries (jar)
- olives

For Sweetening and Seasoning:
- preservative-free instant vegetable stock
- honey, molasses, unrefined sugar
- chives, parsley, mixed herbs (fresh or dried)

Recipes Using On-hand Supplies

Soups
Creamy Carrot Casserole 79 (replace green onions with a leek or two onions)
Creamy Potato Soup 83 (omit fresh celery)
Creamed Millet Soup with Peppers 87 (replace millet flour with semolina or wholewheat flour)

Potatoes
Pan-fried Potatoes 139
Crispy Baked Potatoes 139 (replace Parmesan with any hard cheese)
Apple-Potato Gratin 140 (replace green onions with a small leek and an onion, omit lemon grass)
Bouillon Potatoes 141
Potato Patties 144
Gnocchi with Peppers 149 (replace millet with wheat flour, use canned tomatoes)

Eggs and Cheese
"Kratzete" (Scratched Eggs) 155
Italian Frittata 158
Quark Pancakes with Diced Peppers 161
Fried Cheese with Hot Peppers 163
Cheese Polenta in Tomato Sauce 164

Pasta and Rice
Vegetable Rolls 93 (replace broccoli with grated carrots)
"Spaetzle" Variations 94 (replace spelt with wheat flour)
Noodle Nests au Gratin 97 (use mild cheese for the gratin, and canned tomatoes)
Tomato Risotto 98 (replace tomato juice with vegetable stock, use canned tomatoes)
Cheesy Rice Fritters 101 (replace green onions with a leek and an onion)

Grains and Pulses
Carrot Star 103 (use mild cheese and cream of wheat)
Spelt Dumplings 105 (replace green spelt with another coarse meal or a blend of cream of wheat and bread crumbs)
Pan-fried Bulgur 108 (replace bulgur with rice, almonds with other nuts)

Millet Dumplings with Peppers 106
Millet Pudding with Chive Sauce 107
Red Lentil-stuffed Peppers 112 (replace green onions with leek and onions)

Baked Savories
Polenta-Vegetable Squares 52 (replace cornmeal with cream of wheat, broccoli with carrots; use a hard grating cheese)
Pizza Rounds 170
Potato Quiche 173

Desserts
Quark Dumplings with Cherry Sauce 177
Baked Apple-Nut Pancake 180 (replace walnuts with other nuts)
Apple Fritters with Cinnamon Sugar 181
Fruit-filled Buns 182 (replace prunes with dried apricots or raisins)

How to Recognize Fresh Produce

- Leaves should be crisp and green; be cautious if they have been removed. Older vegetables often have leaves cut back to improve appearance.

- Any cuts should be fresh and juicy. Dry flesh is always a sign of old produce.

- Small lettuces should make you wary; here too, the outer leaves were probably removed.

- Vegetables wrapped in plastic (which may have been chemically treated) retain their appearance for a longer period—but the nutrients still suffer.

- Buying fruit and vegetables in season (see tables page 18–19) and choosing local varieties, increase the likelihood that you are getting fresh local produce.

- As attractive as it may seem, beware of produce sold by street vendors.

- Do not rely on industry classifications; they only categorize size and appearance, not nutritional value. Sample whenever possible—a characteristic, full flavor is still the best indication of quality.

- Your nose will tell you right away if produce is past its prime.

Fruits and vegetables are transported from all over the world to your local produce store so that they are available year round. However, the vitamins in fruit and vegetables are lost during a long transport, prolonged storage and exposure to air and light. To ensure you get the maximum nutrient value from your fruit and vegetables, choose fresh, local produce in their peak season and buy organic whenever possible.

Fruit

Fruit Peak Season	How to Choose	How to Store
Apricot May–August	firm, uniform golden color	ripen in a paper bag; once ripe, refrigerate in a plastic bag for up to 2 days
Banana all year	firm, slightly green at ends or clear yellow with occasional black spots	ripen at room temperature out of direct sunlight
Blueberry May–September	plump, firm, small berries with a slight grey hue	refrigerate in a box for up to 4 days
Cherry April–early August	plump, firm and bright color	eat as soon as possible; refrigerate for no more than 3 days
Grapefruit January–June	smooth, thick skin, rounded or slightly flat at both ends, heavy for its size	store at room temperature for up to 1 week
Grape all year	plump and firm fruit	eat as soon as possible; refrigerate in a plastic or paper bag for up to 4 days
Kiwi all year	uniformly firm and yields to gentle pressure	ripen uncovered, out of direct sunlight or ripen more quickly in a paper bag with a ripe apple, banana or pear; once ripe, refrigerate in a paper or plastic bag for up to 1 week
Lemon all year	fine-textured skin; heavy for its size	store at room temperature or in the refrigerator for several weeks
Mango June–July	tight skin; when ripe, a faint sweet aroma at the stem end and yields to pressure	ripen at room temperature uncovered and out of sunlight; once ripe, refrigerate in a plastic or paper bag for up to 5 days
Melon May–November	evenly ripe fruit; *cantaloupe*: slightly oval, 5" (12 cm) in diameter with a golden background color; *honeydew*: smooth, firm and weighs at least 5 lb (2.3 kg); *watermelon*: symmetrical shape and dull skin	ripen at room temperature; once ripe, refrigerate tightly wrapped in plastic
Orange November–April	firm, round, heavy for size, smooth-textured skin	refrigerate uncovered
Peach May–early October	cream or yellow background color	ripen at room temperature out of direct sunlight or more quickly in a loosely closed paper bag; once ripe, refrigerate in a plastic or paper bag for up to 5 days
Pineapple April–June	plump, with deep green, crisp-looking crown leaves	store at room temperature away from direct sunlight for up to 2 days
Plum June–October January–March	deep color; ripe plums give a little when squeezed	ripen at room temperature out of direct sunlight or more quickly in a loosely closed paper bag; once ripe, refrigerate unwashed in a plastic or paper bag for up to 4 days
Raspberry season varies from region to region	plump, well-shaped berries with no dampness or mold	eat as soon as possible; refrigerate, placing between paper towels on a tray and cover with plastic
Rhubarb March–June	firm, crisp, fresh stalks	refrigerate, unwashed, in a plastic bag for up to 1 week
Strawberry May–July	ripe, unhulled berries	refrigerate in a box for up to 3 days

Vegetables

Vegetable Peak Season	How to Choose	How to Store
Artichoke March–May	tight, compact head with thick, blemish-free leaves; heavy for its size	refrigerate in a closed plastic bag or container with a tight-fitting lid for up to a week
Asparagus April–June	smooth stalk with tight head	buy at the last possible moment; wrap the stem ends in a wet paper towel and store in a plastic bag, or stand the stem ends up in a bit of water
Avocado September–March	ready to eat when it feels slightly soft and the skin is no longer green	refrigerate unwrapped
Beet June–October	round shape, smooth, firm flesh and rich, deep red color	refrigerate in the vegetable drawer in a plastic bag for up to 3 weeks
Belgian endive June–September	firm, crisp head with pure-white leaves and light yellow at the edges and tips; 4"–6" (10–15 cm) long	wrap in a damp paper towel and refrigerate for up to 5 days, protect from light
Broccoli October–April	tightly closed, compact bud clusters and firm, tender stems; deep green (with a hint of purple)	refrigerate unwashed in a plastic bag for up to 3 days
Cabbage May–September	firm heads, soft color, crisp and fresh looking without blemishes; heavy for its size	refrigerate, uncut and unwashed in a plastic bag for up to 1 week
Carrots all year	rich golden-orange color; smooth, clean, firm, well-shaped and even-sized	remove any green tops and refrigerate unwashed in a plastic bag for up to 2 weeks
Cauliflower September–November	clean, firm, snowy-white heads with tight flowerets	refrigerate in a plastic bag for up to 1 week
Celery all year	crisp, tight stalks and fresh-looking leaves	refrigerate in a plastic bag for up to 2 weeks
Chinese cabbage all year	firm, tight head; clean color and crisp texture	wrap in plastic and refrigerate in the bottom drawer for up to 2 weeks
Corn June–September	fresh-looking ear with tight green husk and a fresh, sweet smell; plump, juicy, small, tightly packed kernels	wrap, unhusked, in a damp paper towel and refrigerate in a plastic bag for up to 2 days
Cucumber June–September	small, firm and deep green in color	refrigerate in a plastic bag for up to 1 week; *English cucumbers*: wrap and store in a cool place
Eggplant July–September	firm, heavy, smooth, glossy uniform-colored skin; medium-sized	store unwashed in a dark, humid place
Fennel October–April	firm, crisp white bulb with feathery bright green leaves; stalks at least 10" (25 cm)	refrigerate in a plastic bag for up to 4 days
Kohlrabi June–July	small, smooth bulb and a thin, crisp rind; leaves firm, fresh and green	wrap the bulbs and refrigerate for up to 1 week
Leek October–April	small, clean, and white 2"–3" (5–7.5 cm) from the base with crisp, fresh green tops	cut off roots, discard coarse outer leaves and trim tops; refrigerate in a plastic bag
Lettuce all year	bright color with no blemishes; *iceberg*: crisp, juicy texture; *butter*: soft, delicate leaves; *romaine*: big, stiff upright leaves	rinse with cold water, shake off excess water, wrap in paper towels and refrigerate in a plastic bag for up to 5 days
Mushroom all year	plump, smooth, white with tightly closed caps	buy at the last possible moment; wrap in a paper towel or put in a paper bag and refrigerate for no more than 2 days
Onion all year	hard texture; dry with crackly, unblemished skin and small neck	store unwrapped, in a dry, cool, airy place for up to 2 months; once cut, wrap in plastic and refrigerate for up to 4 days
Peas February–August	fairly large, angular, bright green pod that is packed with medium-sized peas	buy at the last possible moment; refrigerate in a plastic bag for no more than 2 days
Pepper July–November	bright, glossy, firm, well-shaped and thick-fleshed	refrigerate, unwashed, in a plastic bag for up to 5 days
Potato March–July	firm, well-shaped, clean, relatively smooth and free of blemishes, even-colored	store in a dry, cool, airy place for up to 2 months
Pumpkin June–December	feels heavy for its size	store uncovered in the crisper of the refrigerator
Sprouts all year	crisp, fresh, small and brightly colored	buy at the last possible moment
Tomato June–August	smooth, firm, nicely shaped and heavy for its size; bright red	store in a cool place
Zucchini June–August	firm, smooth, glossy, well-shaped unblemished skin; 6"–10" (15–25 cm) long and 1"–2" (2.5–5 cm) in diameter	refrigerate in a plastic bag for up to 5 days

KNOW YOUR VEGETABLES

Vegetables are Healthy

The bounty of the harvest is composed of
75–95% water: this accounts for
vegetables' low calorie content. However,
the remaining 5–25% is rich in vitamins,
minerals, fiber and accessory nutrients
(page 227), making vegetables the food
with the highest nutrient density. Fruit
and vegetables should make up 1/3 of your
daily energy intake. For adults this is
about 2 pounds of "green" food per day.

Healthy Nutrients

- The B group of vitamins, vitamin C
  and beta-carotene (the precursor of
  vitamin A), are strongly represented in
  vegetables.
- Vegetables are important for supplying
  iron, potassium and magnesium (pages
  228 and 229).
- Vegetables contain large amounts of
  roughage in the form of fiber and
  pectin. Not only does roughage promote
  health (page 226) but it also provides
  low-calorie bulk.
- Vegetables are largely made up of
  healthy carbohydrates. These are
  complex sugars that are slowly broken
  down and absorbed into the blood.

Individual Vegetable Groups

- *Brassicas.* Broccoli is by far the leader
  where accessory nutrients (page 227)
  and vitamins are concerned. Broccoli,
  like cauliflower and kohlrabi, can be
  enjoyed raw. Cabbage and Chinese
  cabbage are very tasty in salads. Kale,
  Savoy cabbage and Brussels sprouts are
  generally too bitter to eat raw. Even
  when cabbage is heated it should not be
  "cooked to death," but cooked quickly
  in a wok. Cauliflower and broccoli
  should be steamed.
- *Bulb vegetables.* Onions, garlic, leek, radish
  and daikon radish can be eaten raw.
  Freshly grown radish sprouts are a good
  alternative. Onions, leeks and garlic are
  extremely important in vegetarian
  cooking because of their flavoring
  properties.
- *Fresh pulses.* Fresh peas and beans are rich
  in protein and roughage. Because they
  may contain some harmful elements,
  pulses should always be cooked.
- *Fruity vegetables.* Tomatoes, peppers,
  zucchini, squash and eggplants are
  particularly rich in accessory nutrients.
  Peppers are also high in vitamin C,
  particularly red peppers. Tomatoes and
  peppers are ideal as raw foods. Zucchini
  and squash are extremely mild, making
  them suitable for sensitive stomachs.
  Eggplants have little flavor of their own
  and absorb other flavors.

- *Leaf vegetables.* All varieties with a high
  proportion of leaves tend to have a high
  nitrate content, concentrated in the
  stems, stalks, outer leaves and leaf ribs.
  Buy local field produce and clean these
  types of vegetables properly.
- *Root vegetables.* Carrots, beets and celery
  should be purchased as field crops when
  locally in season.

Tip
Do not sauté eggplants in oil. They suck
it up like a sponge. It is better to sprinkle
them with oil and broil them.

Specialty Vegetables

- *Artichokes* are available fresh or as pickled
  hearts. Fresh artichokes (page 42)
  provide an entertaining eating
  experience. They are served on a plate
  with a finger bowl, a side plate and a
  small bowl with sauce. Leaves are
  removed from the outside, dipped into
  the sauce and the fleshy lower part is
  sucked out. The leaf is then discarded.
  The innermost leaves are "hairy" and
  inedible. Lastly, use a knife and fork to
  eat the heart.
- *Chilis,* also referred to as hot peppers,
  are thin, finger-long red and green
  peppers. There are mild and hot
  varieties. The hot areas are concentrated
  in the seeds and interior sectioning
  membranes. Be careful about contact
  with mucous membranes: chilis can
  really burn!
- *Hearts of palm* are literally cut from the
  heart of a palm. Therefore, they are
  relatively expensive.

• *Okra* is harvested unripe and contains a thick milk-like liquid in the pod. If the pod is cut, the liquid comes out and binds the vegetable. If this is not desired, wipe the pod carefully and blanch it. Okra can also be eaten raw in salads.

Mushrooms

These have a relatively high protein content but are hard to digest. Mushroom protein breaks down faster than meat protein, so old mushrooms that have been stored for a long time should not be eaten. A fresh mushroom dish that has been stored in the refrigerator can be reheated and eaten without problem. Farmed mushrooms are available year round. Clean these with a dry paper towel and then slice as desired. Wash wild mushrooms just briefly, otherwise they will become saturated with water.

Potatoes: The Variety is Important!

Potatoes are usually sorted according to their cooking properties. Potatoes that are firm when cooked (salad potatoes), have a particularly firm, rich consistency. They are ideal for frying, adding to stews and boiling in their skins. They do not break apart, they slice well, but they don't absorb sauces as well as other varieties. Other varieties break apart easily when cooked. In other words, they are ideal when boiled and they will absorb sauces. They are also suitable boiled in their skins, for "gratins" and for baking in foil. Mealy potatoes are indispensable for mashed potatoes, soups and dumplings. As the description implies, they are mealy, tend to break up during cooking and have a crumbly consistency. Choosing the right potato will determine the success of your recipe. Your grocer will be able to tell you which local varieties best meet your needs.

Cooking: Keep the Skins On

Most valuable nutrients like vitamins and minerals are stored directly under the skin. If the potato is peeled raw, the nutrients are partially lost. If potatoes boiled in their skins are peeled afterward, only the peel itself is removed and not the layer underneath. This has the added advantage of removing any undesirable heavy metals like lead and cadmium which can be stored on or in the skin. New potatoes should be thoroughly scrubbed under water if you wish to eat the skin. Use a proper vegetable peeler to peel raw potatoes.

Don't Soak Them

The worst sin for any health-conscious cook is to place peeled potatoes in water because after just 4 hours the sensitive (water-soluble) vitamins B and C have almost disappeared. Peel potatoes immediately before cooking. Then add only 1"–2" (2.5–5 cm) of water to the cooking pot. Potatoes do not need to be completely immersed, as they cook well in steam. Use a pressure cooker (pages 14–15) or a large steamer. You can also reserve the mineral-rich cooking liquid for use in other recipes.

Pierced Potatoes

When baking potatoes, prick them with a fork prior to putting them in the oven. This will keep them from becoming soggy.

Reduce Heavy Metals in Vegetables

• Half of the lead content in vegetables is stored in its leaves and peels. Most of the lead can be removed by washing and then scraping. Peeling or removing outer leaves is even more effective.

• These methods will also reduce up to 50% of mercury content.

• In contrast, cadmium is taken up from the soil and generally stored equally throughout the plant. Peeling will remove only 10% to 15% of this heavy metal.

An Introduction to Lettuce

There are many varieties of lettuce available on the market today.

- *Arugula* tastes nutty and slightly peppery; it stimulates the appetite.
- *Batavia*, also known as "French Crisp," has the neutral taste of loose leaf lettuce, but it resembles iceberg lettuce in its structure and shelf-life.
- *Butter lettuce* has tender, mild-tasting leaves.
- *Corn salad* is high in iron and has the highest vitamin C content of the common salad greens.
- *Frisée lettuce* is a loose variety of endive, sometimes known as curly endive. It has a slightly bitter flavor.
- *Iceberg lettuce* could almost be mistaken for a head of cabbage with its crisp, tightly packed leaves. Unfortunately, it is low in flavor and nutritive value. (Wash this lettuce whole because dirt cannot get inside.)
- *Lollo rosso* is a loose leaf lettuce with tight curls. It has a distinctive red color and pleasant flavor. This lettuce is also available as a green variety.
- *Loose leaf lettuce*, as the name suggests, does not form a head. It has a neutral flavor.

- *Oak leaf lettuce* is a soft variety with a nutty taste. Its name is derived from the shape and color of the leaves.
- *Radicchio* has a somewhat bitter taste. It is also a variety of chicory.
- *Romaine lettuce* has long upright heads with stiff green leaves. Popular in Caesar salads, this is a crispy lettuce that keeps well.

Tips: How to Handle Leaf Lettuce

- Remove the stalk and the ribs from the leaves because the nitrate content is highest here and the vitamin C content is lowest. The green outer leaves are particularly low in nitrates and rich in vitamin C.
- Keep the leaves whole and wash them under running water. Tear them apart only after washing.
- Dry the leaves in a salad spinner. Removing all traces of water will ensure that your dressing has maximum flavor.
- Always prepare lettuce just before eating.

Herbs and Spices are Important

…and not only for flavoring. They improve digestion and make raw food more digestible. Caraway, aniseed and fennel seeds, dill and mint are especially important. If you have difficulty digesting raw salads, flavor them with crushed seeds or chopped herbs. Fresh foods stimulate the digestive juices, so it is best to eat them as an appetizer.

Basic Vinaigrette Recipe

For 4 people:

2 tbsp wine vinegar, 1 tbsp medium hot mustard, 1/2 tsp seasoning salt or sea salt, ground pepper, 4 tbsp of a healthy unrefined oil, 2 tbsp chopped herbs, chopped onions to taste. Beat the vinegar with mustard and spices until creamy, then beat in the oil. Finally fold in the herbs.

Variations: This vinaigrette is milder when prepared with fruit vinegar and more interesting with the addition of crushed garlic and cold-pressed, extra-virgin olive oil.

The ideal dressing for green salads is a vinaigrette (the French word *vinaigre* means vinegar), based on oil and vinegar with lots of fresh herbs like chives, parsley, dill, cilantro and basil.

Vinegar

Selecting a vinegar is primarily a matter of taste. If you love salads, it is worthwhile having different types of vinegar on hand for the sake of variety. Vinegar also keeps well.

There are two different processes for manufacturing vinegar.

Fermented vinegar

An alcoholic liquid (e.g., wine, cider) is fermented by the addition of bacteria and oxygen, producing acetic acid. It generally produces a vinegar with an acid content between 5% and 11% whose specific taste is derived from its base.

White Vinegar

Pure vinegar acid or vinegar "essence" is diluted with water to the desired acid content of 5–15.5%. These vinegars are neutral or sour in taste as they contain no additional flavor.

Basic Vinegar Types:

Cider Vinegar

A strong brown vinegar often used in pickling and well known for its healthful properties.

Distilled Vinegar

Any vinegar produced by alcohol fermentation and having a very sharp taste.

Fruit Vinegar

Produced by fermentation from pure fruit wines. It should not be mixed with distilled vinegar or other additives. Generally available from specialty delicatessens or gourmet shops.

Red and White Wine Vinegar

These may be genuine wine vinegars produced purely from grape wines without additives, or they may be a blend of pure wine vinegar and distilled vinegar. They are pleasant tasting, especially when used in salads.

Specialty Vinegars

The best balsamic vinegar comes from the Italian provinces of Modena and Reggio Emilia. It is produced from Trebbiano grapes, is very aromatic and has a sweetish taste. It is matured for several years in wooden barrels before being sold. There are also a number of flavored vinegars available. Japanese rice vinegar is now widely available. It has a lovely mild taste that enhances the sweetness of both fruits and vegetables. Commercial herb vinegars are available in a number of varieties.

The Right Oil

While choosing vinegar is simply a matter of taste, choosing the right oil involves further consideration. You can choose oils with a neutral flavor or oils with a very distinctive taste. For example, corn oil, sunflower seed oil and wheat germ oil have a neutral taste. Examples of oils with a distinctive taste are walnut oil, olive oil and pumpkin seed oil. Oils differ not only in taste but, more importantly, in their methods of manufacture.

Cold-pressed, unrefined oils

In cold pressing, the oil seeds are ground and then pressed. The highest temperature they reach during this process is no more than 140°F (60°C) which allows all the natural odors, flavors and nutrients (like vitamins and essential fatty acids) to be preserved. Unrefined, organic, cold-pressed oils are far superior to refined oil.

Modern packaging technology has come a long way. These delicate oils have a longer shelf-life than ever before, but they must still be handled with care. Always keep them in dark bottles to prevent deterioration from exposure to light. Cold-pressed, unrefined oils must also be refrigerated.

Because natural unrefined oils are so sensitive to heat it is important to choose an oil that will perform well for each specific recipe. For cold dips and salad dressings we recommend pumpkin seed oil, flax seed oil, canola oil or walnut oil (do not heat them). For gently heated sauces and for baking breads and muffins use organic, cold-pressed high-oleic safflower, high-oleic sunflower or almond oils. For light sautéing use sesame oil or olive oil. Coconut oil and butter are best for frying and baking—as long as they are not overheated.

Always choose cold-pressed, unrefined organic oils. Refining damages the oil to the point where it becomes unhealthy.

For Salads: Oil with Complex Unsaturated Fatty Acids

Complex unsaturated fatty acids (UFAs) found in oils are as important for our bodies as vitamins. They are a basic component of the tissue hormones that are essential to healthy blood pressure, heart rhythm and many other functions. In addition, they tend to lower cholesterol levels.

Vegetable fats contain more highly unsaturated fatty acids than animal fats. When they are heated, the complex UFAs are largely destroyed. Therefore, these high-quality oils should be enjoyed unheated—on salads, for example or, drizzled on top of cooked vegetables instead of butter.

Left: green spelt; right: chickpeas

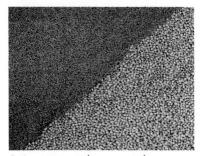

Left: quinoa; right: amaranth

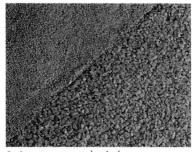

Left: couscous; right: bulgur

Left: buckwheat; right: millet

A Brief Introduction to Grains

Cereal grains contain 70% carbohydrates and 10% proteins. The gluten in the seed is less nutritious than the protein in the germ. Roughage is concentrated in the outer layers. Cereal grains are high in potassium, phosphorus, magnesium, copper and, most of all, iron. All of the B vitamins are present, as are vitamins A and E.

Cereals and Grains

- *Amaranth.* This grain is the tiny seed of an Incan grass. It is exceptionally rich in minerals and protein.
- *Barley.* This grain is as ancient as wheat, has a similar mild taste and good baking properties. Barley is particularly rich in silica, has strengthening, soothing and anticancer properties.
- *Millet.* This ancient grain is usually boiled but rarely baked. It has a mild and delicate taste and has high fluoride and silica content (good for hair, skin and teeth).
- *Oats.* Europe's favorite cereal grain, it has the highest proportion of protein and fat and is very high in iron.
- *Quinoa.* This small grain from the Andes is larger than amaranth. It is very high in iron and protein. Cook it as you would rice.
- *Rye.* This grain is particularly rich in minerals and has a distinctive taste.
- *Spelt.* The "original wheat." It has a hearty taste.
- *Wheat.* The world's most popular bread grain. It has particularly good baking properties, a mildly sweet taste and is rich in nutritious protein.

Specialty Grains

- *Bulgur* is coarsely cracked wheat that has been pre-steamed. It has a pleasantly nutty flavor and cooks in just 15 minutes.
- *Couscous* is very coarsely ground semolina wheat that has also been pre-steamed.

Pulses: Plant Proteins

The seeds of legumes are harvested only when the hull is yellow and dry. They taste best fresh, but dried pulses can be kept for at least a year with proper storage. They should not be kept longer as they can become too dry, requiring a longer cooking time during which they will disintegrate.

- *Beans* come in many varieties and are generally available whole. Eastern cooking has helped popularize mung and soy beans. Red kidney beans are excellent in chili, and black beans have been introduced through the cuisine of South America. White lima beans are the largest.

Tips for Pulses

It is important to salt pulses only after cooking otherwise they will remain tough. Add a little lemon juice to the soaking water to reduce the likelihood of intestinal gas. You should also cook pulses in fresh water.

- *Chickpeas* have a nutty flavor and hold their shape. They are cooked in stews and also roasted as snacks.
- *Dried split peas* are yellow or green and become mushy when cooked.
- *Lentils* are available whole or split. There are brown, green and red lentils in three different sizes.

Health Food

No vegetable has as much nutritious protein as pulses. With up to 37% protein, beans, peas and lentils are a real fitness food. When pulses are combined with milk, eggs or grains, they provide the body with complete essential amino acids. Pulses also contain a significant amount of roughage, more in fact than any other vegetable. Pulses provide minerals like calcium, iron, copper and manganese for daily nutrition.

Soaking is Important

The moisture that dried grains have lost must be restored in order to make them edible. This is best done by long soaking, preferably overnight. Lentils are the only exception. Depending on how old or dry the pulses are, cooking time will be 1–2 hours.

Many Varieties of Rice

Rice is divided into three major groups—long grain, medium grain and short grain. All three groups are available as white rice, brown rice and instant.

- *Long grain* is traditionally used for side dishes and is served granular and loose. Basmati is a nice aromatic variety.
- *Medium grain* has similar cooking properties to short grain rice and is

Make Your Own Thickeners for Sauces

If you grind millet in a food processor or an old coffee grinder, you will have an excellent thickener for sauces—one that does not form lumps, has a neutral taste and is excellent for your skin. Stir into boiling liquid like any other thickener.

Wholewheat noodles

Pasta and egg noodles

Transparent noodles, rice noodles, Chinese egg noodles and soy noodles

ideal for juicy, soft risottos. The best-tasting is Arborio, an Italian variety.

- *Short grain* is used for sweet dishes, rice cakes and puddings; it is rich in starch and cooks to a relatively soft and sticky consistency.

Advantages and Disadvantages?
White rice has been polished and has had its nutritious outer covering removed. Its vitamin, roughage and mineral contents are low. Its only advantages are that it can be stored for an unlimited time and it has a completely neutral taste. Instant or parboiled white rice, however, is polished after being precooked. The roughage content is reduced, but minerals and vitamins move into the kernel during parboiling and are partially preserved.

Brown rice is nutritionally superior to white rice and is therefore the first choice for most vegetarians. It retains its nutritious elements, and it has a strong, nutty taste and good texture. It needs at least 40 minutes of cooking time.

About Noodles

There are almost as many types of noodles as there are noodle shapes.

- *Colored and flavored* noodles may be red from tomatoes or red peppers, green from spinach, dark red from beets, yellow from saffron, black from octopus ink—these add natural colors. Many noodles are now being made with the addition of flavoring agents such herbs, peppers and dried tomato, mushrooms, salmon and even truffles.
- *Chinese egg noodles* are thin like spaghetti but pressed together and formed into a block. They are often available as an

instant product and need only a few minutes in boiling water. They are good for people in a hurry.

- *Egg noodles* are traditionally made of egg dough. These are the typical German noodles. Germany produces soft wheat which requires eggs for binding. Today, egg noodles consist of a mixture of durum and soft wheat. These noodles are more filling and have a somewhat softer consistency. People with high cholesterol levels would do better to choose egg-free pasta.
- *Pasta* refers to a dried dough made of durum semolina wheat. The typical Italian pasta contains only durum semolina wheat, water and salt. These noodles have a firm consistency. They are ideal for people allergic to eggs and are lower in calories than egg pasta products.
- *Rice noodles* are easily digestible and are often confused with transparent noodles. They are manufactured from starch—rice starch. They are ideal for people who cannot tolerate wheat gluten, egg or soy.
- *Soy noodles* contain at least 15% soy flour as well as wheat flour. They are therefore particularly high in protein. Strict vegetarians can use soy noodles to increase their protein intake.
- *Transparent noodles* are made without flour. The small thread-like noodles are transparent because of their high starch content. Uncooked transparent noodles

are pliable and become white during cooking. Apart from rice noodles, they are the lowest in calories of all noodles.

- *Wholewheat noodles* are brown and have plenty of the roughage, vitamins and minerals that are usually missing from "white" varieties. In addition, they have a nutty, earthy taste.

Pineapple: cut out remaining spots in spirals or points.

Coconut: it is best to use a small hacksaw.

What Exactly is in Fruit?

- Fruit is primarily comprised of vitamin C, the B vitamins, beta-carotene and vitamin E.
- Potassium, iron, phosphorus and calcium are the main mineral components. Iron is particularly well absorbed in the presence of vitamin C.
- Fiber in the cell walls and the small seeds of berries provide roughage.
- Carbohydrates are the main element of fruit. In part they consist of complex sugars that are digested slowly and provide long-term energy, as well as simple sugars like glucose, fructose and raw sugar that are absorbed more quickly by the blood.

From Apple to Strawberry

Pomaceous Fruit

- This includes apples and pears. Vitamin content varies greatly between different varieties. Pears are good for acidic stomachs because they are mild and low in acid.

Fruit with Pits

- *Apricots* have unusually high beta-carotene and iron levels which are good for vitality. Their flavor and high acid content also allow them to be combined with savory dishes.
- *Cherries* are high in B vitamins. Sweet cherries should be eaten raw, while sour cherries yield their flavor best when cooked.
- *Nectarines* are smooth-skinned relatives of peaches. Both types of fruit have purging properties and are relatively delicate and mild.
- *Plums* have a noticeable laxative effect, particularly when eaten raw or dried as prunes.

Berries and Grapes

- *Berries* have the highest nutritional content of all fruit.
- *Grapes* have long been known as a medicinal fruit. Their high glucose content makes them useful in relieving fatigue and exhaustion.

Citrus Fruit

- Fruit such as grapefruit, lemons and oranges provide vitamin C in large quantities to help strengthen the immune system. They are ideal to eat during the winter.

The ABCs of Exotic Fruit

- *Chinese* or *Cape gooseberries* have lantern-shaped shells. The small white seeds inside the berry are eaten with the fruit. The flavor is sweet and sour and very strong. This fruit is best eaten raw.
- *Grenadilla* has a hard, smooth shell that reveals a soft, edible pith and tangy berries.
- *Guava* ripens quickly at room temperature. Buy this fruit when it is still firm.
- *Kiwi* tastes refreshingly tart, is soft and has the tiniest of seeds.
- *Kumquat* is Chinese in origin. The skin is pungent-sweet and the pulp is sharply acidic.
- *Lime* is a citrus fruit. It has a green skin, is smaller and rounder than lemon and its juice is milder.
- *Mango* is the queen of the tropical fruits. It smells sweet and aromatic when ripe. The smooth skin is greenish-red and the ripe fruit is yellow, soft and sweet.
- *Papaya* is greenish-yellow when ripe. It has a delicate flavor.
- *Passion fruit* has a chewy, juicy fruit. The flavor is incomparable. Wrinkled fruits are especially flavorful.
- *Pineapple.* Ripe pineapple has an intense smell and should be eaten immediately. To prepare pineapple, cut off the top and bottom of the fruit, place it upright and cut the skin off from the top down.

- *Pitahaya* comes in red or yellow varieties. The red variety has a slightly purple inner flesh, the yellow variety contains white flesh. They have a mild blackberry taste; the texture is almost pear-like.
- *Prickly* or *Cactus pear* has many small spines (use gloves to peel it). There are seeds throughout the fruit.
- *Rambutan* is a relative of the lychee, from South East Asia. The interior of the fruit has a sweet jelly-like quality and contains a kernel the size of a hazelnut.
- *Salak palm* has a white-fleshed interior that contains one seed. This fruit tastes sweet and sour.
- *Star fruit* yields beautiful stars when cut into slices. It is yellow right through when ripe, has a thin peel that can be eaten and is translucent. It tastes refreshingly sweet and crisp.
- *Tamarillo* has a pleasant bittersweet flavor similar to tomato. It has a thick substantial texture which is excellent in cooked preparations.

Dried Fruit: Healthy Tidbits

Drying is the simplest, most primitive method of preserving fruit. Because drying is done without additives, vitamins are lost in the process. Therefore, dried fruit is not a substitute for fresh. But it's ideal for sweet and healthy snacking or when a shot of energy is needed.

- The drying process concentrates mineral content.
- Dried fruit provides roughage. Prunes are commonly used to relieve constipation.

Fructose concentration also increases. Therefore, dried fruit is not a low-calorie item but rather an effective energy booster. Drying initiates an enzymatic browning process, making the fruit unattractively brown. The addition of sulfur prevents discoloration, but those allergic to sulfur should eat only the brown, untreated fruit. Preservatives like ascorbic acid are sometimes added to help preserve fruit with a high water content. Dried fruit that is too dry and hard can be soaked in water for 1–2 hours, just as our ancestors did.

Nuts and Seeds

These are extremely important in vegetarian cooking. Their flavor enhances our food and their high protein and fat content makes our food filling in a healthy way. They are high in minerals, vitamins A, C, E, K, and the B vitamins.

The ABCs of Nuts and Seeds

- *Almonds* are an important ingredient in baking and savory dishes.
- *Brazil nuts* have a high fat content and taste delicious. They are difficult to crack and shell.
- *Cashews* have the least fat and the highest carbohydrate content of all nuts—hence their sweetish taste.
- *Coconuts* have less fat than cashews and are the lowest in calories of all nuts. You can check for freshness by shaking them.
- *Hazelnuts* and *walnuts* have a very high fat content.
- *Macadamia nuts* contain no digestible carbohydrates, only roughage. They have a delicate crunchy taste and the highest fat content of any nut (73%).
- *Peanuts* have the most protein and are less than 50% fat. Their flavor is so distinctive that it can dominate a dish.
- *Pecans* are similar to walnuts but more delicate in flavor.
- *Pine nuts* are soft and can be crushed in a mortar very easily. They are shelled and are so delicate in flavor that they go very well with many recipes.
- *Pistachios* have a pleasant taste and are popular as a decoration on sweet dishes. Unfortunately they are quite expensive.
- *Pumpkin seeds* are green when skins have been removed. They are an excellent garnish with their fruity taste and their attractive color.
- *Sesame seeds* come in light, black and wholegrain sesame (slightly bitter) varieties.
- *Sunflower seeds* are rich in complex unsaturated fatty acids and are very affordable.
- *Walnuts* have the highest proportion of complex unsaturated fatty acids.

Pine nuts and pistachios

Sesame seeds and sunflower seeds

Pecans and walnuts

Cashews and macadamia nuts

HERBS, EDIBLE FLOWERS, SPICES AND AROMATICS

Herbs are Healthy

Few plants have as high a vitamin and mineral content as herbs. This is not the only reason that herbs are so nutritious, however. Fragrant and flavorful essential oils (made with herbs) also have a soothing effect on the body. They stimulate the digestive juices and increase our appetite. In addition, herbs have distinct flavors which allow us to reduce the amount of added salt, processed seasonings or pepper. They enhance the natural taste of food without overpowering it.

Tips for Using Herbs in the Kitchen

Freshly picked herbs taste best and their vitamin content is higher than dried herbs.
- When harvesting and storing herbs, avoid crushing or breaking them. Herbs lose nutritional value when they are damaged.
- Chop or prepare herbs as close as possible to the time of use.
- Add herbs to a dish just before serving—this preserves their tender structure, their fragrance and their nutritional value.
- Always wash the entire herb, gently dab it with a paper towel and only then pick off the leaflets.
- A chopping knife is the best tool for finely chopping herbs. Never process herbs; it makes them fibrous and unattractive.
- Add frozen herbs to the pot while they are still frozen, if possible, so that they lose the least nutritional value and flavor.

Quick Overview of Herbs

- *Basil* has a spicy, slightly peppery taste. The leaves are easily bruised and are best cut lengthwise—never chopped. Basil is best when used fresh. It stimulates the appetite and digestion.

- *Chervil* has a taste similar to parsley and also brings to mind aniseed. Its gentle flavor goes well with fresh salads and green sauces. It gives the famous chervil soup its distinctive taste. Add chervil only at the end of the cooking process. The spring herb chervil is very rich in vitamin C and has a cleansing effect.
- *Chives* are rich in vitamin C and essential oils that stimulate digestion and strengthen the stomach.
- *Cilantro* is the parsley of the Orient. The seeds of the cilantro plant are known as coriander. This herb gives Indian cooking its distinctive flavor.
- *Dill* is a popular, delicate herb. It has a taste similar to fennel, goes well with cucumber and beets and is especially good in fresh salads. Dill is very high in vitamin C.
- *Lavender* is the herb of France's Provence district. Because it is very aromatic, its leaves are suitable for seasoning.
- *Lemon balm* has a strong lemony taste. Its delicate leaves are particularly popular as a garnish on desserts and its fresh fragrance is also a perfect complement to salads and sauces.
- *Lovage* is also known as the "Maggi herb," named after the popular European soup condiment.
- *Marjoram* was originally a Mediterranean herb. Its small, tough leaves have a strong minty fragrance. This herb also tastes good dried. Marjoram strengthens the stomach and relieves cramps. Add it to food only toward the end of the cooking process.
- *Mint* is primarily used as a tea and as a medicinal herb for relief from gallstone pain and indigestion.
- *Oregano* is similar to marjoram, but has a stronger, less cultivated flavor. It releases its flavor during cooking.
- *Parsley* grows all over the world. It is very rich in vitamins and therefore should always be added only after cooking.
- *Pimpernel* has tender, serrated leaves on a long stalk. It has a mild taste and is very rich in vitamins.
- *Rosemary* was originally a Mediterranean herb. Its tough needles have a resinous, bitter taste. Rosemary can also be dried. The camphor-like oils and tannin

Basil

Savory

Tarragon

Chervil

Cilantro

Lovage

Mint

Pimpernel

Rosemary

Sage

Thyme

agents in rosemary stimulate blood pressure and revive the spirits.

- *Sage* has soft, hairy, silver-green leaves with a unique, intense, bitter-lemon fragrance.
- *Savory* makes pulses more digestible. It has a peppery fragrance and a stronger taste than its relative, oregano.
- *Sorrel* is very rich in vitamins and minerals and has blood purifying and purging effects. Sorrel tastes best when the leaves are sautéed in butter and then puréed.
- *Tarragon* is one of the classic herbs. Its delicately bitter, slightly peppery fragrance is best released by cooking, so cook half of the tarragon with the dish and add the second half just before serving. Tarragon goes with sauces, salads and spring vegetables. This herb has a diuretic effect, stimulates digestion and is known to relieve rheumatism.
- *Thyme* is another Mediterranean herb. It has a spicy taste and retains much of its flavor even when dried. The tiny leaves release their full flavor only when cooked—as with oregano, add it before cooking and cook it with the food. Thyme has an antiseptic effect, relieves cramps, assists in the digestion of fat and relieves coughs.

Introduction to Spices

Like herbs, spices can benefit our general well-being. They have a medicine-like pharmacological effect. Their essential oils also stimulate the appetite and enhance the digestibility of many dishes. Crush fresh spices in a mortar immediately before using them. You can also use a pepper mill or coffee grinder. Soft spices like juniper or pimento can be crushed with the flat side of a knife. Some important spices and their effects are listed below.

- *Bay* stimulates the appetite.
- *Caraway* stimulates digestion.
- *Chili/cayenne pepper* stimulates circulation and is an antiseptic.
- *Cinnamon* stimulates the appetite and digestion, and strengthens the stomach.
- *Cloves* are easily digestible.
- *Coriander* stimulates digestion.
- *Cumin* strengthens the stomach.
- *Curry* is a mixture of spices (including turmeric, chili, coriander, cumin) available in various strengths.
- *Fennel* relieves pain and cramps and has a calming effect.

- *Ginger* stimulates the appetite and perspiration, and is easily digestible.
- *Juniper* promotes perspiration and has a diuretic effect. It helps prevent gout.
- *Lemon grass* stimulates the appetite and digestion.
- *Mustard seed* stimulates digestion and has antiseptic qualities.
- *Paprika* contains three times as much carotene as carrots and has a stabilizing effect on circulation. The capsaicin content stimulates the appetite and kills bacteria.

Cooking With Essential Oils

Essential oils are commonly used in scented lamps and potpourri—but the idea that one can cook with them is new. We do use herbs, spices and flowers as natural foods, but we can also keep essential oils of lavender or rose readily at hand.

Buying Essential Oils

It is best to buy natural essential oils for culinary use from a health food store. They should be certified organic, and must be produced without chemicals. It is extremely important that they be 100% pure essential oils.

Use of Essential Oils

Five drops of essence of basil is enough to produce an effective mixture when added to 1 cup cold-pressed, extra-virgin olive oil. If you add a teaspoon of this fragrant oil to a ratatouille, for example, it will smell as though it were freshly prepared on the shores of the Mediterranean. One teaspoon of the oil is enough for four servings.

If you use the essential oil without cooking oil, never add it directly to the dish, but always into a spoon first. It is often enough to add a drop to the spoon, allow it to drip off and then stir the spoon through the food. Always add the essential oil after cooking. Common essential oils are: basil, thyme, rosemary, pepper, coriander and lime.

Edible Flowers

Of course, we cannot eat all flowers—but certainly a lot more than you might think. Since they are usually quite flavorful, a few small petals sprinkled on a salad is often enough unless the flowers form the focal point of the meal. It is important that you use only organically grown flowers guaranteed to be free of animal droppings. Flowers from florists are often treated—don't use them in salads.

- The flowers of herbs can generally be eaten. The flowers of borage, mugwort, lavender, marjoram, nasturtium, thyme and hyssop are particularly tasty.
- Ornamental flowers such as roses, violets, dahlias, hibiscus, orange blossoms, magnolias and sunflowers can also be used.
- In the garden, enjoy daisies, dandelions, marigolds, elder, jasmine, fennel and zucchini blossoms.

Sprouts: Lighter than Seeds

Sprouting reduces the carbohydrate content of the seed by half. Fat, too, is reduced during sprouting. Consequently the seed's caloric content decreases—it becomes "lighter."

What Happens During Sprouting?
- The seed's protein composition is altered; it becomes more easily digestible.
- Vitamin content rises significantly. This applies particularly to vitamins E, C, B_1, B_2, niacin and biotin. Only folic acid decreases.
- Mineral content increases.
- Roughage increases.
- In pulses, the percentage of harmful ingredients decreases. Briefly, the seeds become more digestible and their nutrient content expands during sprouting. The pulses taste better, are softer and retain a delicious crunch.
- The nitrate content of sprouts remains low when temperatures are maintained between 63° and 77°F (17°–25°C) and the sprouts are grown in water. Before eating, sprouts should be briefly blanched in boiling water or stir fried in a wok to eliminate unwanted germs which can develop in a moist environment. The nitrate content in sprouts reaches its peak during the first days and can be reduced by a sprouting time of 4 to 6 days and by adding more light after the second day.

How to Grow Sprouts
Sprouts will only grow from healthy seeds. Commercial seeds have usually been treated and are not suitable for sprouting.
- When shopping, request seeds for sprouting so that you can be assured of success.
- Check the seeds, wash them in a large bowl, and remove anything that floats to the top.
- Four factors are involved in the sprouting process: water, temperature, light and air. Water prepares the seeds for sprouting. Depending on the type of seed, they need to be soaked for several hours (see table).

Instructions for Growing Sprouts

Seed Type	Soaking Time (in hours)	Sprouting Time (in days)	Special Nutrients and Characteristics
Alfalfa	5–6	5	Vitamin B_2
Barley	12	2–3	Silica
Beans	12	5	Protein, inedible when raw
Chickpea	12	3	Protein, bitter if left too long
Cress	6	8	Vitamin C
Lentil	12	3	Protein, easy to grow
Flax	4	2	Discard slime
Millet	8	3	Protein, fluoride
Mung Bean	12	5	Protein, easy to grow
Mustard	12	6–12	Stimulates digestion
Oat	4	2–3	Iodine, fluoride
Pea	12	3	Protein
Pumpkin	12–16	3	Remove shells after sprouting
Radish	4	2	Protects from molds (antibacterial)
Rye	12	2–3	Fluoride
Soy bean	12	3	Protein, some slime
Wheat	12	2–3	Unsaturated fats, carotene

- Soak 1 part seeds in 8 parts water: the water content will increase from 10% to more than 70%. Don't discard the soaking water; it has absorbed valuable nutrients and can be used in cooking.
- Place the plump, soaked seeds in a jar or sprouting bowl. Cover the bottom of the sprouting bowl with a thin layer of seeds. The jar should not be more than 1/4 full. Only then will enough light and air reach the seeds. This space also leaves enough room for the sprouts to grow.
- Sprouts need to be rinsed with clean water about twice a day. This increases the oxygen supply and prevents mold growth. Use a water temperature close to lukewarm; ice-cold water inhibits sprouting.
- Sprouting containers have perforations in the bottom because the rinse water must be able to fully drain. Jars must be closed with cheesecloth and placed upside down on a rack (this design can be bought ready-made as a sprouting jar in health food stores).
- Regular daylight is sufficient for sprouts—pumpkin seeds do better in a darker environment.
- After just one day, you will see the first sprout tips. They are only ripe after having reached a certain length (see table); only then will nutrient content and taste be at their best.
- Now comes the harvest. Use sprouts when they're fresh. If you have an excess, keep them in the fridge in a clean, tightly closed container for up to 2 days. Cool temperatures slow down growth. By the way, sprouts may also be frozen.

Warning: Molds
Molds can grow quickly in a moist environment. So, proper airing and rinsing of sprouts is extremely important. One trick is to add a few radish seeds to every jar of sprouts—they have antibacterial properties.

All in all, sprouts are a very economical, nutritionally complete alternative—especially during the winter months when fresh organic vegetables can be scarce. These are as fresh as you will ever get.

Tofu: Soy Baking Cheese

The word *tofu* is Japanese and consists of the words *to*, the bean, and *fu* meaning fermentation or curdling. Yellow soy beans are soaked, puréed, cooked and filtered. This process separates the solid from the liquid components. The soy milk produced in this way is naturally curdled and the developing soy "cheese" is then pressed. When blended, tofu can be used in many recipes as a substitute for cheese or quark.

Tofu: The Ultimate Protein

In vegetarian cooking, tofu has gained increasing importance because it supplies pure plant protein. In addition:
- It contains B vitamins and vitamin E.
- It supplies iron, phosphorus and potassium.
- Tofu contains all 8 essential amino acids, which the body needs but cannot produce itself.

Tips for Tofu Marinades

Cut the tofu into cubes or slices 1/2" (1 cm) thick (depending on the dish) and marinate them in one of the following sauces:

- Spicy tomato sauce
- Blend of olive oil, pressed garlic, salt, pepper, and finely chopped basil
- Soy sauce mixed with some vegetable stock
- Pumpkin seed oil stirred into soy sauce

The marinated tofu can be fried in a pan, put into casseroles, stuck on skewers with vegetables and barbecued, or simply diced into salads (the basil marinade is particularly well suited for this).

- Tofu is low in calories: it has only about 90 calories per 2/3 cup (100 g).
- Tofu has no cholesterol.
- The abundantly present acid decreases cholesterol and other dangerous fat deposits in the blood, blood vessels and organs.
- Tofu is second only to eggs in lecithin content.

How to Prepare Tofu
- Discard any liquid after opening the package. Rinse the tofu briefly under cold water. Dab it dry with a paper towel.
- As tofu absorbs flavors slowly, season or marinate it for quite a while before baking or frying it.

More Specialty Ingredients
- *Miso* is a fermented paste commonly made from soy beans or rice. It is used for flavoring.
- *Rice paper* consists of thin leaves of rice starch which require moistening before use. They serve as wraps for spring rolls and similar dishes.
- *Seaweed* plays an important role in Japanese cooking. As *nori* it is used in sushi making.
- *Soy* is an important source of protein in Eastern vegetarian cooking. It is also used in industrially produced baked goods.
- *Soy sauce* is produced by fermenting soy beans. Sometimes this is done in combination with wheat or rice. Soy sauce's flavor and color develop through the fermentation process and with the addition of brine. Check the ingredients on the bottle. If you find sugar, color, corn syrup, artificial seasonings and preservatives, you have an unnatural product.

Condiments and Seasonings
Amid a flood of prepared condiments, a few tried and true natural products can be used for seasoning food.
- *Ketchup* is a thick sauce made from tomatoes. Its sweet and sour flavor comes from sugar, vinegar, onions,

garlic, ginger, cloves and other spices. Always buy natural ketchup.
- *Tabasco* is a red liquid extract made from chili pods. It should be used in drops and will complement hot and spicy dishes and drinks.
- *Tomato paste* is a pure, unseasoned, spreadable tomato concentrate without seeds and skins.
- *Worcestershire sauce* is a brown liquid derived from mustard, vinegar, salt, pepper, sugar, ginger, cloves, tamarind and other spices.
- *Vegetable stock* figures prominently in vegetarian cooking. It often adds a well-seasoned taste. Vegetable stock powder, derived from yeast extracts, herbs and vegetable concentrates, is a substitute for the time-consuming homemade variety. Always shop for vegetable stock that does not contain chemical preservatives.
- *Yeast flakes* are available in the following varieties: engevita, brewer's and nutritional. Nutritional yeast flakes have the best flavor—like a mild cheese. Their high vitamin B content makes them valuable for the vegan diets and for people suffering from stress. *Important:* Do not cook yeast with the dish, but add it when serving.

Milk

Milk Demystified

Organically produced milk has a prominent place in some vegetarian diets. If you completely reject milk and other dairy products, you may have difficulty obtaining enough calcium. Dairy products can also provide an interesting twist to vegetarian cooking. Here are the valuable nutrients in milk:

- *Calcium* from milk contributes to healthy teeth and bones.
- *Lactose* is the carbohydrate component of milk. It is important for cheese production.
- *Milk fat* is easy to digest because of its fine distribution of tiny droplets and because it provides essential linoleic acid.
- *Milk protein* complements whole grains.
- *Vitamin A* is plentiful in milk. It is important for beautiful skin and healthy eyes.
- *Vitamin B_2*, the growth vitamin, plays an important role in metabolism.
- *Vitamin B_{12}* is important for forming red blood cells and is only available from animal-based foods (and vegetables marinated in lactic acid). For this reason, dairy products are important for vegetarians.

Milk Processing

- First, milk is homogenized. Fat droplets and protein are distributed evenly in the milk, so the cream separates and rises to the top. During this process, the fat content (3.5% for whole milk) is adjusted.
- During pasteurization, the milk is heated to about 160°F (70°C) for a few seconds to gently kill any germs.
- UHT milk, however, is quickly heated to ultra high temperatures without being exposed to air. It keeps, unopened, for three months.
- Unpasteurized milk has not been heated and contains all the valuable nutrients of raw milk. Because it may still contain unwanted or questionable components, laws pertaining to the sale of unpasteurized milk vary among countries. Proper storage is critical.
- You should always choose organically produced milk and milk products as these are the safest and healthiest sources.

Tip

Whole milk contains a large number of fat-soluble vitamins, and its calcium is particularly well absorbed. Use lower fat milk only if you need to lose weight.

Dairy Products for Better Health

As milk "sours" it becomes easier to digest and develops health-promoting qualities. Sour milk products may be tolerated by people who can otherwise not digest pure milk.

- *Buttermilk.* This is the liquid which is left behind during the manufacturing of butter. It is rich in protein and lecithin and low in calories.
- *Crème fraîche.* Thick tart cream.
- *Kefir.* A sour milk drink, produced by fermenting milk. Kefir is slightly carbonated and mildly alcoholic.
- *Sour cream.* A dairy product soured with bacteria; it contains 7–14% fat.
- *Whey.* This is the liquid which develops during cheese making. It hardly has any fat, but contains valuable protein.
- *Whipping cream.* The thick cream which has been skimmed off the milk, with a minimum of 30% fat.
- *Yogurt.* Milk inoculated with special yogurt cultures and incubated.

Cheese

Cheese: The Delicious Power Pack

Cheese is basically concentrated milk or, according to cheese regulations, "fresh products or products in different stages of maturation produced from coagulated milk." Therefore cheese contains high concentrations of all the healthy nutrients found in milk. Lactose is converted to lactic acid by bacteria or rennet, so there are hardly any carbohydrates left in cheese.

Cheese is particularly high in calcium, which is indispensable to bones and teeth.

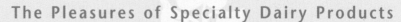

The Pleasures of Specialty Dairy Products

Recipes in this book feature two specialty dairy products you may not be familiar with:

- Quark is a traditional fresh cheese from Germany. It is quickly becoming popular in this country and can now be found in many health food stores and grocery stores. Depending on the recipe, you can usually substitute baking cheese for quark, or any of the following: cream cheese, ricotta, sour cream or tofu.

- Crème fraîche is a thick European-styled cream with a tart edge. Make your own by using one of the following methods. It is well worth the time. *Sour cream method:* Mix 1 cup (250 ml) heavy (whipping) cream with 1/2 to 1 cup (125–250 ml) sour cream. Let the mixture stand at room temperature, uncovered, for several hours (overnight is best). Cover when thick. It will keep for 1 week in the fridge. *Buttermilk method:* Mix 1 tbsp buttermilk into 1 cup (250 ml) heavy (whipping) cream. Let the mixture stand at room temperature, uncovered, for several hours (overnight is best). Cover when cream has thickened. The cream will keep in the fridge for 1–2 days.

Just 2 oz (60 g) of Swiss cheese will meet the daily calcium requirements of an adult woman. Cheese is an alternative for people who don't like milk or cannot tolerate it, but still need to get calcium in their diet. Eating too much cheese may have disadvantages.

- Cheese can be quite salty at times which is not good for people with high blood pressure. Luckily, more and more low-sodium varieties are becoming available.
- Some cheeses can be high in hidden fats. This is a critical consideration when an individual's overall fat consumption is already high.

How to Distinguish Different Varieties

The overwhelming variety of cheeses can be classified according to their water content. The hardest cheeses are comprised of the least amount of water—less than 57%, whereas the softest cheeses are made of more than 73% water. Here are the categories, listed according to hardness:

- *Fresh or unripened cheeses* from cow, sheep and goat's milk (e.g., quark, baking cheese, cream cheese and Ricotta).
- *Hard cheeses* (e.g., Parmesan, Romano and Asiago) may be stored for a long time and have a robust flavor.
- *Semi-hard or firm cheeses* (e.g., Cheddar, Gouda, Edam and Emmenthal) are somewhat milder and are suitable for sandwiches, salads and cooking.
- *Semi-soft cheeses* (e.g., Oka, Feta, Monterey Jack and Mozzarella) are softer still, and vary greatly in taste.
- *Soft cheeses* (e.g., Limburger, Camembert, Muenster, Brie and Roquefort) also vary greatly. Either they have been inoculated with molds, like Camembert, Brie and

Roquefort, or they have a moist surface and an intense aroma and flavor like Muenster and Limburger.

Cheese May Have Less Fat Than You Think

The fat content listed on dairy products produced in Canada refers to percentage by weight. You will find that most cheese is significantly lower in fat than luncheon meats (which usually contain 35% fat!). Some dairy products and their fat levels:

- Quark 0%
- Baking cheese 0.4%
- Dry-curd cottage cheese 0.4%
- Yogurt 0–5%
- Sour cream 7–14%
- Ricotta 14.5%
- Mozzarella (partially skimmed) 21.3%
- Feta 26%
- Gouda 29%
- Cream cheese 32%
- Whipping Cream 33%
- Cheddar averages about 34.5%

Eggs

About Eggs

Cholesterol has given eggs a bad name during recent years. This is a pity, because eggs provide several valuable nutrients. Only those who have an unbalanced fat metabolism need worry about cholesterol.

Egg white is almost 90% water. It contains hardly any fats or carbohydrates. It is rich in minerals like potassium, calcium, chlorine and sulfur. Sulfur is detectable in old eggs by its unpleasant smell.

Egg yolk is high in protein. One-third of the yolk consists of fats. These fats contain both cholesterol and lecithin which are needed for our general

metabolism and particularly in our neurological metabolism and the growth of cell membranes.

- The yolk's vitamin content is very high, especially in the fat-soluble vitamins A, D and E. The water-soluble vitamins B_1 and B_2 are also present, as are niacin, pantothenic acid and biotin.
- Eggs contain the minerals calcium, iron, phosphorus and sulfur. The high iron content (7.2 mg per 100 g) is notable and important to the vegetarian diet.
- An egg's valuable nutrients are readily available—up to 95% of the nutrients will be used by the body. Protein, lecithin, iron and the fat-soluble vitamins in eggs are a perfect complement to plant foods. Eggs combine with potatoes for an especially high-grade protein.

Storing Eggs Properly

- The cooler the better: 45°–50°F (7°–10°C) is the perfect temperature. Eggs will keep for up to four or five weeks in the fridge.
- Eggs breathe, so store them in a non-airtight container to keep them as fresh as possible.
- Eggs absorb odors, so never store them close to strong-smelling foods.

Checking for Freshness

- When broken, the fresh yolk is spherical and separates easily from the egg white. An old egg has a flat yolk and is slightly runny.
- When boiled, the yolk of a fresh egg is centered, away from the shell.
- A fresh egg will sink to the bottom of a 10% salt solution—an old egg will float.

The fresh egg sinks in a salt solution.

The old egg floats.

A fresh egg: the yolk is spherical.

An old egg: the yolk is flat.

MENU SUGGESTIONS

When guests are coming...

- Asian Vegetable Stir Fry 124
- Asparagus Quiche 172
- Cheese-Spinach Pie 160
- Cheese Terrine 195
- Chinese Fondue 205
- Beans and Tomatoes with
  Cheese Crust 115
- Millet Dumplings with Peppers 106
- Millet Pudding with Chive Sauce 107
- Pizza Rounds 170
- Potato Quiche 173
- Savory Asparagus-Spinach Pudding 159
- Savory Spelt Tart 175
- Squash Quiche 174
- Stuffed Pepper Slices 195
- Summer Raclette 207

Elegant full menu suggestions

- Artichokes with Tomato Sauce 42
- Eggplant Medley 45
- Rhubarb Cooler 189

- Salsa Verde 77
- Zucchini-Egg Roll 169
- Quark Dumplings with Cherry Sauce
  (1/2 recipe) 177

Classic European

- Herb Soup with Baked Custard 86
- Polenta-Mushroom Slices 103
- Stuffed Swiss Chard Rolls 119
- Tomato Sauce 72
- Quark-Fruit Dessert (1/2 recipe) 186

Mediterranean

- Crispy Moons with Tomato Sauce 106
- Delicately Marinated Vegetables 55
- Mediterranean Medley 129
- Saffron-Orange Risotto with
  Pea Pods 98
- Fresh fruit

Exotic

- Asian Vegetable Stir Fry 124
- Exotic Carrot Soup 86
- Spring Rolls 198
- French Provincial Melon-Rice Pudding
  (1/2 recipe) 186

Quick

- Bruschetta 52
- Cheese Carpaccio 49
- Fried Rice 101
- Fruit salad

Economical

- Chinese Vegetable Soup 82
- Creamed Pumpkin with Tortellini 132
- Quark Dumplings with
  Cherry Sauce 177

For fitness (menu #1)

- Spelt Quiche 105
- Wild Herb Salad with Nettle Gouda 55
- Yogurt Shake 190

For fitness (menu #2)

- Millet Dumplings with Peppers 106
- Sweet and Sour Zucchini Salad 63
- Quark-Fruit Dessert 186

Using supplies on hand

- Carrot Star 103
- Creamed Millet Soup with Peppers 87,
  (use a mild grating cheese and wheat
  semolina or wheat flour instead of
  millet flour)
- Apple Fritters with Cinnamon
  Sugar 181

For 2 servings (menu #1)

- Artichokes with Tomato Sauce 42
- Coconut-Rice Ring
  (in mini ring form) 99
- Kiwi Sour 189
- Quark-Fruit Dessert 186

For 2 servings (menu #2)

- Alfalfa Appetizer 44
- Basil "Spaetzle" with Gouda 164
- Ice cream

For 2 servings (menu #3)

- Mushroom Carpaccio 49
- Pan-fried Stuffed Eggs 156
- French Provincial Melon-Rice
  Pudding 186

For 2 servings (menu #4)

- Bruschetta 52
- Kohlrabi Medallions 121
- Marinated Zucchini 41
- Quark Dumplings with
  Cherry Sauce 177

Low in calories (menu #1)

- Delicately Marinated Vegetables 55
- Stuffed Zucchini 132
  (replace cream with milk)
- Chilled Cherry Sauce 187
  (without almonds and dumplings)

Low in calories (menu #2)

- Mushroom Consommé 88
- Puréed Potatoes 142
  (without sesame seeds)
- Steamed Vegetables with
  Parsley Sauce 123
- Fresh fruit

For spring

- Asparagus with Creamed Quark 41
- Fresh Spring Vegetables with Cheese 120
- Rhubarb Cooler 189
- Strawberries with ice cream

For summer

- Chilled Fruited Zucchini Soup 187
- Cheese in Carrot-Watercress Salad 62
- Tomato Lasagna 128

For fall

- Mushroom Carpaccio 49
- Wild Rice Pumpkin 85
- Kiwi Sour 189
- Apple Fritters with Cinnamon Sugar 181

In the chill of winter

- Corn Salad with Red Lentils and Egg 58
- Orange-Date Soufflé 183
- Exotic Punch 189

Entertaining at the barbecue

- Bulgur Salad 56
- Colorful Vegetables with Egg Dip 48
- Couscous Mix 57
- Dips 74–77
- Summer Pasta Salad with Light Vinaigrette 61
- Wild Herb Salad with Nettle Gouda 55
- Vegetarian barbecue recipes 208–211

Serving a cold buffet

(Quantities before the parentheses are for 10 servings; those enclosed in the parentheses are for 20 servings)

In the Spring

- Cheese in Carrot-Watercress Salad 62 2x (4x)
- Cream of Radish Soup 91 2x (4x)
- Crunchy Potato Salad 196 2x (4x)
- Fruit Clafouti 185 1x (2x)
- Marinated Zucchini 41 2x (4x)
- Olive-Tomato Dip 75 2x (3x)
- Stuffed Pepper Slices 195 2x (4x)
- Vegetable Terrine 46 1x

(when serving 20, add 1x Asparagus Quiche 172)

In the Spring/Summer

- Bruschetta 52 2x (4x)
- Cheese-Spinach Pie 160 1x (2x)
- Couscous Mix 57 2x (4x)
- Delicately Marinated Vegetables 55 2x (4x)
- Eggs in Aspic 157 1x (2x)
- Fruit Basket (when serving 20, add 2x Roasted Pepper and Avocado Salad 64)
- Pasta Shells with Avocado Stuffing 53 1x (when serving 20, use Apricot Quiche 174, instead)

In the Summer

- Bulgur Salad 56 2x (4x)
- Cheese Terrine 195 1x
- Chilled Cherry Sauce with Quark Dumplings 187 2x (4x) (when serving 20, add Herb Tortilla with Pepper Sauce 159)
- Colorful Vegetables with Egg Dip 48 2x (4x)
- Layered Salad 197 2x (4x)
- Pepper Boats 48 2x (4x)
- Summer Pasta Salad with Light Vinaigrette 61 2x (4x)
- Tomato Quiche 173 1x (2x) (with Pepper Sauce) 159

Serving a hot and cold buffet

In the Fall

- Cheese Ball Salad 59 1x (2x)
- Giant Stuffed Mushrooms 137 3x (5x)
- Millet Pudding with Chive Sauce 107 1x
- Mushroom Consommé 88 2x (4x)
- Pancake Tower 181 1x (when serving 20, add 2x Eggs in Sorrel Sauce 156)
- Salsa Verde 77 2x (4x)
- Spicy Bean Salad 66 2x (3x)

- Wild Rice Pumpkin 85 1x, Sorrel Sauce 156

In the Fall/Winter

- Avocado-Basil Dip 74 2x (4x)
- Exotic Carrot Soup 86 2x (4x)
- Fruity Radicchio Salad 58 2x (4x)
- Mustard Fruit 213 1x
- Orange-Date Soufflé 183 1x (when serving 20, add Savory Spelt Tart 175)
- Wild Rice-Pineapple Salad 56 2x (4x)
- Winter Pasta 47 1x
- Zucchini-Egg Roll 169 1x (2x)

In the Winter

- Black & White Pudding 178 1x
- Borscht 81 2x (4x)
- Corn Salad with Red Lentils and Egg 58 2x (4x)
- Creamy Nut Dip 77 2x (4x)

MENU SUGGESTIONS

- Mushroom Carpaccio 49 2x (4x)
- Orange-Endive Flower 59 2x (4x)
- Stuffed Potato Roll 148 1x (2x)

Serving finger food with wine

- Beet Rounds with Dip 43
- Bruschetta 52
- Cheese Terrine 195
- Curried Chickpea Fritters 117
- Muffins 12
- Pasta Shells with Avocado Stuffing 53
- Pizza Rounds 170
- Polenta-Vegetable Squares 52
- Potato Pancakes 169
- Sprout Pockets 198
- Spring Rolls 198
- Stuffed Pepper Slices 195
- Tomato with Wine Noodles 53

In a hurry

- Amaranth-Mushroom Fry 111
- Artichoke-Orange Cocktail 45
- Avocado-Basil Dip 74
- Cheese Ball Salad 59
- Cheese Carpaccio 49
- Cheese Polenta in Tomato Sauce 164
- Couscous with Ratatouille 109
- Cream of Radish Soup 91
- Creamy Potato Soup 83
- Italian Frittata 158
- "Kratzete" (Scratched Eggs) 155
- Leek Pasta with Three-cheese Sauce 166
- Pizza Potatoes 140
- Quark Dumplings with Cherry Sauce 177
- Tacos 51

- Tomato Risotto 98
- Tomato-Yogurt Salad 64

On a budget

- Apple Fritters with Cinnamon Sugar 181
- Apple-Potato Gratin 140
- Baked Apple-Nut Pancake 180
- Baked Strawberry Pudding 184
- Borscht 81
- Bruschetta 52
- Bulgur Pilaf 108
- Bulgur Salad 56
- Cabbage with Peppers 133
- Carrot Star 103
- Cheesy Rice Fritters 101
- Cherry Trifle 185
- Chili sans carne 114
- Chinese Fondue 205
- Chinese Vegetable Soup 82
- Colorful Vegetables with Egg Dip 48
- Corn Salad with Cream Cheese 66
- Couscous with Ratatouille 109
- Creamed Millet Soup with Peppers 87
- Creamy Potato Soup 83
- Crispy Moons with Tomato Sauce 106
- Crunchy Potato Salad 196
- Delicately Marinated Vegetables 55
- Essence of Beet Soup 88
- Fennel with Tomato Sauce 68
- Fruit-filled Buns 182
- Fruity Waldorf Salad 65
- Greek Potato Casserole 80
- Herbed Quark Soufflé 161
- Italian Frittata 158
- "Kratzete" (Scratched Eggs) 155
- Marinated Zucchini 41
- Mild Lentil Soup 83
- Millet Dumplings with Peppers 106
- Millet Omelet with Root Vegetables 154
- Muesli-Apple Buns 199
- Mushroom Consommé 88
- Noodle Nests au Gratin 97
- Pan-fried Potatoes 139
- Polenta-Mushroom Slices 103
- Polenta-Vegetable Squares 52
- Potato Goulash 145
- Potato Mousse with Zucchini 147
- Potato Pancakes 169
- Potato Patties 144
- Potato Quiche 173
- Quark Pancakes with

- Diced Peppers 161
- Quark Dumplings with Cherry Sauce 177
- Red Cabbage with Millet Gratin 135
- Red Lentil-stuffed Peppers 112
- Savoy Cabbage with Roast Chickpeas 85
- Spelt Dumplings 105
- Stuffed Beets 51
- Stuffed Cucumbers in Tomato Sauce 130
- Stuffed Kohlrabi with Green Sauce 123
- Stuffed Oven Potatoes 146
- Tomato Lasagna 128
- Tomato Risotto 98
- Tomato-Yogurt Salad 64
- Vegetable Bouillon with Sesame Spirals 89
- Vegetable Rolls 93
- Vegetable Soup with Cornmeal Dumplings 84
- Winter Pasta 47

Non-dairy and egg-free meals

- Artichoke-Orange Cocktail 45
- Asian Vegetable Stir Fry 124
- Barbecued Corn 209
- Bannock 209
- Bruschetta 52
- Bulgur Pilaf 108
- Chili sans carne 114
- Chinese Vegetable Soup 82
- Confetti Aspic 47
- Corn Salad with Red Lentils and Egg 58
- Couscous-Berry Mix 200
- Creole Rice 100
- Curried Squash 69
- Dal 112
- Delicately Marinated Vegetables 55
- Eggplant Medley 45
- Essence of Beet Soup 88
- Exotic Carrot Soup 86
- Fennel with Tomato Sauce 68
- Fresh Mint Peas 116
- Fried Rice 101
- Fruity-Spicy Adzuki Bean Soup 81
- Garlicky Carrots 211
- Gnocchi with Peppers 149
- Hearty Eggplant Slices 208
- Kohlrabi with Bay Leaves 211
- Marinated Zucchini 41
- Minestrone 79
- Muesli Bars 199
- Mushroom Carpaccio 49
- Mushroom Consommé 88

- Olive-Tomato Dip 75
- Pan-fried Bulgur 108
- Pasta Shells with Avocado Stuffing 53
- Pear-Mustard Dip 74
- Potato Goulash 145
  (replace clarified butter with oil)
- Saffron-Orange Risotto with
  Pea Pods 98
- Tacos 51
- Tofu Ragout with Chinese Cabbage 134
- Tomato Risotto 98
- Tomato Sauce 72
- Tomato-Tofu Kabobs 208
- Vegetable Bouillon with Sesame
  Spirals 89
- Vegetable Kabobs 130
- Wild Rice-Pineapple Salad 56

It needs to be easy

- Alfalfa Appetizer 44
- Artichokes with Tomato Sauce 42
- Asparagus with Creamed Quark 41
- Cheese Polenta in Tomato Sauce 164
- Cheese-Spinach Pie 160
- Couscous with Ratatouille 109
- Creole Rice 100
- Eggplant Medley 45
- Elegant Egg Terrine 153
- Greek Potato Casserole 80
- Oat Crêpes 155
- Pan-fried Bulgur 108
- Pepper Boats 48
- Polenta-Vegetable Squares 52
- Spelt Dumplings 105
- Spring Vegetables with
  Herbed Cheese Crust 162

Entertaining for brunch

(Bread basket, butter, different jams, honey, cheese platter)
- Apricot-Tomato Jam 222
- Asparagus Quiche 172
- Bruschetta 52
- Cheese-Spinach Pie 160
- Chocolate Spread 220
- Essence of Beet Soup 88
- Millet Pudding with Blueberries 178
- Muffins 12
- Orange-Endive Flower 59
- Pancake Tower 181
- Pepper Boats 48
- Pizza Rounds 170
- Quark-Fruit Dessert 186

- Raw Vegetables with Dips 74–77
- Shakes 190–191
- Squash Quiche 174
- Stuffed Pepper Slices 195
- Tomato Quiche 173
- Uncooked Berry Jam 222
- Zucchini-Almond Spread 220

Children are hungry

- Apple Fritters with
  Cinnamon Sugar 181
- Baked Apple-Nut Pancake 180
- Baked Fruit Salad 184
- Basil "Spaetzle" with Nettle Gouda 164
- Black & White Pudding 178
- Bouillon Potatoes 141
- Cheese Ball Salad 59
- Cheese Fondue 204
- Cheesy Rice Fritters 101
- Cherry Trifle 185
- Children's Raclette 206
- Creamy Potato Soup 83
- Fruit-filled Buns 182
- Grilled Brie Sandwiches 167
- Layered Salad 197
- Noodle Nests au Gratin 97
- Pancake Tower 181
- Polenta-Vegetable Squares 52
- Potato Pancakes 169
- Quark Dumplings with
  Cherry Sauce 177
- Quark Pancakes with Diced Peppers 161
- Rice Pudding with Raspberry Sauce 179
- Shakes 190–191
- Stuffed Pepper Slices 195
- Tomato Lasagna 128
- Tomato Sauce 72

Gift giving

- Apricot Chutney 217
- Apricot Quiche 174
- Apricot-Tomato Jam 222
- Berries in Spicy Syrup 213
- Carrot-Rhubarb Sauce 223
- Cherry-Pineapple Sauce 223
- Chocolate Spread 220
- Cucumber Relish 214
- Delicately Marinated Vegetables 55
- Mixed Pickles 216
- Muffins 12
- Mushroom Flavoring Sauce 214
- Mustard Fruit 213
- Olive Spread 218

- Onion Spread 221
- Peanut Butter 221
- Pesto 218
- Plum-Mango Chutney 217
- Plum Vinegar 219
- Potato Quiche 173
- Squash Quiche 174
- Tomato Ketchup 215
- Uncooked Berry Jam 222
- Vegetable Loaf 175
- Zucchini-Almond Spread 220

Planning a picnic

(In addition to mixed green salad)
- Bulgur Salad 56
- Cheese-Spinach Pie 160
- Cheesy Stuffed Tomatoes 197
- Colorful Vegetables with Egg Dip 48
- Confetti Aspic 47
- Couscous Mix 57
- Crunchy Potato Salad 196
- Dips 74–77
- Dressings 76
- Eggplant Rolls with Creamed Millet 50
- Fruit Clafouti 185
- Fruit-filled Buns 182
- Fruit Salad with Crispy Quinoa 201
- Layered Salad 197
- Pepper Boats 84
- Polenta-Vegetable Squares 52
- Quark-Fruit Dessert 186
- Ratatouille-Potato Salad 69
- Spicy Bean Salad 66
- Sprout Pockets 198
- Summer Pasta Salad with
  Light Vinaigrette 61
- Tomato-Yogurt Salad 64
- Vegetable Salad 62
- Vegetable Terrine 46
- Wild Rice-Pineapple Salad 56

The Recipes

Appetizers and Snacks

Asparagus with Creamed Quark

Ingredients for 2 servings:

1 lb (500 g) green asparagus
salt
1–2 tbsp lemon juice
2 egg whites
1 3/4 cup (200 g) quark
 (see page 32)
2 tbsp cream
1 bunch of mixed herbs
1 clove of garlic
some pistachios

Preparation time: 40 min
Calories per serving: 190
24 g protein, 5 g fat,
12 g carbohydrate

- Wash and clean the asparagus. Cook the stalks in a little boiling salted water for 20 minutes then drain. Drizzle lemon juice over the asparagus and let cool.

- Beat the egg whites until stiff. Blend the quark with the cream and salt.
- Wash and finely chop the herbs. Peel and mince the garlic. Fold the chopped herbs and garlic into the egg whites and then into the quark. Chop the pistachios and sprinkle them over the quark. Pour the dressing over the asparagus before serving.

Tip

Never soak asparagus. Wash the asparagus stalks under cold running water, shaking them gently to release sand from the tips. Be careful not to overcook asparagus. Place the asparagus in boiling water, stalks first, and then gently submerge the stalks to cook the tips.

Marinated Zucchini

Ingredients for 2 servings:

5 small zucchini
2 tbsp cold-pressed,
 extra-virgin olive oil
salt
1 clove of garlic
a few basil leaves
2 tsp lemon juice
pepper, freshly ground
oil for the aluminum foil

Preparation time: 20 min
Calories per serving: 190
8 g protein, 12 g fat,
12 g carbohydrate

- Preheat broiler. Wash and clean the zucchini and cut in half lengthwise. Sprinkle the cut surfaces lightly with olive oil and salt. Place the zucchini on lightly oiled aluminum foil (shiny side up) with the cut surfaces up.

- Brown for 6–8 minutes under the broiler, not too close to the element.
- In the meantime, peel and mince the garlic. Wash and finely chop the basil. Mix the garlic with basil, lemon juice and pepper then spread on the hot zucchini halves. Serve the zucchini warm or cold with wholegrain bread.

Tip

If you have an oven without a broiler, you can bake the zucchini on the highest rack at 450°F (230°C) for 4–5 minutes. For a smoother flavor, substitute balsamic vinegar for the lemon juice.

Artichokes with Tomato Sauce

Ingredients for 4 servings:

4 artichokes (about 1/2 lb
 (250 g) each)
1–2 tbsp lemon juice
1/2 cup (100 ml) vegetable stock
1 lb (500 g) ripe tomatoes
salt
2 tbsp tomato paste
pepper, freshly ground
1/2 cup (100 g) goat's-milk
 cream cheese
1 tbsp cold-pressed,
 extra-virgin olive oil
2 tsp capers

Preparation time: 40 min
Calories per serving: 240
6 g protein, 2 g fat,
11 g carbohydrate

- Wash the artichokes and cut the stems off just below the head. Cook the artichokes with the lemon juice and stock for 30 minutes. The artichokes are done when a leaf can be easily removed.
- Meanwhile, wash and prick the tomatoes and steam them over boiling water for 5 minutes. Peel and press them through a large-meshed sieve. Stir the thick juice into the stock, together with the tomato paste and pepper.
- Fold the cheese, oil and 1 tsp of the capers into the sauce and purée. Add salt and pepper to taste. Add the remaining capers to the tomato sauce and serve with warm or cooled artichokes.

Baked Vegetables with Amaranth Batter

Ingredients for 4 servings:

1/2 cup (120 g) amaranth
 (or substitute wholewheat flour)
salt
3 eggs
1/2 cup (120 g) yogurt
1 tsp caraway
1 tsp turmeric
pepper, freshly ground
1/3 lb (150 g) broccoli
1 red pepper
1/2 lb (250 g) small mushrooms
a few lemon slices
clarified butter for frying

Preparation time: 40 min
Calories per serving: 480
12 g protein, 37 g fat,
25 g carbohydrate

- Grind the amaranth to a fine, flour-like consistency. Mix it with a little salt, the eggs, the yogurt and the herbs until it forms a thick batter and let it sit for 15 minutes.
- Meanwhile, clean, wash and pat the vegetables dry. Separate the broccoli tops, cut the pepper into strips and leave the mushrooms whole.
- Heat the clarified butter to 325–375°F (160–190°C). (Bubbles should appear when a wooden spoon is placed in it.)
- Dip the vegetable pieces into the batter. Place the battered vegetables immediately into the hot clarified butter and cook until golden brown. Drain briefly on a paper towel. Serve hot with lemon slices.

Beet Rounds with Dip

Ingredients for 2 servings:

1/4 cup (30 g) walnuts
salt
pepper, freshly ground
2/3 cup (150 g) yogurt
1 tsp cold-pressed walnut oil
 (or substitute extra-virgin olive oil)
3 medium-large beets
1 egg
8 tbsp non-instant oats
clarified butter for frying

Preparation time: 45 min
Calories per serving: 480
16 g protein, 27 g fat,
41 g carbohydrate

- To make the dip, finely chop the walnuts and stir them into the yogurt. Stir in oil and season with salt and pepper.
- Peel the beets and cut into slices 1/2" (1 cm) thick. Cook the slices in a pot with a little salted water for 20 minutes then allow to cool.
- Beat the egg. Dip the beet slices in the egg one by one, then in the oats. Press the oats well into both sides.
- Heat a little clarified butter in a frying pan. Fry the beet slices until crisp on both sides then drain on a paper towel.

Variation

These rounds can also be made from other root vegetables. If you have a sweet tooth try baked apple slices or bananas. Creamed cottage cheese or raspberry sauce can be used as a dip.

Tip

Beets provide potassium. The greens can also be eaten— they are rich in vitamins A and C and potassium, and are a good source of iron and calcium.

Alfalfa Appetizer

Ingredients for 2 servings:

1/2 lb (250 g) alfalfa sprouts
2 oz (50 g) corn salad
2 pink grapefruit
1 bunch of radishes
1/4 cup (50 g) crème fraîche
 (see page 32)
4 tbsp milk
1–2 tsp tomato ketchup
Worcestershire sauce
salt
pepper, freshly ground

Preparation time: 30 min
Calories per serving: 240
9 g protein, 13 g fat,
30 g carbohydrate

- Rinse and dry the sprouts.
  Wash and clean the
  corn salad.
- Peel the grapefruit
  (including the white pith)
  with a sharp knife and

separate the segments. Leave
some segments whole for
decoration, cut the rest into
halves or thirds, depending
on their size.
- Wash, clean and thinly slice
  the radishes.
- Stir together the crème
  fraîche, milk and ketchup
  until smooth. Flavor with
  Worcestershire sauce, salt
  and pepper.
- Loosely mix the sprouts,
  corn salad, grapefruit pieces
  and radishes. Arrange them
  decoratively on two plates,
  add the dressing to the salad
  and garnish with the
  remaining grapefruit
  segments.

Variation

For a spicier appetizer, try a
mix of alfalfa and radish
sprouts.

Hearts of Palm Cocktail

Ingredients for 4 servings:

1 egg
1/2 lb (250 g) cherry tomatoes
1 small can of hearts of palm
half a lettuce
1 bunch of chives
salt
pepper, freshly ground
2 tbsp cold-pressed,
 extra-virgin olive oil
2 tbsp dry vermouth
 (or substitute vegetable stock)
4 good lettuce leaves for garnish

Preparation time: 30 min
Calories per serving: 120
3 g protein, 9 g fat,
2 g carbohydrate

- Hard boil the egg, rinse in
  cold water and allow to cool.
  Wash and halve the
  tomatoes. Reserve 4 halves

for the garnish. Drain the
hearts of palm, reserving the
liquid. Cut hearts of palm in
1/2" (1 cm) thick slices.
Wash the lettuce and cut
into thin strips. Wash and
chop the chives.
- Mix the tomatoes, hearts of
  palm slices and lettuce. Mix
  the hearts of palm liquid
  with salt, pepper, chopped
  chives, oil and vermouth
  then fold carefully into the
  salad.
- Line four bowls with one
  lettuce leaf each. Dish the
  salad into each bowl.
- Chop the egg white then
  press the yolk through a fine
  sieve. Cut the reserved
  tomato halves into quarters
  then distribute the yolks,
  whites and tomatoes over the
  salad.

Artichoke-Orange Cocktail

Ingredients for 4 servings:

1 bunch of rucola
1/4 lb (125 g) portulaca
2 oranges
1/2 lb (250 g) carrots
1 small jar artichoke hearts (about 5)
juice of 1/2 lemon
4 tbsp cold-pressed, extra-virgin olive oil (or substitute cold-pressed pumpkin seed or flax oil)
1/2 tsp hot mustard
salt

Preparation time: 20 min
Calories per serving: 240
73 g protein, 19 g fat,
16 g carbohydrate

- Wash and clean the rucola and portulaca. Tear the larger pieces of rucola into smaller pieces.
- Peel the oranges (including the white pith) with a sharp knife and separate into segments.
- Wash, peel and julienne the carrots. Remove the artichoke hearts from the liquid and cut them into thin slices.
- Mix the lemon juice, olive oil and mustard then add salt. Mix the rucola, portulaca, some of the orange pieces, grated carrots and some of the artichoke hearts with the dressing.
- Spread the remaining orange segments and artichoke hearts on the salad.

Tip
Watercress or corn salad can be used instead of rucola and portulaca.

Eggplant Medley

Ingredients for 4 servings:

1 3/4 lb (875 g) eggplants
1/2 lb (250 g) pitted green olives
1 lb (500 g) ripe tomatoes
4 tbsp lemon juice
salt
pepper, freshly ground
2 cloves of garlic
2 thick bunches of basil
2 tbsp cold-pressed, extra-virgin olive oil

Preparation time: 45 min
Calories per serving: 170
4 g protein, 11 g fat,
12 g carbohydrate

- Wash the eggplants, bake for 25–30 minutes in a preheated oven at 400°F (200°C) until blisters begin to form on the skin. Rinse under cold water, peel, remove stems and cut the flesh into small pieces.
- Thinly slice the olives. Blanch the tomatoes, then let sit for a minute. Remove the skins and cut the flesh (without seeds) into small pieces.
- Mix everything together and season with lemon juice, salt and pepper.
- Peel and finely chop the garlic. Wash the basil and cut the leaves into strips. Mix garlic, basil and oil with the salad. Serve with a wholewheat baguette.

Tip
By puréeing the eggplants and olives, the resulting paste makes a good dip for raw vegetables or boiled potatoes.
Instead of using olive oil, try hazelnut oil, walnut oil, flax oil or pumpkin seed oil. Each adds a distinct flavor to the recipe.

Vegetable Terrine

Ingredients for 4 molds or 8 cups:

4 eggs
1 bunch of fresh basil
2 avocados
1 lime
10 sheets agar-agar (vegetable gelatin)
1 1/4 cups (300 ml) cold
 vegetable stock
salt
soy sauce
pepper, freshly ground
1/4 lb (125 g) mild chili peppers
 (adjust to taste)
1/3 lb (150 g) freshly cooked
 asparagus
20 small cherry tomatoes

Preparation time: 20 min
(+6 hrs setting time)
Calories per mold: 360
14 g protein, 32 g fat,
8 g carbohydrate

- Hard boil the eggs, rinse in cold water and let cool. Wash the basil and remove the leaves.
- Remove the avocado from the peel with a spoon. Squeeze the lime. Purée the basil, avocado and lime juice.
- Prepare the agar-agar according to instructions and melt over low heat. Add the cold vegetable stock one spoonful at a time. Mix with the avocado purée and add salt, soy sauce and pepper.
- Clean the peppers and drain the asparagus. Cut the peppers and the asparagus into small pieces. Fold both into the avocado mixture.
- Line the molds or cups with plastic wrap. Spoon half of the mixture into the molds.
- Blanch the tomatoes, rinse in cold water and peel. Discard the skins and add the tomatoes to the mixture. Add the other half of the avocado mixture to the molds.
- Peel and slice the eggs. Arrange the egg slices on top of the molds. Serve with a vinaigrette (page 22).

Confetti Aspic

Ingredients for a regular loaf pan
or similar sized mold
(4 servings):

1 bunch of mixed fresh herbs
1 lemon
1/2 lb (250 g) carrots
1/2 lb (250 g) small zucchini
3/4 cup (150 ml) vegetable stock
seasoning salt
1 lb (500 g) tomatoes
1/2 cup (100 g) corn
12 sheets agar-agar
 (vegetable gelatin)

Preparation time: 1 hr
(+6 hours setting time)
Calories per serving: 110
9 g protein, 1 g fat,
16 g carbohydrate

- Wash the mixed herbs.
  Thinly slice the lemon then
  boil both in water for
  20 minutes. Pour the liquid
  through a sieve. Peel the

carrots, cook for 10 minutes
in the liquid and remove with
a slotted spoon. Wash and
clean the zucchini, cut into
small pieces, cook for
5 minutes in the liquid then
remove.
- Add the vegetable stock to
  the liquid, season well with
  salt then strain.
- Cut tomatoes into small pieces.
- Soften the agar-agar in cold
  water for about 10 minutes.
  Heat 1 cup of the liquid and
  dissolve the agar-agar in it
  then add the remaining
  liquid.
- Pour a layer of liquid into
  the baking dish and
  refrigerate until set. Add the
  vegetables then pour the rest
  of the liquid over them and
  refrigerate for about six
  hours. Serve with a herbed
  yogurt sauce.

Winter Pasta

Ingredients for a regular loaf pan
(4 servings):

1/2 lb (250 g) carrots
1/2 lb (250 g) broccoli
1 leek
6–8 large Savoy cabbage leaves
2 1/3 cups (600 ml) vegetable stock
1/2 cup (100 g) cornmeal
1/3 cup (100 g) cream
4 eggs
salt, freshly ground pepper
nutmeg, freshly grated
coconut oil or butter for the pan

Preparation time: 40 min
(+1 hr baking time)
Calories per serving: 240
13 g protein, 16 g fat,
9 g carbohydrate

- Preheat oven to 375°F
  (190°C). Lightly oil the
  baking dish.
- Wash the vegetables. Peel and
  cut the carrots in half

lengthwise. Cut the broccoli
into flowerets, peel the stalk
and cut it into strips. Chop
the leek.
- Bring 1 1/4 cups (300 ml)
  stock to a boil, cook the
  carrots for 5 minutes, add the
  broccoli and leek, cook for
  another 5 minutes, remove the
  vegetables. Top up the stock
  to 1 1/4 cups (300 ml).
- Blanch the cabbage leaves in
  the stock for 3 minutes.
- Top the stock up to 1 1/4
  cups (300 ml), add the
  cornmeal, bring to a boil
  then remove from heat and
  cool. Fold in the cream and
  eggs, season with the spices.
- Line the baking dish with
  some of the cabbage leaves.
  Add vegetables and corn.
  Cover with cabbage leaves,
  then with aluminum foil.
- Bake for 1 hour. Serve with a
  tomato sauce.

Pepper Boats

Ingredients for 4 servings:

1/2 cup (100 g) quark
  (see page 32)
1/2 cup plus 2 tbsp (150 g)
  extra-thick yogurt
1/4 cup (50 g) Feta cheese
salt, freshly ground pepper
1–2 tsp agar-agar flakes
  (vegetable gelatin)
1/4 cup (60 g) whipping cream
2 tbsp pine nuts
1 bunch of mixed herbs
  (e.g., chives, parsley, sorrel)
1 clove of garlic
1 tbsp cold-pressed, extra-virgin
  olive oil (or substitute cold-
  pressed pumpkin seed or flax oil)
1 yellow and 1 red pepper

Preparation time: 30 min
(+12 hrs setting time)
Calories per serving: 200
9 g protein, 15 g fat,
7 g carbohydrate

- Cream the quark with the
  yogurt and Feta cheese using
  a food processor then add
  salt and pepper. Dissolve the
  agar-agar in 2 tbsp water and
  heat until it melts. Mix with
  2 tbsp of the cheese mixture
  then add to the remainder of
  the mixture and refrigerate.
- Whip the cream until stiff.
  When the cheese mixture
  begins to set, fold in the
  cream. Coarsely chop the
  pine nuts. Wash the herbs,
  peel the garlic and mince
  both. Fold into the mixture
  with the oil.
- Wash and clean the peppers,
  fill with the mixture and let
  set in the refrigerator
  overnight. Cut into eighths
  with a wet knife.

Colorful Vegetables with Egg Dip

Ingredients for 3 servings:

1/3 lb (150 g) carrots
1 lb (500 g) small new potatoes
1/3 lb (150 g) asparagus (use
  white and green if available)
1/2 lb (250 g) sugar-snap peas
1 young kohlrabi
3 green onions
2 tbsp cold-pressed, extra-virgin
  olive oil
salt, freshly ground pepper
4 tbsp lemon juice
2 eggs
1/2 cup (125 g) quark
  (see page 32)
1 tsp mustard
1/2 bunch each of parsley,
  pimpernel and chives
3 tbsp whipped cream

Preparation time: 1 1/4 hrs
Calories per serving: 360
179 g protein, 13 g fat,
32 g carbohydrate

- Preheat oven to 375°F
  (190°C). Wash, clean and
  peel the vegetables. Peel the
  potatoes, if desired. Mix the
  oil with salt, pepper and
  lemon juice then toss with
  the potatoes, kohlrabi and
  carrots. Wrap the potatoes,
  kohlrabi and carrots in
  separate aluminum foil
  packages. Bake the potatoes
  and kohlrabi for 40–55
  minutes on the middle rack
  (test for doneness), carrots
  for 35 minutes.
- Blanch the peas and onions
  in simmering salted water for
  5 minutes. Boil the asparagus
  for 15 minutes.
- Soft boil the eggs. Purée
  them with quark and
  mustard when cooled. Wash
  and finely chop the herbs.
  Fold herbs, salt, pepper and
  cream into the dip.

Cheese Carpaccio

Ingredients for 4 servings:

1 small head of oak leaf lettuce
12 black olives
1 small jar of artichoke hearts
salt
pepper, freshly ground
1 tsp mild mustard
1 pinch caraway
1/3 lb (150 g) Parmesan, Asiago,
  or Pecorino cheese, sliced
  very thinly

Preparation time: 20 min
Calories per serving: 240
2 g protein, 9 g fat,
4 g carbohydrate

- Remove the leaves from the lettuce head and wash. Cut out the thick ribs (use the core elsewhere).
- Spread the lettuce leaves on four flat plates. Segment the olives and remove the pits.
- Drain the artichoke hearts and reserve the liquid. Halve the artichokes and cut into narrow segments.
- Prepare a seasoned marinade in a cup with the artichoke liquid, a little salt, pepper, mustard, caraway and olive oil.
- Place 1 tbsp marinade on the lettuce leaves. Place the cheese on the lettuce, scatter olives and artichokes then add the remaining marinade. Serve with a wholewheat baguette.

Variation

For a different look and flavor, use Belgian endive instead of the lettuce. Belgian endive has delicate, pale leaves and a mildly bitter taste.

Mushroom Carpaccio

Ingredients for 2 servings:

1/4 lb (125 g) brown mushrooms
1/4 lb (125 g) shiitake mushrooms
  (or substitute oyster mushrooms)
1 tsp lemon juice
2 bunches of cilantro
2 tsp balsamic vinegar
2 tbsp cold-pressed, extra-virgin
  olive oil
seasoning salt
pepper, freshly ground
1 pinch dried basil
1/2 tsp green peppercorns

Preparation time: 20 min
Calories per serving: 110
1 g protein, 8 g fat,
5 g carbohydrate

- Wipe the mushrooms with a dry cloth. Slice them thinly and sprinkle with a little lemon juice.
- Wash the cilantro, remove the leaves and chop.
- Prepare a marinade from the vinegar, oil, seasoning salt and basil.
- Place the mushroom slices decoratively on two plates and add the marinade. Scatter the peppercorns over the mushrooms and let the carpaccio sit for at least 15 minutes. Garnish with cilantro.

Tip

Substitute your favorite oils and vinegars. Whenever possible, choose cold-pressed, unrefined organic oils—they provide a rich source of nutrients that are needed for many body functions such as circulation, hormone production, cell division, brain development and immune response.

Eggplant Rolls with Creamed Millet

Ingredients for 14 rolls:

14 preserved vine leaves
1 large eggplant
salt
pepper, freshly ground
4 tbsp cold-pressed,
 extra-virgin olive oil
1 onion, chopped
1 clove of garlic, crushed
1/2 cup (100 g) millet
1 cup (500 ml) vegetable stock
1/2 cup (100 g) herbed cream cheese
1/4 lb (125 g) cherry tomatoes
1–2 tbsp balsamic vinegar
butter for greasing the baking sheet

Preparation time: 1 3/4 hrs
Calories per roll: 57
2 g protein, 3 g fat,
6 g carbohydrate

- Wash, drain and wipe dry the vine leaves. Wash the eggplant, cut in half crosswise, then cut lengthwise into slices about 1/2" (1 cm) thick. Salt the slices and let them "perspire" for 1 hour.
- Rub the salt and water from the eggplant slices with a paper towel then sprinkle with pepper and 3 tbsp olive oil. Brown them on a greased baking sheet under the broiler for about five minutes on each side.
- Sauté the onion and garlic in the remaining oil, add the millet and stock. Cook over low heat for 30 minutes and allow to cool. Fold the cream cheese into the millet and season to taste.
- Arrange the vine leaves side by side. Wash and halve the cherry tomatoes. Add some of the creamed millet to the eggplants and place two tomato halves on each. Roll the vine leaves, place upright and sprinkle with the vinegar. The eggplant rolls can be eaten lukewarm or cold.

Stuffed Beets

Ingredients for 2 servings:

2 large beets
1/4 cup (40 g) spelt
1 cup (250 ml) vegetable stock
salt
2 tbsp lemon juice
1/2 cup (75 g) smoked cheese
1 bunch of dill
4 tbsp sour cream
pepper, freshly ground

Preparation time: 1 1/4 hrs
Calories per serving: 290
16 g protein, 14 g fat,
26 g carbohydrate

- Wash and peel the beets. Cook the spelt in the vegetable stock over low heat for 50 minutes. Boil the beets in salted water for 50 minutes or until cooked. Remove the beets from the water with a slotted spoon.
- Allow the beets and the spelt to cool.
- Hollow out the beets and sprinkle them with lemon juice. Cut the cheese into tiny cubes. Wash the dill, shake dry and finely chop the tips. Stir the dill and some pepper into the sour cream. Mix with the spelt and cheese then fill the beets.
- Purée the beet flesh with the remaining sour cream, season with lemon juice, salt and pepper. Add to the stuffed beets.

Tip

For variety, try stuffing other root vegetables like yams and potatoes. Choose small vegetables to serve as an appetizer or a snack.

Tacos

Ingredients for 6 taco shells:

1/3 lb (150 g) corn salad
2 oz (50 g) iceberg lettuce
1 green pepper
1 large sour apple
1 tsp lemon juice
10 stuffed green olives
1 bunch of chives
2 tbsp grapeseed oil (you may substitute cold-pressed pumpkin seed, flax or extra-virgin olive oil)
2 tbsp raspberry vinegar (or substitute balsamic vinegar)
1/3 cup (75 ml) vegetable stock
salt
pepper, freshly ground
6 taco shells

Preparation time: 30 min
Calories per taco: 160
74 g protein, 4 g fat,
26 g carbohydrate

- Clean and wash the corn salad, iceberg lettuce and green pepper. Cut the iceberg lettuce into thin strips. Cut the green pepper into quarters and remove seeds and insides then slice into julienne strips. Wash and dry the apple, cut it into quarters and remove the core. Slice the apple quarters into thin strips and sprinkle with lemon juice.
- Slice the olives into rings. Wash and chop the chives. Mix the oil with the vinegar and the stock to make a dressing. Season with salt and pepper.
- Mix all salad ingredients carefully, then fold in the dressing. Serve the salad in the taco shells.

Bruschetta

Ingredients for 4 servings:

4 slices of rye bread
3–4 ripe tomatoes
some basil leaves
2 cloves of garlic
4–6 tbsp cold-pressed
 extra-virgin olive oil
salt, freshly ground pepper

Preparation time: 10 min
Calories per serving: 230
4 g protein, 13 g fat,
24 g carbohydrate

- Cut each slice in half. Toast the bread with some olive oil.
- Blanch the tomatoes and let them sit for a minute. Remove the skin and seeds and cut the tomato flesh into large pieces. Wash and finely chop the basil leaves and mix them with the tomatoes.
- Peel the garlic cloves and cut them in half.
- Rub the bread well with the garlic and sprinkle with olive oil. Place the tomatoes on the bread and press in gently. Lightly salt the bread and grind pepper over it. Bruschetta tastes good warm or cold.

Tip

A hearty, non-crumbly bread and very good, extra-virgin olive oil are important for bruschetta. Olives, cheese or slices of garlic can be placed on the bread.

Variation

Pesto (p. 218) can be spread on bread and topped with tomatoes and a light drizzle of oil for a spicier bruschetta.

Polenta-Vegetable Squares

Ingredients for 3 servings:

1 cup (125 g) cornmeal
1/3 cup (100 g) sour cream
1 cup (250 ml) vegetable stock
1 carrot
1/4 lb (125 g) broccoli
1 small red pepper
1 tsp butter
2 tbsp Parmesan cheese,
 freshly grated
2 eggs
salt, freshly ground white pepper
paprika
butter for the baking pan

Preparation time: 45 min
Calories per serving: 480
21 g protein, 19 g fat,
55 g carbohydrate

- Mix the cornmeal with the sour cream and the vegetable stock and bring to a boil, stirring continuously. Simmer for 15 minutes over low heat, stirring only occasionally.
- Grease a small baking pan. Preheat oven to 325°F (160°C). Wash and clean the carrots, broccoli and pepper. Grate the carrot. Chop the broccoli into pieces as large as the carrot gratings. Cut the pepper into small pieces.
- Heat the butter and sauté the vegetables for 2–3 minutes. Mix the vegetables, Parmesan cheese and eggs into the cornmeal and season to taste with salt, pepper and paprika. Spread the cornmeal in the baking pan and bake for 15 minutes on the middle rack.
- Leave the polenta in the pan for a short time, then cut into squares and serve.

Tomatoes with Wine Noodles

Ingredients for 4 servings:

8 medium-sized vine-ripened
 tomatoes
salt
3/4 cup (200 ml) dry white wine
1/4 cup (45 g) orzo
2 tsp cold-pressed, extra-virgin
 olive oil (or substitute cold-
 pressed pumpkin seed or flax oil)
white pepper, freshly ground
a few stalks of chervil
2 tbsp Cheddar cheese
 (or any strong hard cheese)

Preparation time: 20 min
Calories per serving: 130
4 g protein, 4 g fat,
12 g carbohydrate

- Wash the tomatoes, cut off
 tops to make a small lid and
 hollow them out. Lightly salt
 the inside of the tomato.

Turn tomatoes upside down
to drain.
- Bring the wine to a boil with
 a little salt. Add the noodles
 and boil for 5 minutes or
 until *al dente* (cooked but
 firm). Drain, mix with olive
 oil and pepper and let cool.
- Wash the chervil and remove
 the leaves from the stalks.
 Save some leaves for
 decoration and coarsely chop
 the remaining leaves. Grate
 the cheese and stir into the
 noodles with the chopped
 chervil. Season and fill the
 tomatoes with the mixture.
- Place a lid on each tomato
 and decorate with chervil.

Tip
This appetizer retains the flavor
of the wine but the alcohol
evaporates during cooking.

Pasta Shells with Avocado Stuffing

Ingredients for 4 servings:

8 large pasta shells
salt
1 lime
1 shallot
1 bunch of parsley or cilantro
1 avocado
pepper, freshly ground

Preparation time: 30 min
Calories per serving: 260
7 g protein, 13 g fat,
28 g carbohydrate

- Cook the noodles until they
 are *al dente* (cooked but
 firm), rinse with cold water
 then drain.
- Squeeze the juice of half a
 lime over the noodles. Peel
 and finely chop the shallot.
 Wash the herbs and remove
 the stems.

- Set aside half of the leaves
 and chop the remainder. Peel
 the avocado and remove the
 pit. Cut into small pieces.
 Squeeze the juice from the
 remaining half lime and mix
 it immediately with the
 shallots and herbs. Season
 with salt and pepper.
- Fill the noodles with the
 mixture and garnish with the
 remaining herbs.

Tip
This finger food is a well-
suited accompaniment to an
aperitif. The avocado contains
vegetable fat and is very mild,
slowing the absorption of
alcohol by the blood.

Variation
Red or green noodles make an
attractive and tasty alternative
to regular pasta.

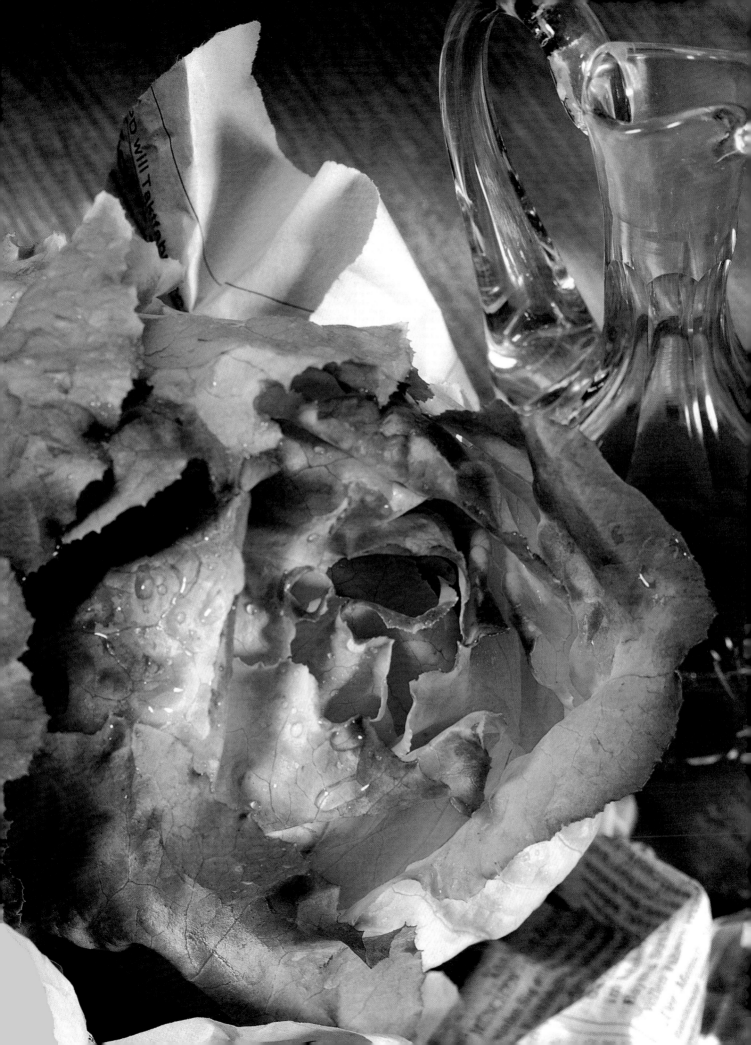

Salads

Delicately Marinated Vegetables

Ingredients for a 10 cup
(2.5 l) stoneware pot:

2 lb (1 kg) small mushrooms
3 lemons
2 cloves of garlic
2 tsp salt
6 peppercorns
2 bay leaves
2 sprigs of thyme
2 tbsp cold-pressed,
  extra-virgin olive oil
1/2 lb (250 g) carrots
1 leek

Preparation time: 1 hr
Calories: 400
24 g protein, 16 g fat,
44 g carbohydrate

- Wipe and dry-scrub the mushrooms. Squeeze the lemons. Peel and press the garlic.

- Bring the lemon juice, garlic, 1 3/4 cups (400 ml) water, salt, peppercorns, bay leaves, thyme and olive oil to a boil.
- Add a quarter of the mushrooms to the liquid, return to the boil then remove them with a slotted spoon. Repeat with the remaining mushrooms. Clean the carrots and cut them into 1/2" (1 cm) thick slices. Cook for 5 minutes in the liquid.
- Clean the leek and cut it into slices 1/2" (1 cm) thick.
- Remove the carrots with a slotted spoon and return the liquid to a boil. Boil the leek in the liquid for 5 minutes. Place the vegetables in the stoneware pot and pour the liquid over them. These vegetables will keep for about 2 weeks when covered and stored in a cool place.

Wild Herb Salad with Nettle Gouda

Ingredients for 4 servings:

2 oz (50 g) sorrel
1/4 lb (125 g) dandelion leaves
  (clean them before weighing)
1 bunch of radishes
1 kohlrabi with leaves still attached
2 tbsp fruit vinegar
2 tbsp cold-pressed,
  extra-virgin olive oil
3 tbsp vegetable stock
pepper, freshly ground
salt
Worcestershire sauce
4 tbsp sunflower seeds
1/3 lb (150 g) nettle Gouda
  (or substitute medium Gouda)
Daisies for decoration

Preparation time: 45 min
Calories per serving: 260
15 g protein, 20 g fat,
7 g carbohydrate

- Wash, clean and drain the sorrel. Wash and clean the dandelions and cut into bite-sized pieces. Wash, clean and slice the radishes. Peel and coarsely grate the kohlrabi. Wash the soft kohlrabi leaves, chop them finely and set aside.
- Mix the vinegar, oil and vegetable stock to make a dressing and season with pepper, salt and a few drops of Worcestershire sauce. Add the kohlrabi leaves.
- Carefully mix the salad ingredients and toss with the dressing. Dry roast the sunflower seeds, allow them to cool slightly and sprinkle them over the salad. Grate the Gouda coarsely and scatter on the salad. Garnish with the daisies.

Bulgur Salad

Ingredients for 4 servings:

1 clove of garlic
1/4 cup (250 g) bulgur
salt
1 small eggplant
4 tbsp cold-pressed,
 extra-virgin, olive oil
1/2 lb (250 g) small zucchini
1 shallot
10 black olives
1 bunch of fresh basil
Mediterranean dressing
 (recipe page 76)
2 eggs

Preparation time: 40 min
Calories per serving: 400
7 g protein, 16 g fat,
4 g carbohydrate

• Peel and mince the garlic.
 Place the bulgur and garlic in
 2 cups (500 ml) boiling
 water, add 1 tsp salt and cook

over low heat for 5–10
minutes, then allow to cool.
• Slice the eggplant, salt the
 slices and allow to "perspire"
 for 10 minutes. Dry the
 eggplant slices with paper
 towels. Heat the oil in a pan
 and cook the eggplant slices
 on both sides until they are
 crisp. Drain on paper towels.
• Wash and clean the zucchini.
 Cut the zucchini and
 eggplant into medium-sized
 pieces. Peel and finely chop
 the shallot. Quarter and pit
 the olives. Wash the basil
 and cut into strips.
• Mix all ingredients then add
 the Mediterranean dressing.
 Hard boil the eggs for
 8 minutes, rinse in cold
 water then peel, halve and
 place them on the salad.

Wild Rice-Pineapple Salad

Ingredients for 2 servings:

1/2 cup (100 g) wild rice
1 3/4 cups (400 ml) vegetable
 stock
1/2 pineapple
1/2 lb (250 g) sauerkraut
1 small radicchio
1 tbsp pumpkin seeds
1 tbsp lemon juice
2 tsp mild mustard
2 tbsp nut or seed oil (e.g., cold-
 pressed walnut oil or flax oil)
salt
pepper, freshly ground

Preparation time: 1 1/4 hr
Calories per serving: 190
6 g protein, 6 g fat,
26 g carbohydrate

• Cook the rice in the
 vegetable stock over low heat
 for 50 minutes.

• Remove the fruit from the
 pineapple and reserve the
 juice. Cut the fruit into
 small pieces.
• Finely chop the sauerkraut.
 Wash, clean and drain the
 radicchio. Reserve 4 good
 leaves and cut the remainder
 into very fine strips.
• Dry roast the pumpkin seeds
 until they turn light brown.
 Mix the rice, pineapple,
 sauerkraut and shredded
 radicchio.
• Blend the pineapple juice,
 lemon juice, mustard, oil,
 salt and pepper for the
 dressing.
• Mix the salad and dressing.
 Place the radicchio leaves on
 two plates, add the salad and
 the roasted pumpkin seeds.

Couscous Mix

Ingredients for 4 servings:

4 tbsp lemon juice
1 cup (200 g) couscous
1 2/3 cups (375 ml) whey
 (from the health food store, or
 substitute buttermilk)
5 tbsp cold-pressed, extra-virgin
 olive oil (or substitute cold-pressed
 pumpkin seed or flax oil)
salt, freshly ground pepper
1 clove of garlic
1 bunch of parsley
1 bunch of cilantro (optional)
2/3 lb (300 g) zucchini
1 red pepper
2/3 lb (300 g) tomatoes
1 bunch of green onions
1/2 lb (250 g) dry Ricotta cheese
 (or substitute Feta)

Preparation time: 30 min
Calories per serving: 450
17 g protein, 22 g fat,
47 g carbohydrate

- Place the lemon juice in a bowl
  with the couscous, oil, salt,
  pepper and half of the whey.
  Let sit for 15–20 minutes.
- Peel and mince the garlic.
  Wash and coarsely chop the
  parsley and cilantro.
- Wash the vegetables. Clean the
  zucchini and cut into small
  pieces. Halve the red pepper,
  remove the stem and seeds then
  chop into small pieces. Slice the
  tomatoes into thin wedges.
  Chop the onions into small
  segments.
- Fold all vegetables into the
  couscous, crumble the cheese
  over it and arrange the salad in
  a bowl.
- Add the remaining whey just
  before serving.

Tip

Whey and olives contain lactic
acid; garlic and onions contain
antibacterial compounds, and red
pepper and tomatoes are full of
beta-carotene. This salad has a
stimulative effect and helps the
body ward off bacterial infections.

Fruity Radicchio Salad

Ingredients for 4 servings:

1/3 lb (150 g) blue cheese
2 oranges
1 small radicchio
1 red onion
3 celery stalks
1 clove of garlic
3 tbsp cold-pressed, extra-virgin
  olive oil (or substitute cold-
  pressed pumpkin seed or flax oil)
4–5 tbsp lemon juice
salt
pepper, freshly ground
1 pinch paprika
1 pinch ginger powder
2 tbsp sesame seeds
  (or substitute sunflower seeds)

Preparation time: 1 1/4 hr
Calories per serving: 220
11 g protein, 14 g fat,
12 g carbohydrate

- Cut the cheese into small cubes. Peel and quarter the oranges, cut the quarters into thin slices and save all the juice. Wash the radicchio and cut into fine strips. Peel the onions and slice into rings. Wash and thinly slice the celery. Peel and mince the garlic.
- Prepare a marinade from the oil, lemon and orange juice, garlic and herbs.
- Carefully mix all ingredients except for the radicchio and the marinade. Cover and leave in the fridge for at least 1 hour.
- Dry roast the sesame seeds. Before serving, toss the radicchio with the salad and scatter the sesame seeds over it.

Tip
Radicchio is an excellent source of vitamins A and C.

Corn Salad with Red Lentils and Egg

Ingredients for 2 servings:

2 eggs
1/2 cup (100 g) red lentils
1 1/4 cups (300 ml) vegetable
  stock
4 slices of bread for toasting
1/4 lb (125 g) corn salad
1 sprig of basil
2 tbsp red wine vinegar
2 tsp cold-pressed, extra-virgin
  olive oil (or substitute pumpkin
  seed or flax oil)
salt
pepper, freshly ground
2 tbsp butter
2 tbsp black sesame seeds
1 small tart apple
  (e.g., Granny Smith)

Preparation time: 30 min
Calories per serving: 640
26 g protein, 36 g fat,
54 g carbohydrate

- Hard boil the eggs, peel them and set them aside. Simmer the lentils in the vegetable stock over low heat for 6 minutes. Toast the bread.
- Wash and clean the corn salad and shake it dry. Wash and finely chop the basil. Place the lentils in a sieve—save the liquid and mix it with vinegar, oil, salt, pepper and basil to make a dressing.
- Butter the toast and spread it with sesame seeds. Cut into small squares.
- Peel, core and cut the apple into matchstick-sized pieces. Mix the apple with the corn salad, lentils and dressing and place on a plate. Garnish the salad with the toast squares and the egg.

Cheese Ball Salad

Ingredients for 4 servings:

1/2 lb (250 g) Roma tomatoes
2/3 lb (300 g) Mozzarella
1/2 iceberg lettuce
1 bunch of fresh basil
1/2 cup (115 g) sour cream
  (or substitute yogurt)
2 tbsp cold-pressed,
  extra-virgin olive oil
1 tbsp cold-pressed, unrefined
  pumpkin seed or flax oil
4 tbsp lemon juice
salt
pepper, freshly ground

Preparation time: 30 min
Calories per serving: 260
16 g protein, 19 fat,
5 g carbohydrate

- Wash the tomatoes and remove the stems. Slice the tomatoes and layer them in a bowl.
- Cut the Mozzarella into bite-sized chunks. Place over the tomatoes.
- Tear the iceberg lettuce into bite-sized pieces then wash and drain them thoroughly. Place the lettuce on the cheese.
- Wash the basil, remove leaves from the stems and chop finely. Whisk the sour cream with basil, oils, lemon juice and herbs. Pour the dressing over the salad.

Variation

For a more piquant salad, try a stronger cheese like Emmenthal or Gruyère. Or, crumble small amounts of Feta or blue cheese over the tomatoes.

Orange-Endive Flower

Ingredients for 2 servings:

1 Belgian endive
2–3 oranges
1 bunch of chives
1/4 cup (50 g) yogurt
seasoning salt
pepper, freshly ground
2 tbsp chopped pistachios

Preparation time: 20 min
Calories per serving: 210
8 g protein, 8 g fat,
28 g carbohydrate

- Remove leaves from the endive and wash.
- Peel the oranges and separate the segments. Reserve the juice.
- Wash and chop the chives.
- Squeeze some orange juice into the yogurt, add chives, season with salt and pepper.

- Drain the endive leaves well and arrange on two plates in the shape of a star.
- Distribute the orange segments between the endive leaves and sprinkle the sauce over the salad. Scatter the remaining chives and the pistachios on the salad.

Tip

Belgian endive has acid-binding and diuretic effects. Both the endive and the oranges provide plenty of vitamin C and fiber.

Variation

Mix a salad of Belgian endive, apple or beet, and carrot for a tasty and visually appealing alternative.

Buckwheat Salad with Lemon Sauce

Ingredients for 4 servings:

1 cup (200 g) buckwheat
salt, freshly ground pepper
1/2 lb (250 g) cherry tomatoes
1/3 cup (80 g) firm Brie or
 Camembert cheese
1 head of green leaf lettuce
1 kohlrabi
1 small onion
1 clove of garlic
1 bunch of fresh basil
2 tbsp lemon juice
2 tbsp cold-pressed walnut oil
1 tsp yeast flakes
some vegetable stock
seasoning salt

For the lemon sauce:
peel and juice of 1/2 lemon
salt, freshly ground pepper
1 tbsp sour cream
2 tsp horseradish blended with cream
 (adjust to taste)
1/2 cup (125 g) whipping cream

Preparation time: 45 min
Calories per serving: 430
14 g protein, 20 g fat,
46 g carbohydrate

- Cover buckwheat with water and boil for 2 minutes. Drain the buckwheat and rinse in cold water. Cook the buckwheat again in 1 3/4 cups (400 ml) salted water for 15 minutes. Drain, rinse in cold water and let cool.
- Wash and halve the tomatoes. Cut the cheese into small chunks. Clean and pat dry the lettuce. Arrange on four plates. Peel and coarsely grate the kohlrabi. Mix it with the tomatoes, remaining lettuce, cheese and buckwheat.
- Peel and mince the onion and garlic. Wash and finely chop the basil. Stir the lemon juice with 3 tbsp water, oil, yeast, onion, garlic, vegetable stock, salt, pepper and basil. Toss salad with the marinade and arrange on the plates. Mix the ingredients for the lemon sauce, pour over the salad and serve.

Summer Pasta Salad with Light Vinaigrette

Ingredients for 4 servings:

1/3 lb (150 g) bow noodles
salt
1/2 lb (250 g) young spinach
   leaves
2/3 lb (300 g) small zucchini
1 bunch of fresh basil
1 clove of garlic
12 pitted green olives
1/2 cup (100 ml) vegetable stock
3 tbsp lemon juice
pepper, freshly ground
3 tbsp grated Parmesan cheese

Preparation time: 30 min
Calories per serving: 200
10 g protein, 5 g fat,
29 g carbohydrate

- Cook the noodles until *al dente* (cooked but firm) in salted water. Rinse in cold water and drain.
- Wash the spinach and zucchini. Sort the spinach and remove any hard stalks. Clean and thinly slice the zucchini. Wash the basil and remove the leaves. Peel and coarsely chop the garlic.
- Purée the basil leaves in a blender with the garlic, olives, stock and lemon juice to make a dressing. Season well with salt and pepper.
- Carefully mix all prepared ingredients, toss with the dressing and garnish with the Parmesan cheese.

Tip

Vary the color and shape of the pasta for a festive meal or to appeal to children.

Quinoa with Radishes

Ingredients for 4 servings:

1 1/4 cup (250 g) quinoa
   (or substitute millet or couscous)
3 1/2 tbsp cold-pressed,
   extra-virgin olive oil
4 tbsp lemon juice
salt
2 bunches of radishes
2/3 cup (150 g) Ricotta
2 bunches of chives
3 cloves of garlic
1 large cucumber
1/2 cup (125 ml) vegetable stock
2 tbsp fresh mint in strips
   (or substitute lemon balm)
white pepper, freshly ground

Preparation time: 30 min
Calories per serving: 400
15 g protein, 16 g fat,
51 g carbohydrate

- Sauté the quinoa in 1/2 tbsp olive oil. Add 1 tbsp of the lemon juice to 1 3/4 cups (400 ml) water and pour over the quinoa. Add 1 tsp salt and bring to a boil. Boil the quinoa for 15 minutes, then allow to cool uncovered.
- Meanwhile, clean, wash and quarter the radishes. Break the cheese into chunks. Wash and chop the chives. Peel and mince the garlic. Wash the cucumber, halve it lengthwise and grate.
- Loosely mix all ingredients. Mix the remaining lemon juice with the stock, the remaining oil, mint, salt and pepper. Fold in and season.

Tip

Radishes, with their mustardy flavor, are a source of potassium and vitamin C.

Vegetable Salad

Ingredients for 4 servings:

1 lb (500 g) broccoli
salt
1 lb (500 g) Roma tomatoes
3 sprigs each of basil and thyme
1 bunch of parsley
2 hard-boiled eggs
2/3 cup (150 g) crème fraîche
  (see page 32) or yogurt
3 tbsp lemon juice
pepper, freshly ground

Preparation time: 30 min
Calories per serving: 230
9 g protein, 19 fat,
8 g carbohydrate

- Wash the broccoli and separate into flowerets. Blanch the flowerets in a little salted water for 3 minutes, drain well and save the water.

- Wash and dry the tomatoes, remove the stems and slice.
- Wash the herbs and remove the leaves from the stems. Reserve some of the herbs for decoration and finely chop the rest.
- Purée the eggs with the crème fraîche and the lemon juice then blend with some of the liquid from the broccoli. Add the herbs and season to taste.
- Layer the broccoli flowerets and the tomato slices, adding a little of the creamed herb sauce between each layer.
- Pour the remaining sauce on the salad and decorate with herbs.

Variation
Add fresh, chopped carrots for a crunchier, more colorful salad.

Cheese in Carrot-Watercress Salad

Ingredients for 4 servings:

3 tsp chopped pine nuts
3 tbsp lemon juice
2 tbsp cold-pressed nut or seed oil
1/3 cup (80 ml) dry cider
  (or substitute apple juice)
2 tbsp mild mustard
seasoning salt
2/3 lb (300 g) carrots
1 tart apple
1/2 lb (250 g) watercress
2 bunches of chives
2/3 lb (300 g) mini Mozzarella balls
  (available from specialty
  delicatessens, or substitute
  Mozzarella chunks)

Preparation time: 20 min
Calories per serving: 330
18 g protein, 20 g fat,
14 g carbohydrate

- Dry roast the pine nuts. Set aside to cool.
- Mix the lemon juice, oil, cider, mustard and seasoning salt to make a dressing.
- Wash, peel and grate the carrots. Wash, quarter, core and grate the apple.
- Mix the grated carrot and apple with half of the dressing.
- Wash, clean and shake the watercress dry and mix with the remaining dressing.
- Place the carrots in the middle of four plates and arrange the watercress in a ring around them.
- Wash the chives and cut into sections. Roll the Mozzarella balls in the chives. Distribute the cheese balls on top of the salad.

Red Cabbage Salad

Ingredients for 4 servings:

1 lb (500 g) red cabbage
  (about 1/2 a head)
3 tbsp lemon juice
1 tbsp cold-pressed pumpkin seed
  oil (or substitute cold-pressed flax
  oil or extra-virgin olive oil)
salt
pepper, freshly ground
3 oranges
1/4 cup (50 g) buckwheat grains
1/3 cup (100 g) whipping cream
2 tbsp sour cream
1–2 tsp mild mustard

Preparation time: 45 min
Calories per serving: 220
5 g protein, 12 g fat,
25 g carbohydrate

- Wash the cabbage, cut it into thin strips then steam for 15 minutes.
- Drain the cabbage and save the liquid. Mix 4 tbsp of the steaming liquid with 2 tbsp lemon juice, oil, salt and pepper. Add this mixture to the red cabbage and leave to cool.
- Peel and quarter the oranges, cut the sections into thin slices. Squeeze the juice from two segments into a cup and set aside.
- Roast the buckwheat in a pan then let it cool. Whip the cream until semi-stiff, add the sour cream and the mustard, season with the remaining lemon and orange juice, salt and pepper.
- Mix the cabbage with the remaining orange pieces. Pour the dressing over the salad and garnish with buckwheat grains.

Sweet and Sour Zucchini Salad

Ingredients for 4 servings:

1 lb (500 g) small zucchini
1/2 pineapple
1/4 lb (125 g) sauerkraut
  (from the health food store)
1 bunch of dill
1 1/3 cups (300 g) sour cream
seasoning salt
white pepper, freshly ground

Preparation time: 30 min
Calories per serving: 180
6 g protein, 8 g fat,
20 g carbohydrate

- Clean and dry the zucchini. Slice the zucchini into julienne strips.
- Peel the pineapple and cut out the hard core. Cut the fruit into strips. Save the juice.
- Cut the sauerkraut into small pieces across the fibers. Wash the dill, remove the tips and chop them.
- Mix the sour cream with the dill and pineapple juice until blended, season with salt and pepper. Mix the zucchini, pineapple and sauerkraut with the dressing.

Tip

Sauerkraut from the health food store is particularly mild and digestible. Regular canned sauerkraut is generally much more sour, so rinse it thoroughly with cold water and drain it before use.

Tomato-Yogurt Salad

Ingredients for 2 servings:

1 clove of garlic
1 lb (500 g) small tomatoes
2 sprigs of basil
1 cup (200 g) yogurt
1/2 cup (100 g) Ricotta
1/2 cup (100 g) quark
 (see page 32)
salt
pepper, freshly ground

Preparation time: 20 min
Calories per serving: 260
20 g protein, 15 g fat,
15 g carbohydrate

- Halve the garlic clove and
  rub it on the inside of a
  salad bowl. Wash the
  tomatoes, cut it into
  quarters or eighths, removing
  the stems. Wash the basil
  and remove the leaves. Halve
  the larger leaves.

- Purée the yogurt with the
  Ricotta and quark, season
  well with salt and pepper and
  place in the salad bowl.
- Arrange the tomatoes around
  the yogurt in a star shape
  with the basil leaves between.

Tip

This basic recipe can be varied
in many ways. It tastes
delicious with radishes,
peppers, celery, cucumber or
zucchini, broccoli or fresh
lettuce. The salad is more
filling with cold cooked pulses
like chickpeas or red beans, or
with cooked grains like quinoa,
rice or millet. The salad is even
more nutritious and tasty when
garnished with 1–2 tbsp cold-
pressed walnut oil, flax oil or
pumpkin seed oil and chopped
nuts.

Roasted Pepper and Avocado Salad

Ingredients for 4 servings:

3 red peppers
1 tbsp cold-pressed,
 extra-virgin olive oil
salt, freshly ground pepper
1/2 cup (125 g) dry Ricotta
2 tbsp (25 g) herbed cream cheese
2 sprigs of thyme
2 cloves of garlic
3 tbsp lemon juice
3 tbsp cold-pressed, extra-virgin
 olive oil (or substitute cold-
 pressed pumpkin seed or flax oil)
2 avocados
1/2 lb (250 g) yellow or red
 cherry tomatoes

Preparation time: 1 hr
Calories per serving: 360
9 g protein, 31 g fat,
11 g carbohydrate

- Brush the peppers with olive
  oil and broil them on all

sides until the skins turn
black. Salt the peppers, cover
them with a wet towel, skin
them and cut the flesh into
long strips. Arrange them on
a plate.
- Blend the Ricotta with the
  cream cheese, salt and pepper.
  Cut into 4–6 portions and
  shape them into balls.
- Wash the thyme and remove
  the leaves. Peel and mince the
  garlic. Mix 2 tbsp lemon juice
  with salt, pepper, thyme,
  garlic and olive oil to make a
  marinade.
- Halve the avocados and cut
  the flesh into narrow
  segments. Arrange the
  avocados among the peppers
  then drizzle the remaining
  lemon juice over top.
- Clean, wash and halve the
  cherry tomatoes. Arrange
  them on the plate and pour
  the marinade over the salad.
  Place cheese balls on top.

Fruity Waldorf Salad

Ingredients for 4 servings:

1/2 lb (250 g) red grapes
 (seedless if possible)
1/3 lb (150 g) seedless white
 grapes
1 orange
1/3 red apple
1/2 lb (250 g) celery
1/4 cup (50 g) walnut halves
1/3 cup (75 g) lemon yogurt
1/4 cup (50 g) crème fraîche
 (see page 32)
salt
pepper, freshly ground
1–2 tbsp lemon juice
Worcestershire sauce

Preparation time: 30 min
Calories per serving: 240
4 g protein, 14 g fat,
26 g carbohydrate

- Wash grapes and remove
 from stems. Halve the red
 grapes and remove the seeds.
 Segment the orange,
 squeezing the juice from one
 segment. Put some segments
 aside.
- Wash, quarter, core and cut
 the apple into matchstick-
 sized pieces. Gently mix the
 fruit.
- Wash, clean and thinly slice
 the celery. Add to the fruit.
- Roast the walnuts and let
 cool. Set four good walnut
 halves aside and chop the
 rest.
- Blend the lemon yogurt with
 the crème fraîche. Season
 with salt and pepper. Fold
 the nuts and the dressing
 into the fruit mixture.
 Season with lemon juice and
 Worcestershire sauce.
 Garnish the salad with nuts
 and oranges.

Mild Sprout Salad

Ingredients for 2 servings:

1 1/2 cups (100 g) wheat sprouts
1 small lettuce (e.g., lollo rosso)
1 zucchini
2 carrots
1/2 lb (250 g) spinach
juice of 2 oranges
2 tbsp crème fraîche
 (see page 32)
2 tsp cold-pressed, extra-virgin
 olive oil (or substitute cold-
 pressed nut or seed oils like
 walnut oil or flax oil)
1 tsp mustard
salt
pepper, freshly ground
2 tbsp nutritional yeast
2 tbsp yellow crisp flax seeds
 (or substitute sesame or
 sunflower seeds)

Preparation time: 30 min
Calories per serving: 210
14 g protein, 11 g fat,
18 g carbohydrate

- Rinse the wheat sprouts and
 drain well. Wash and dry the
 lettuce and arrange on a
 plate.
- Wash the zucchini. Peel the
 carrots. Coarsely grate
 zucchini and carrots.
- Wash and clean the spinach,
 remove the stalks and tear
 the larger leaves apart.
- Mix sprouts, zucchini,
 carrots and spinach then
 arrange on two plates.
- Beat the orange juice with
 the crème fraîche and the oil,
 season with mustard, salt
 and pepper. Add the yeast
 flakes.
- Pour the sauce over the salad
 and serve.

Tip

Be sure to choose crisp, fresh
sprouts. Grow them yourself
or buy them immediately
before use.

Corn Salad with Cream Cheese

Ingredients for 4 servings:

3 cobs of corn (or substitute about
 1 cup frozen corn)
salt
1 large carrot
1 bunch of chives
1 small head of iceberg lettuce
1 red onion
2/3 cup (150 g) herbed cream
 cheese
1/2 cup (100 g) buttermilk
pepper, freshly ground

Preparation time: 35 min
Calories per serving: 220
8 g protein, 13 g fat,
14 g carbohydrate

- Husk and wash the corn
 cobs. Boil the corn in lightly
 salted water for about
 20 minutes.

- Stand the corn upright on a
 cutting board and remove the
 kernels by slicing downward
 all the way around.
- Wash, peel and grate the
 carrots. Wash and chop the
 chives. Wash the lettuce, tear
 into bite-sized pieces and
 drain. Peel and thinly slice
 the onion.
- Blend the cream cheese with
 buttermilk and add the
 chives. Season the dressing
 with pepper and salt. Loosely
 mix the corn, grated carrots,
 lettuce and onion and toss
 them with the dressing.

Tip

Make your own herbed cream
cheese with fresh herbs from
the garden. Snip basil, oregano,
dill or chives into 2/3 cup
softened cream cheese. Add
1/2 clove of crushed garlic and
mix well.

Spicy Bean Salad

Ingredients for 4 servings:

1 1/3 lb (650 g) green beans
1/2 cup (100 ml) vegetable stock
3 cobs of corn
1 clove of garlic
3 green onions
1 bunch of fresh basil
3 tbsp pine nuts
4 tbsp cold-pressed, extra-virgin
 olive oil (or substitute cold-
 pressed pumpkin seed or flax oil)
1/2 cup (60 g) Parmesan cheese,
 freshly grated
4 red chili peppers

Preparation time: 45 min
Calories per serving: 310
12 g protein, 19 g fat,
22 g carbohydrate

- Wash and clean the beans.
 Bring the vegetable stock to a
 boil and simmer the beans
 over low heat for 20 minutes
 or until cooked *al dente*.

- Meanwhile, clean the corn and
 cut the raw kernels off the cob
 with a large knife, slicing from
 top to bottom.
- Peel and coarsely chop the
 garlic. Clean and wash the
 green onions and cut into
 rings. Grind the garlic and
 basil in a mortar (or food
 processor) with the pine
 nuts and add the oil. Beat
 the mixture with the
 Parmesan cheese and the
 lukewarm bean liquid and
 pour over the corn. Add the
 warm beans and the green
 onions.
- Clean the chili peppers, cut
 into thin half rings, add to
 the salad. Serve lukewarm
 with bread.

Tip

Experiment using different
herbs—substitute sprigs of
cilantro for the fresh basil.

Crunchy Asparagus and Sugar-snap Pea Salad

Ingredients for 4 servings:

2 lb (1 kg) thick white asparagus
  (or substitute green)
4 tbsp lemon juice
salt
1 pinch sugar
2 eggs
1 1/2 lb (750 g) sugar-snap peas
1–2 tbsp white wine vinegar
4 tbsp cold-pressed,
  extra-virgin olive oil
2 tsp mild mustard
1 bunch of tarragon

Preparation time: I hr
Calories per serving: 260
8 g protein, 12 g fat,
9 g carbohydrate

- Wash and trim the asparagus and cut into pieces about 2" (5 cm) long. Mix the lemon juice with a little water, 1 tsp salt and the sugar. Cook the asparagus pieces in this liquid for about 20 minutes. Let them cool in the liquid.
- Hard boil the eggs for about 7–8 minutes then peel and cut into eighths.
- Wash the peas, trim the ends and remove any stems.
- Remove asparagus from the liquid and cook the peas in this liquid for 6 minutes. Mix the vegetables gently.
- Season the liquid with the vinegar, oil, mustard and salt and mix into the warm vegetables.
- Wash the tarragon, set some aside, remove leaves, chop and mix into the salad. Garnish the salad with the eggs and serve decorated with the remaining tarragon.

Tip
The salad will also taste wonderful with grilled Feta instead of the eggs.

Fennel with Tomato Sauce

Ingredients for 4 servings:

4 medium-large fennel
1 tbsp herbes de Provence in oil
  (or substitute 1 tsp mixed dried
  herbs mixed with 1 tsp oil)
3 tomatoes
2 tbsp cold-pressed, extra-virgin olive
  oil (or substitute cold-pressed
  pumpkin seed or flax oil)
salt
2 tsp soy sauce
pepper, freshly ground
1 heaping tbsp sesame seeds
aluminum foil

Preparation time: 45 min
Calories per serving: 170
8 g protein, 7 g fat,
11 g carbohydrate

- Preheat oven to 375°F (190°C).
  Wash the fennel and cut off the
  points where it was previously
  cut. Remove the green outer
  leaves and set them aside. Cut
  the fennel in half lengthwise.
- Lightly grease the shiny side of
  four pieces of aluminum foil
  with olive oil, then sprinkle
  with the herbes de Provence.
  Place two pieces of fennel with
  the cut side down on the herb-
  oiled aluminum foil. Wrap the
  foil around the fennel. Bake the
  fennel for 15–20 minutes.
- Meanwhile, blanch the
  tomatoes, let them sit for a
  minute and then skin them.
  Finely chop the tomato flesh
  and the fennel. Add the oil and
  season the tomato sauce with
  salt, soy sauce and pepper.
- Unwrap the fennel, slice it
  thinly and place it in the sauce.
  Let it rest for a short time and
  sprinkle with sesame seeds
  before serving.

Tip
Fennel stimulates the appetite and
aids digestion.

Ratatouille-Potato Salad

Ingredients for 4 servings:

1 lb (500 g) potatoes
3/4 lb (375 g) eggplants
2 zucchini
2 tomatoes
1 large bunch of fresh basil
1/3 lb (150 g) Mozzarella cheese
3 tbsp balsamic vinegar
salt
pepper, freshly ground
4 tbsp cold-pressed, extra-virgin olive oil (or substitute cold-pressed pumpkin seed or flax oil)
2 cloves of garlic
aluminum foil

Preparation time: 50 min
Calories per serving: 520
26 g protein, 26 g fat,
46 g carbohydrate

- Wash the vegetables. Cook the potatoes, unpeeled, in a little water, then peel and slice. Slice the eggplants about 1/2" (1 cm) thick and broil in a foil-lined pan.
- Cut the eggplants into small chunks. Wash and finely grate the zucchini. Wash the tomatoes and cut them into pieces, removing the stem area. Wash the basil and remove the leaves. Cut the larger leaves into strips, leave the smaller ones whole.
- Cut the Mozzarella into large pieces. Blend the vinegar, seasonings and oil. Peel and mince the garlic, then add to the sauce.
- Let the potatoes sit in the sauce for about 15 minutes, then add the remaining ingredients. Serve with wholewheat rolls.

Curried Squash

Ingredients for 3 servings:

1 1/2 lb (750 g) winter squash
2 onions
2–3 tbsp cold-pressed sesame oil (or substitute extra-virgin olive oil)
salt
chili pepper
1 tsp caraway
2 tsp turmeric
1/2 tsp powdered ginger
1 pinch nutmeg
3 tbsp (50 ml) dry white wine (or substitute vegetable stock)
1 1/2 tbsp green pumpkin seeds

Preparation time: 30 min
Calories per serving: 330
8 g protein, 17 g fat,
24 g carbohydrate

- Peel the squash and remove the interior, including the seeds. Cut the squash into large pieces.
- Peel the onions and cut into small pieces.
- Heat the oil in a large frying pan, sauté the onions and squash for 10 minutes, stirring continuously. Add the spices during this time.
- When the squash is almost cooked, add the wine and remove from heat.
- Coarsely chop the pumpkin seeds and dry roast them but be careful not to brown them. Season the squash and serve sprinkled with pumpkin seeds.

Tip
Experiment with different kinds of squash. To start, try acorn, buttercup or butternut squash.

Dips and Sauces

Sage and Lemon Butter

Ingredients for 4 servings:

16 sage leaves
1/2 cup (100 g) butter
1/2 cup (125 ml) vegetable stock
2 tbsp lemon juice
4 egg yolks
1 pinch pepper, freshly ground
salt

Preparation time: 10 min
Calories per serving: 260
3 g protein, 27 g fat,
6 g carbohydrate

- Briefly sauté the sage in melted butter.
- Add the remaining ingredients one by one. Beat well with a whisk and heat to just below the boiling point. Season with salt and pepper. Serve with tender vegetables and new potatoes.

Cream of Chives

Ingredients for 4 servings:

1 clove of garlic, crushed
1 cup (250 g) cream
1/2 cup (125 ml) vegetable stock
salt
2 tbsp grated almonds
2 bunches of chives

Preparation time: 15 min
Calories per serving: 200
30 g protein, 19 g fat,
3 g carbohydrate

- Cook the cream with the stock, salt, almonds and garlic for about 10 minutes or until it has thickened.
- Wash and chop the chives. Set some aside, stir the rest into the sauce.
- Bring the sauce to a boil. Sprinkle the sauce with chives and serve with potatoes, rice or steamed vegetables.

Creamed Pumpkin and Carrot Sauce

Ingredients for 4 servings:

1 lb (500 g) pumpkin
1/2 lb (250 g) carrots
2 tbsp unrefined, organic sesame oil (or substitute extra-virgin olive oil)
salt
pepper, freshly ground
ginger powder
a few drops of lemon juice
3 tbsp currants
3/4–1 cup (200 g) sour cream or extra-thick yogurt
2 tbsp (30 g) coarsely chopped pumpkin seeds

Preparation time: 30 min
Calories per serving: 210
6 g protein, 13 g fat,
18 g carbohydrate

- Cut the pumpkin into large pieces and remove the peel.

Scrub and finely chop the carrots.
- Heat the oil in a saucepan, add the carrots and pumpkin and sauté for 6–7 minutes over medium heat. Purée well with a blender or food processor.
- Season the sauce with salt, pepper, ginger and lemon juice. Add the currants.
- Warm everything in the saucepan then gently stir in the sour cream or yogurt. Garnish with pumpkin seeds and serve. The sauce is a good accompaniment for pasta, particularly ravioli, and for barbecued vegetables.

Variation
Substitute butternut or buttercup squash for a slightly sweeter sauce.

Dips and Sauces

Sage and Lemon Butter

Ingredients for 4 servings:

16 sage leaves
1/2 cup (100 g) butter
1/2 cup (125 ml) vegetable stock
2 tbsp lemon juice
4 egg yolks
1 pinch pepper, freshly ground
salt

Preparation time: 10 min
Calories per serving: 260
3 g protein, 27 g fat,
6 g carbohydrate

- Briefly sauté the sage in melted butter.
- Add the remaining ingredients one by one. Beat well with a whisk and heat to just below the boiling point. Season with salt and pepper. Serve with tender vegetables and new potatoes.

Cream of Chives

Ingredients for 4 servings:

1 clove of garlic, crushed
1 cup (250 g) cream
1/2 cup (125 ml) vegetable stock
salt
2 tbsp grated almonds
2 bunches of chives

Preparation time: 15 min
Calories per serving: 200
30 g protein, 19 g fat,
3 g carbohydrate

- Cook the cream with the stock, salt, almonds and garlic for about 10 minutes or until it has thickened.
- Wash and chop the chives. Set some aside, stir the rest into the sauce.
- Bring the sauce to a boil. Sprinkle the sauce with chives and serve with potatoes, rice or steamed vegetables.

Creamed Pumpkin and Carrot Sauce

Ingredients for 4 servings:

1 lb (500 g) pumpkin
1/2 lb (250 g) carrots
2 tbsp unrefined, organic sesame oil (or substitute extra-virgin olive oil)
salt
pepper, freshly ground
ginger powder
a few drops of lemon juice
3 tbsp currants
3/4–1 cup (200 g) sour cream or extra-thick yogurt
2 tbsp (30 g) coarsely chopped pumpkin seeds

Preparation time: 30 min
Calories per serving: 210
6 g protein, 13 g fat,
18 g carbohydrate

- Cut the pumpkin into large pieces and remove the peel.

Scrub and finely chop the carrots.
- Heat the oil in a saucepan, add the carrots and pumpkin and sauté for 6–7 minutes over medium heat. Purée well with a blender or food processor.
- Season the sauce with salt, pepper, ginger and lemon juice. Add the currants.
- Warm everything in the saucepan then gently stir in the sour cream or yogurt. Garnish with pumpkin seeds and serve. The sauce is a good accompaniment for pasta, particularly ravioli, and for barbecued vegetables.

Variation
Substitute butternut or buttercup squash for a slightly sweeter sauce.

Tomato Sauce

Ingredients for 4 servings:

2 lb (1 kg) tomatoes
1 onion
1 clove of garlic
2 sprigs of thyme
2 tbsp cold-pressed,
 extra-virgin olive oil
salt
pepper, freshly ground
1/2 cup (100 ml) vegetable stock
nutritional yeast

Preparation time: 30 min
Calories per serving: 88
3 g protein, 4 g fat,
10 g carbohydrate

- Wash the tomatoes and cut out the stalks. Cut the tomatoes into large pieces. Peel and mince the onion and garlic. Wash the thyme and remove the leaves.
- Heat the oil in a saucepan, sauté the onions and garlic until translucent. Add the tomatoes, salt and pepper. Pour in the vegetable stock and add the thyme.
- Simmer the sauce, uncovered, over medium heat until it has reduced by half. Purée the sauce in a blender or food processor until it is creamy. Season with the yeast. This tomato sauce complements pasta, rice or any type of dumpling.

Tip

Tomatoes are an excellent source of vitamin C. This antioxidant helps prevent free-radical damage in the body, strengthens tissues and aids in the absorption of other nutrients.

Cheese-Cucumber Sauce

Ingredients for 4 servings:

1 cucumber
2–3 sprigs dill
3/4–1 cup (200 g) soft cheese
 (e.g., Brie or Camembert)
3 tbsp blue cheese
 (e.g., Gorgonzola)
1 tbsp butter
3 tbsp crème fraîche
 (see page 32)
1–2 tbsp millet flour (or substitute
 wheat flour stirred into water)
salt
pepper, freshly ground

Preparation time: 15 min
Calories per serving: 290
15 g protein, 22 g fat,
7 g carbohydrate

- Wash, peel and coarsely grate the cucumber. Wash and finely chop the dill. Remove the rinds from both cheeses and cut into chunks.
- Sauté the grated cucumber in the butter. Stir in the crème fraîche and simmer for 3 minutes. Add the cheese and melt it into the sauce.
- Stir the millet flour into the sauce and bring it to a boil. Season with a little salt, pepper and the dill. Serve with potatoes, pasta or cooked grains.

Tip

Not every cheese melts well in sauce. Soft cheeses and blue cheeses melt the fastest. The best firm cheeses for melting are Fontina, Emmenthal and Gruyère.

Parsley-Bread Sauce

Ingredients for 4 servings:

3 bunches of parsley
3 slices day-old wholewheat
 or rye bread
1 onion
3 tbsp butter
1 1/4 cups (300 ml) vegetable stock
1 1/4 cups (300 g) cream
1 tsp horseradish sauce

Preparation time: 20 min
Calories per serving: 400
6 g protein, 34 g fat,
16 g carbohydrate

- Wash the parsley and purée in a blender or food processor. Cut the bread into pieces. Peel and mince the onion.
- Sauté the bread and onion in half of the butter then add the stock and cream. Blend well.

- Add the remaining butter, parsley and horseradish to the sauce and let it sit for a short time. Serve this cream sauce with steamed vegetables, dumplings and potatoes.

Tip

Herbs have a strong flavor but little substance. Therefore, a herb sauce needs an additional binding agent. Day-old bread is substantial and has a relatively neutral flavor. It has fewer calories than ground almonds or pine nuts, which can also be used to thicken sauces.

Tip

Parsley inhibits tumor-cell growth and helps heal anemia. It also helps remedy digestive complaints and has been used extensively as a diuretic.

Roast Vegetable Cream Sauce

Ingredients for 4 servings:

1/2 parsnip
2 carrots
1/2 leek
2 onions
1/4 lb (125 g) mushrooms
1 large tomato
2 tbsp tomato paste
1/2 cup (100 ml) dry red wine (or
 substitute vegetable stock)
soy sauce
1/2 cup (100 g) crème fraîche
 (see page 32)
1–2 tsp nutritional yeast (or to
 taste)

Preparation time: 30 min
Calories per serving: 160
3 g protein, 11 g fat,
9 g carbohydrate

- Wash and peel the parsnip and carrots and cut into large pieces. Wash the leek and slice into thick rings. Peel and quarter the onions. Clean the mushrooms. Wash the tomatoes, cut in half and remove the stalk area.
- Dry roast the onions in a saucepan. Add the remaining vegetables and roast well. Add the tomato paste.
- Pour in the red wine, about 1 3/4 cups (400 ml) water and 1–2 tbsp soy sauce. Simmer covered for 15 minutes over medium heat. Drain the vegetables and save the liquid.
- Purée the vegetable mixture with the crème fraîche. Add to the liquid and heat again. Season to taste with yeast and soy sauce. Serve with steamed vegetables, pasta, gnocchi and dumplings.

Hot Pepper Dip

Ingredients for 4 servings:

2–3 onions
2 cloves of garlic
1/3 cup (75 ml) vegetable stock
paprika
1 tbsp hot pepper paste (or
 substitute tomato paste)
salt
pepper, freshly ground
1 chili pepper
2 red peppers
2/3 cup (150 g) cream
2 tbsp balsamic vinegar

Preparation time: 20 min
Calories per serving: 160
3 g protein, 12 g fat,
9 g carbohydrate

• Peel and coarsely chop the
 onions and garlic. Cook
 them in the vegetable stock
 for about 5 minutes along
 with the paprika, pepper
 paste, salt and pepper.

• Let the liquid boil down and
 allow the vegetables to cool.
 Clean and slice the chili
 pepper. Clean and dice the
 red peppers. Blend or process
 the pepper, chili and the
 onion-vegetable mix. Press
 through a sieve.
• Season the dip well. Whip
 the cream until partly stiff
 then combine with balsamic
 vinegar. Serve with
 dumplings, boiled potatoes
 and barbecued food.

Tip
Wear gloves when handling
chili peppers; the seed oils can
burn your skin. Hot peppers
are rich in vitamin C. They
also promote digestion, clear
the sinuses and cleanse the
body by inducing perspiration.

Pear-Mustard Dip

Ingredients for 4 servings:

1 ripe yellow pear
2 tbsp sesame seeds
1/2 bunch of dill
1 tbsp mild mustard
1–2 tbsp lemon juice
seasoning salt

Preparation time: 15 min
Calories per serving: 50
2 g protein, 3 g fat,
4 g carbohydrate

• Pour boiling water over the
 pear and remove the skin.
 Remove the core. Dry roast
 the sesame seeds. Wash and
 chop the dill.
• Purée the pear with mustard
 and lemon juice. Stir in the
 sesame seeds and season the
 dip with salt. Serve with
 barbecued and marinated
 vegetables and rice dishes.

Avocado-Basil Dip

Ingredients for 4 servings:

2 bunches of basil
1 lemon
1 ripe avocado
2/3 cup (150 g) sour cream
 or extra thick yogurt
1/3 cup (100 g) cream
2 tsp mild mustard
pepper, freshly ground

Preparation time: 15 min
Calories per serving: 240
3 g protein, 24 g fat,
5 g carbohydrate

• Wash the basil and finely
 chop the leaves.
• Squeeze the lemon into a
 mixing bowl. Halve the
 avocado, scoop out the flesh
 from both halves, blend with
 lemon juice and add the
 remaining ingredients.

Tzatsiki

Ingredients for 4 servings:

1/2 cucumber
1 bunch of parsley
2 cloves of garlic
1 tbsp cold-pressed, extra-virgin
 olive oil (or substitute cold-
 pressed pumpkin seed or flax oil)
1 1/2 cups (350 g) quark
 (see page 32)
2/3 cup (150 g) yogurt
salt
white pepper, freshly ground
lemon juice

Preparation time: 15 min
Calories per serving: 95
13 g protein, 2 g fat,
6 g carbohydrate

- Wash and grate the
  cucumber. Purée the garlic
  with parsley leaves and oil.
- Mix quark with yogurt. Drain
  the grated cucumber and mix
  with remaining ingredients.

Kefir-Radish Cream

Ingredients for 4 servings:

3 bunches of radishes
1 cup (200 g) kefir (available from
 the health food store)
1/2 cup (100 g) cream
1 pinch sugar
salt
pepper, freshly ground

Preparation time: 15 min
Calories per serving: 140
4 g protein, 10 g fat,
7 g carbohydrate

- Cut the radishes into large
  pieces and blend them with
  the kefir.
- Combine the cream with a
  few drops of lemon juice and
  the sugar and whip until
  stiff. Fold into the radishes.
- Season with the spices and
  refrigerate. Serve with raw
  vegetables, boiled potatoes or
  salads.

Olive-Tomato Dip

Ingredients for 4 servings:

1 cup (150 g) each black
 and green olives
1 sprig of thyme
1 bunch of parsley
1/3 cup (75 g) peeled almonds
2/3 lb (300 g) firm tomatoes
salt
pepper, freshly ground
paprika

Preparation time: 10 min
Calories per serving: 310
6 g protein, 29 g fat,
7 g carbohydrate

- Pit the olives. Wash the
  parsley and thyme, remove
  their leaves and process with
  the olives and almonds to
  form a paste.

- Blanch the tomatoes. Remove
  the skins and seeds and chop
  the remaining fruit into
  small pieces. Stir the tomato
  pieces into the almond-olive
  paste and season well with
  spices. This dip is a nice
  addition to baked potatoes,
  flat breads and raw
  vegetables.

Tip
Always buy the best, freshest
olives you can afford.
Experiment with different
types (e.g., Kalamata, Italian)
either as a snack or in cooking.
Olives are an excellent source
of healthy fat. They reduce the
need for additional salt in any
recipe as they have a naturally
salty flavor.

Mediterranean Dressing

Ingredients for 4 servings:

2 tbsp lemon juice
1/2 cup (125 ml) cold
  vegetable stock
1/2 tsp seasoning salt
  (or substitute sea salt)
pepper, freshly ground
1 clove of garlic
1 tsp cold-pressed,
  extra-virgin olive oil
2 tsp cold-pressed, unrefined nut
  or seed oil
1 sprig of basil

Preparation time: 10 min
Calories per serving: 57
0 g protein, 2 g fat,
7 g carbohydrate

• Mix the lemon juice, stock,
  seasoning salt and pepper.
• Peel and mince the garlic and
  add it to the sauce.

• Whisk together the oils.
  Wash the basil, cut the leaves
  into fine strips and stir into
  the dressing. Serve with
  vegetable salads, pasta, grain
  and potato salads.

Tip
Different herbs including
oregano, marjoram, rosemary,
parsley and thyme complement
your various Mediterranean
dishes. You can also use this
dressing as a dip for bread.

Variation
By using vinegar instead of
lemon juice and 1 tsp mustard,
this dressing becomes a light
vinaigrette. Make a creamy salad
dressing by substituting cream
for the stock.
  Hazelnut, walnut, flax and
pumpkin seed oil are rich in
healthy fats and nutrients if
unrefined and unheated.

Creamy Lemon Dressing

Ingredients for 4 servings:

2/3 cup (150 g) sour cream
2/3 cup (150 g) lemon yogurt
  (or substitute natural yogurt with
  1 tbsp each of lemon juice and
  sugar stirred in)
4 tbsp orange juice
1 bunch of dill
1/2 tsp salt

Preparation time: 10 min
Calories per serving: 75
3 g protein, 5 g fat,
4 g carbohydrate

• Combine the sour cream,
  yogurt and orange juice and
  blend until smooth.
• Wash and finely chop the
  dill. Season the dressing with
  dill and salt. Serve with fruit
  salads and other sweet and
  sour salads such as Waldorf
  salad.

Cocktail Sauce

Ingredients for 4 servings:

2 tbsp natural ketchup
1/3 cup (75 g) quark
  (see page 32)
2/3 cup (150 g) cream
salt
pepper, freshly ground
Worcestershire sauce

Preparation time: 5 min
Calories per serving: 140
3 g protein, 12 g fat,
3 g carbohydrate

• Beat the ketchup with the
  quark until smooth. Slowly
  fold in the cream.
• Season with salt, pepper and
  Worcestershire sauce. The
  cocktail sauce will keep for
  2–3 days in the refrigerator.
  Serve with subtly flavored
  salads, and salads containing
  fruit.

Salsa Verde

Ingredients for 4 servings:

1 bunch of parsley
1 bunch of fresh basil
1 cup (200 ml) vegetable stock
2–3 tbsp Parmesan cheese,
 freshly grated
1/4 cup (30 g) bread crumbs
3 tbsp cold-pressed, extra-virgin
 olive oil (or substitute cold-
 pressed pumpkin seed or flax oil)
1 hard-boiled egg yolk
salt
pepper, freshly ground

Preparation time: 10 min
Calories per serving: 120
4 g protein, 9 g fat,
6 g carbohydrate

- Wash the herbs and remove stems. Purée leaves in a food processor and gradually add the stock.
- Add the Parmesan cheese, bread crumbs, oil and egg yolk then season with salt and pepper. Serve with eggs, cucumbers, boiled potatoes, pasta and vegetables.

Variation

Frankfurter Green Sauce:
Use one bunch each of dill, parsley, sorrel, lemon balm, borage, tarragon, pimpernel and lovage. Finely chop the herbs. Press the yolks of four hard-boiled eggs through a sieve, blend in 3 tbsp oil,
1/2 cup (125 ml) vegetable or herb stock, 1 1/3 cups (300 g) sour cream, salt, pepper and the finely chopped herbs. Add finely chopped egg white.

Creamy Nut Dip

Ingredients for 4 servings:

1/4 cup (40 g) chopped hazelnuts
1 bunch of parsley
1/4 cup (40 g) chopped almonds
1/2 cup (100 g) pitted black olives
2/3 cup (150 ml) vegetable stock
2 tbsp tomato paste
1/4 cup (50 g) crème fraîche
 (see page 32)
salt
pepper, freshly ground
1–2 tsp Amaretto liqueur, to taste

Preparation time: 15 min
Calories per serving: 290
5 g protein, 26 g fat,
6 g carbohydrate

- Dry roast the nuts and then let them cool. Wash the parsley and remove the stems. Finely chop the nuts with the parsley and olives in a blender or food processor.

- Add stock, tomato paste and crème fraîche to the mixture then add Amaretto to taste.
- The sauce will keep for 2–3 days in the refrigerator if kept in a tightly closed jar. This dip makes a good accompaniment to mushrooms, tastes good spread on bread, or with grilled vegetables.

Tip

This dip is full of healthy fats. For a more subtly flavored dip, try pine nuts instead of the hazelnuts. Or, experiment with different nuts and seeds to create new taste combinations (e.g., sesame seeds and pecans). You can also substitute 1 tsp honey for the Amaretto.

Soups and Casseroles

Creamy Carrot Casserole

Ingredients for 4 servings:

1 3/4 lb (875 g) potatoes (about 5)
1 1/3 lb (600 g) carrots (about 8)
2 bunches of green onions
1 clove of garlic
4 tsp butter
salt
pepper, freshly ground
1 pinch ground lemon grass
 (from an Asian grocery)
1/2 cup (125 ml) vegetable stock
1/2 cup (125 g) cream
1/4 cup (50 g) raisins
1 cup fresh or frozen corn
2 eggs
1 tbsp sesame seeds

Preparation time: 1 hr
Calories per serving: 480
12 g protein, 20 g fat,
58 g carbohydrate

- Peel the potatoes and cut into medium-sized pieces. Wash and peel the carrots and cut into sticks. Wash the green onions and cut into 1" (2.5 cm) lengths. Peel and mince the garlic.
- Sauté the potatoes and carrots in butter. After 7 minutes add the corn, onions, salt, pepper, lemon grass and garlic. Stir in the vegetable stock and cream.
- Cook the casserole for 15 minutes. Add the raisins and allow them to heat up.
- Meanwhile, boil the eggs for 7 minutes, rinse in cold water and peel. Dry roast the sesame seeds until they are light brown.
- Serve with halved eggs and sprinkle with sesame seeds.

Minestrone

Ingredients for 4 servings:

1/3–1/2 cup bow noodles
salt
2 carrots
1/2 lb (250 g) each of
 yellow and green beans
2/3 lb (300 g) zucchini
2 large tomatoes
1 bunch of mixed herbs
1–2 cloves of garlic
3 tbsp cold-pressed,
 extra-virgin olive oil
6 cups (1 1/2 l) vegetable stock
2 cups (250 g) shelled peas
pepper, freshly ground
2–3 tbsp Parmesan cheese,
 freshly grated

Preparation time: 1 hr
Calories per serving: 230
16 g protein, 4 g fat,
33 g carbohydrate

- Cook the noodles *al dente* in plenty of salted water. Wash the vegetables. Cut the carrots into fine strips, the beans into pieces and the zucchini into strips. Wash the tomatoes and cut into large pieces, removing the stalk. Wash and finely chop the herbs. Peel and mince the garlic.
- Sauté the garlic and beans in oil. Add the stock and simmer covered for about 15 minutes.
- Add the carrots and peas and simmer for another 15 minutes. Add the zucchini and tomatoes, simmer everything for about 5 minutes more. Add herbs and noodles to the soup, season and serve with Parmesan cheese.

Greek Potato Casserole

Ingredients for 4 servings:

1 bunch of parsley
2 tsp salt
1 pinch pepper, freshly ground
1 pinch oregano
1 pinch cinnamon
1 3/4 lb (875 g) potatoes for boiling
3 tbsp cold-pressed,
  extra-virgin olive oil
1 onion
1/2 lb (250 g) zucchini
1/2 lb (250 g) tomatoes
1/2 cup (100 g) dry Ricotta cheese
1/2 cup (100 g) sour cream
1/2 cup (100 g) cream

Preparation time: 45 min
Calories per serving: 400
11 g protein, 16 g fat,
38 g carbohydrate

- Wash and finely chop the
  parsley. Mix salt with pepper,
  oregano, cinnamon and parsley.
- Wash the vegetables. Peel and
  thinly slice the potatoes. Heat
  the oil in a large saucepan,
  brown the potatoes, sprinkle the
  herb mixture over top, cover
  and cook over low heat.
- Meanwhile, peel the onions and
  cut into small pieces, add them
  to the potatoes and sprinkle
  with some of the remaining
  herb mixture.
- Slice the zucchini, add to the
  saucepan and season with the
  remaining herb mixture.
- Blanch the tomatoes, remove
  the skins, cut them into
  quarters and remove the stalk
  area and seeds. Top the
  vegetables with the tomato
  pieces and cook for 15 minutes.
- Blend the cheese, sour cream
  and cream then spread on the
  vegetables and cook again for
  5–10 minutes.

Important
With this casserole, cooking is
already in progress during
preparation, so always keep the lid
on.

Fruity-Spicy Adzuki Bean Soup

Ingredients for 4 servings:

1 1/4 cups (250 g) adzuki beans
  (or substitute kidney beans)
1 onion
1 chili pepper
1 red and 1 green pepper
2 tbsp cold-pressed,
  extra-virgin olive oil
3 1/4 cups (750 ml) vegetable
  stock
2 medium-sized potatoes
salt
pepper
1 pineapple
2–3 tbsp lemon juice
1 tbsp sugar
paprika
Worcestershire sauce

Preparation time: 1 hr
(+12 hrs soaking time)
Calories per serving: 450
4 g protein, 5 g fat,
46 g carbohydrate

- Soak the beans in cold water overnight.
- Peel and mince the onion. Wash, clean and finely chop the chili pepper. Wash, clean and thinly slice the peppers.
- Heat the oil and sauté the onion, chili pepper and peppers. Drain the soaked beans and add to the chopped onion. Add the vegetable stock and simmer for 40 minutes.
- Meanwhile wash, peel and dice the potatoes, and add them to the soup. Cook for about 25 minutes.
- Peel the pineapple, cut it into small pieces and add to the soup with lemon juice and sugar. Bring to a boil and season with paprika and Worcestershire sauce.

Borscht

Ingredients for 4 servings:

1/2 lb (250 g) onions
1 lb (500 g) tomatoes
2 cloves of garlic
5 medium-sized beets
3 celery stalks
5 medium-sized potatoes
1 lb (500 g) cabbage
2 tbsp clarified butter
6 cups (1 1/2 l) vegetable stock
pepper, freshly ground
1 pinch sugar (optional)
2 tbsp lemon juice
1 bunch of parsley
2 stalks of dill
2/3 cup (150 g) sour cream or
  extra thick yogurt

Preparation time: 1 hr
Calories per serving: 400
13 g protein, 12 g fat,
62 g carbohydrate

- Peel and thinly slice the onions. Blanch the tomatoes, remove skins and chop. Peel and mince the garlic.
- Wash, peel and coarsely grate the beets. Clean and thinly slice the celery. Wash and peel the potatoes and cut into medium-sized pieces. Clean the cabbage and cut into fine strips.
- Sauté onions in the clarified butter until translucent. Add the vegetables and sauté for 15 minutes.
- Pour in the stock, season with salt, pepper, lemon juice and sugar, if desired. Cook for another 30 minutes.
- Wash and coarsely chop the herbs, set some aside and add the rest to the soup. Serve the soup with sour cream or thick yogurt, and the rest of the herbs.

Creamy Corn and Tomato Soup

Ingredients for 2 servings:

1 fresh cob of corn
1/2 cup (125 ml) vegetable stock
1 tbsp butter
3/4 cup (60 g) cream of wheat
1 cup (200 ml) milk
2 tomatoes
2 egg yolks
2 tbsp finely chopped parsley

Preparation time: 45 min
Calories per serving: 360
12 g protein, 16 g fat,
31 g carbohydrate

• Husk the corn and simmer
  the cob in vegetable stock
  for 15 minutes. Remove
  from heat, take out the corn
  and reserve the stock. Hold
  the corn upright and cut the
  kernels off from top to
  bottom using a sharp knife.

• Heat the butter and brown
  the cream of wheat, add the
  corn liquid and the milk,
  and simmer for 10 minutes.
• Blanch the tomatoes, remove
  skins, seeds and stalks and
  cut into pieces.
• Beat the egg yolks in a cup
  with a little of the soup,
  then stir into the soup. Do
  not boil the soup again, or
  the egg will coagulate.
• Add the parsley, corn and
  tomatoes and heat gently.

Variation

On cold evenings, spice up this
wonderful late summer soup
with a few chopped green
chilies, or a dash of cayenne
pepper or paprika.

Chinese Vegetable Soup

Ingredients for 4 servings:

1/3 lb (150 g) transparent noodles
1 red pepper
2/3 lb (300 g) small mushrooms
1 bunch of green onions
1/4 Chinese cabbage
4 cups (1 l) vegetable stock
3/4 cup (100 g) bamboo shoots
  (canned)
2 1/2–3 cups (160 g) bean sprouts
1 cup (200 g) fresh or frozen corn
a few drops Tabasco sauce
salt
pepper, freshly ground
1–2 tsp soy sauce
2 tbsp chives

Preparation time: 30 min
Calories per serving: 260
11 g protein, 3 g fat,
44 g carbohydrate

• Pour boiling water over the
  noodles, cover and set aside
  for 4 minutes.
• Wash the peppers and cut
  into strips. Clean the
  mushrooms and cut them
  into bite-sized pieces. Wash
  the green onions and slice
  them at an angle in long
  sections. Wash the cabbage
  and cut into strips.
• Place all the vegetables
  (except bamboo shoots and
  sprouts) and stock in a
  saucepan. Simmer for
  15 minutes.
• Rinse the bamboo shoots,
  cut into bite-sized pieces and
  heat them in the soup. Add
  the sprouts and noodles then
  season with Tabasco, salt,
  pepper and soy sauce.
  Sprinkle chives on top.

Creamy Potato Soup

Ingredients for 2–3 servings:

1 small leek
2 medium-sized carrots
1 celery stalk
1 large onion
1 sprig of thyme
5 mashing potatoes
2 tbsp cold-pressed,
 extra-virgin olive oil
1–2 bay leaves
3 juniper berries
1/2 tsp peppercorns
salt
4 cups (1 l) vegetable stock
1 bunch of chives
1/2 cup (100 g) sour cream or
 thick yogurt

Preparation time: 45 min
Calories per serving: 520
13 g protein, 21 g fat,
69 g carbohydrate

- Wash the leek and cut into rings. Clean the carrots and celery and cut them into strips. Peel and slice the onion. Wash the thyme and remove the stems. Peel the potatoes and cut them into large pieces.
- Sauté the leek, carrots, celery, potatoes and onion in oil. Add thyme, bay leaves, peppercorns, salt and vegetable stock.
- Bring the soup to a boil and simmer for about 15 minutes.
- Purée the soup in a blender or food processor.
- Wash and finely chop the chives, add them to the soup. Fold the sour cream or thick yogurt into the soup or place a dollop on each serving.

Mild Lentil Soup

Ingredients for 4 servings:

1/2 lb (250 g) potatoes
 (1 large or 2 small)
5 cups (1 1/4 l) vegetable stock
1 cup (200 g) red lentils
1 clove of garlic
1 pinch saffron powder
1/2 tsp curry powder
1 pinch caraway
3 tbsp lemon juice
3 tbsp grated almonds
salt
pepper, freshly ground
2/3 cup (150 g) dry Ricotta cheese
2 tbsp cold-pressed,
 extra-virgin olive oil
1 bunch of chives

Preparation time: 40 min
Calories per serving: 380
21 g protein, 18 g fat,
36 g carbohydrate

- Wash and peel the potatoes and cut them into small pieces. Boil with the stock and lentils until cooked.
- Peel and mince the garlic. Dissolve the saffron in I tsp hot water then add it to the soup with curry powder, caraway and garlic.
- Stir in the lemon juice and the almonds then season with salt and pepper.
- Grind pepper over the Ricotta. Chop the cheese into small pieces, add to the hot oil and sauté until crisp.
- Chop the chives. Sprinkle the cheese and chives over the soup and serve.

Tip
You can substitute green or brown lentils for the red ones. Green and brown lentils have a stronger flavor and require a longer cooking time than red lentils.

Vegetable Soup with Cornmeal Dumplings

Ingredients for 2 servings:

1 cup (150 g) coarse cornmeal
  or corn grits
2 cups (450 ml) milk
2 tsp Parmesan cheese, freshly grated
salt, freshly ground pepper
2 tbsp herbed cream cheese
1 lb (500 g) mixed fresh vegetables
  (e.g., green beans, carrots, celery,
  leek, cauliflower, peas, tomatoes)
2 medium potatoes
1 bunch of thyme and parsley
2 tbsp butter
2 cups (500 ml) vegetable stock
soy sauce

Preparation time: 45 min
Calories per serving: 620
27 g protein, 14 g fat,
98 g carbohydrate

- Stir the cornmeal into the milk
  and bring to a boil. Simmer for
  7 minutes over low heat, stirring
  occasionally. Mix with the
  Parmesan cheese, salt and cream
  cheese, leave to cool then shape
  into about 30 dumplings.
  (This is best done by holding
  one tablespoon in each hand and
  "passing" the cornmeal mix from
  one spoon to the other.)
- Wash the vegetables. Cut the
  beans into 2–3 pieces each and
  thinly slice the carrots, celery
  and leek. Cut the cauliflower into
  small flowerets.
- Shell the peas. Blanch the
  tomatoes, let sit for a minute,
  remove the skins and cut into
  cubes. Wash and peel the
  potatoes and cut into small
  pieces. Wash and finely chop the
  herbs.
- Heat the butter, sauté the
  vegetables and potatoes briefly,
  then add the vegetable stock.
  Add the herbs and cook over
  moderate heat for 15 minutes.
- After 5 minutes add the
  cornmeal dumplings. Season the
  soup with salt, pepper and soy
  sauce.

Savoy Cabbage with Roast Chickpeas

Ingredients for 4 servings:

1/2 lb (250 g) chickpeas
1 small Savoy cabbage
1 cup (200 ml) tomato juice
salt, freshly ground pepper
3 tbsp quick-cooking
 rolled oats
1 clove of garlic
4 tbsp cold-pressed,
 extra-virgin olive oil
1 tbsp mild curry powder
1/2 cup (100 g) crème fraîche
 (see page 32)
3 tbsp sour cream
1 handful of alfalfa sprouts

Preparation time: 2 hrs
(+12 hrs soaking time)
Calories per serving: 480
21 g protein, 23 g fat,
41 g carbohydrate

• Soak chickpeas overnight. The next day, drain and add fresh water. Boil the chickpeas for 1 3/4 hours or until cooked.
• Meanwhile, quarter, wash and shred the cabbage. Heat the tomato juice, add the cabbage, season with pepper and salt, and cook for 30 minutes. Stir in the oats.
• Peel the garlic and press with the flat side of a knife. Roast the drained chickpeas in oil with garlic, salt and curry powder until light brown.
• Mix the chickpeas with the cabbage, let it heat up then serve in bowls. Mix the crème fraîche with the sour cream, place a dollop on each portion and garnish with the sprouts.

Wild Rice Pumpkin

Ingredients for 6 servings:

1 small pumpkin
 (5 1/2–6 1/2 lbs (2.5–3 kg))
salt, freshly ground pepper
paprika
1 1/4 cups (250 g) wild rice
2 cups (500 ml) vegetable stock
1 bunch of green onions
2/3 lb (300 g) small zucchini
1 lb (500 g) roma tomatoes
1 clove of garlic
1 cup lentil sprouts
 (or substitute bean sprouts)
1/2 cup (100 g) crème fraîche
 (see page 32)

Preparation time: 2 1/4 hrs
(including 1 1/2 hrs
cooking time)
Calories per serving: 310
13 g protein, 1 g fat,
510 g carbohydrate

• Wash the pumpkin and cut out a lid. Remove the stringy pulp and seeds from inside and score the inner flesh all the way around. Rub the flesh with a mixture of salt, pepper and paprika.
• Cook the rice in the stock for 15 minutes. Preheat the oven to 400°F (205°C).
• Wash and chop the green onions. Wash the zucchini and cut into thick slices. Cut the tomatoes into small pieces. Peel and mince the garlic.
• Mix the rice with the vegetables and add the sprouts. Fill the pumpkin with this mix. Place the lid on the pumpkin and bake on the middle rack for 80 minutes or until the pumpkin and rice are fully cooked. Garnish with crème fraîche before serving.

Exotic Carrot Soup

Ingredients for 4 servings:

1 lb (500 g) carrots
1 onion
1 clove of garlic
2 oranges
1 tsp clarified butter
1 pinch coriander
2 cups (500 ml) vegetable stock
1/4 cup (50 g) raisins
salt, freshly ground pepper
Worcestershire sauce
cilantro (or substitute parsley)

Preparation time: 25 min
Calories per serving: 150
3 g protein, 4 g fat,
25 g carbohydrate

- Wash and peel the carrots and chop into small pieces. Peel and coarsely chop the onion and garlic. Finely grate about 1/2 tsp orange peel. Halve the oranges and squeeze out the juice.
- Heat the clarified butter, sauté the onion and garlic until translucent. Add the carrots and grated orange peel then season with the coriander. Add the orange juice and enough vegetable stock to just cover the carrots.
- Cook the carrots for 10 minutes. Purée the carrots in the stock. Bring the purée to a boil again with the remaining stock and raisins.
- Season the soup well with salt, pepper and Worcestershire sauce. Garnish with cilantro and serve.

Herb Soup with Baked Custard

Ingredients for 4 servings:

2 eggs
1/2 cup (100 ml) milk
salt, freshly ground white pepper
nutmeg, freshly grated
2–3 green onions
1/4 lb (125 g) chervil
1/2 bunch of parsley
2 tbsp sorrel
1 potato, peeled and chopped
3 1/4 cups (750 ml) vegetable stock
3 tbsp millet flour
1 cup (200 g) cream
chervil for garnish
butter for the baking dish

Preparation time: 1 hr
Calories per serving: 260
7 g protein, 21 g fat,
22 g carbohydrate

- Preheat oven to 325°F (160°C). Fill a shallow pan (large enough to hold a baking dish) with 1" (2.5 cm) of water and set it in the oven. Grease the baking dish.
- Beat the eggs and milk then season with salt, pepper and nutmeg. Pour the egg mix into the dish. Set the dish in the water-filled pan and bake for 40 minutes, or until a knife inserted in the center comes out clean. Cut the egg custard into bite-sized pieces.
- Rinse and chop the green onions. Finely chop the herbs.
- Boil the stock with the potato and onions. Cook gently for 15 minutes until potatoes are very soft.
- Add the chopped herbs and the millet flour, purée and bring to a boil again. Add the custard pieces to the soup. Whip the cream until stiff and fold into the soup. Garnish with chervil.

Cream of Pea Soup with Croutons

Ingredients for 4 servings:

3/4 cup (150 g) dried green peas
3 1/2 cups (800 ml) vegetable stock
1 onion
1 clove of garlic
3 tbsp butter
1 lb (500 g) fresh or frozen peas
1/2 cup (100 g) sour cream
1/2 cup (100 g) cream
salt, freshly ground pepper
nutmeg, freshly grated
2 slices dark rye bread

Preparation time: 1 hr
(+12 hrs soaking time)
Calories per serving: 330
8 g protein, 24 g fat,
22 g carbohydrate

- Soak the dried peas overnight in 1 3/4 cups (400 ml) vegetable stock.
- The next day, peel and finely chop the onion and garlic, and sauté in 1 tbsp butter.
- Add the soaked peas and the rest of the stock and cook for 40 minutes or until everything is soft. Add the frozen peas, cook for another 10 minutes, then blend with the mixture.
- Add the sour cream and the cream. Heat the soup and season with salt, pepper and nutmeg.
- Break the bread into bite-sized pieces. Heat the remaining butter and sauté the bread until golden brown. Serve the soup in four bowls and sprinkle with croutons.

Tip
For a lighter soup, substitute 1/2 cup vegetable stock for the sour cream and the cream.

Creamed Millet Soup with Peppers

Ingredients for 4 servings:

2 onions
3 tbsp butter
1 tsp paprika
1/2–2/3 cup (80 g) millet flour
 (or substitute wholewheat flour)
2 cups (500 ml) cold vegetable stock
1 1/3 lb (650 g) red peppers
1/2 cup (125 g) cream
5 tbsp tomato paste
salt, freshly ground pepper

Preparation time: 30 min
Calories per serving: 290
6 g protein, 20 g fat,
25 g carbohydrate

- Peel and finely chop the onions. Heat the butter and sauté the onions. Dust with paprika and millet flour and sauté lightly.
- Remove the saucepan from the stove and add the vegetable stock, stirring continuously and beating with a whisk to prevent the formation of lumps. Simmer the soup for 5 minutes.
- Meanwhile, remove stalks and seeds from the peppers and purée in a blender or food processor.
- Whip the cream until it begins to stiffen. Stir the peppers and tomato paste into the soup and heat again but do not boil. Season the soup with salt and pepper, fold in the cream and serve.

Tip
Serve with a hearty bread, and garnish with a sprig of basil or cilantro.

Mushroom Consommé

Ingredients for 4 servings:

1 lb (500 g) mushrooms
1 tbsp dried mushrooms
salt
4 cups (1 l) vegetable stock
1 bay leaf
1–2 pimentos
1 tsp thyme leaves
2 peppercorns
1–2 tbsp medium sherry, or to taste

Preparation time: 2 1/2 hrs
(+12 hrs resting time)
Calories per serving: 24
4 g protein, 0.4 g fat,
1 g carbohydrate

- Wipe the mushrooms clean (wash only if very dirty). Chop mushrooms in a food processor until crumbly.

- Mix the mushrooms with salt and leave them overnight in a cloth-covered bowl in a cool place. Bring the mushroom mix to a boil in a large saucepan together with the stock, herbs and spices and simmer for 2 hours.
- Line a strainer with cheesecloth. Strain the soup and thoroughly squeeze out all the liquid. Flavor with the sherry and serve.

Tip
The longer the mushrooms sit in the stock, the more flavor they will develop.

Important
Mushrooms must not be left in an airtight container, and the temperature during storage should be no higher than 53°F (10°C).

Essence of Beet Soup

Ingredients for 4 servings:

2 lb (1 kg) beets
1 onion
1/2 leek
1 carrot
1/2 lb (250g) celery
1 tbsp butter
6 juniper berries
1 bay leaf
pinch chili pepper flakes
salt
pepper, freshly ground
1 lemon

Preparation time: 40 min
Calories per serving: 170
6 g protein, 4 g fat,
27 g carbohydrate

- Wash and peel the beets and cut them into large pieces. Peel and halve the onion. Wash, clean and finely cut the leek, carrot and celery.

- Sauté the onion in the saucepan with the cut surfaces down. Add the butter and sauté the remaining vegetables briefly. Add 4 cups (1 l) water.
- Add the juniper berries, bay leaf and pepper flakes, and salt lightly. Simmer for 30 minutes.
- Strain the vegetable liquid through a fine strainer and reheat. Season to taste with salt, pepper, a little lemon juice and vegetable stock.
- Sprinkle a little grated lemon rind over the soup and serve.

Tip
The cornmeal dumplings (page 84) or the baked custard (page 86) can be added to this soup.

Vegetable Bouillon with Sesame Spirals

Ingredients for 4 servings:

1 onion
1 bay leaf
3–4 cloves
vegetables for stock (e.g., carrot,
  onion, celery) or substitute
 4 cups (1 l) prepared vegetable stock
1/2 fennel bulb
1 1/2 lb (750 g) ripe tomatoes
salt
1 tsp peppercorns
3–4 juniper berries
1 egg
1/3 cup (50 g) flour
1/2 cup (100 ml) milk
clarified butter for frying
1 tsp black sesame seeds
  (or substitute white sesame seeds
  or sunflower seeds)
1 bunch of parsley

Preparation time: 1 hr
Calories per serving: 180
8 g protein, 6 g fat,
22 g carbohydrate

- Peel the onion and pin the bay
  leaf to it using the cloves. Wash
  and coarsely chop the remaining
  vegetables.
- Bring the vegetables to a boil in
  a pot with 4 cups (1 l) water,
  1 tsp salt, peppercorns and
  juniper berries. Lower the heat
  and simmer the vegetables for
  30 minutes. Strain the bouillon.
- Mix a smooth batter using the
  egg, flour, milk and a pinch of
  salt. Allow it to rest for
  5 minutes. Heat a little clarified
  butter in a coated frying pan and
  make thin pancakes from the
  batter. Scatter sesame seeds on
  the crêpes before the dough sets
  in the pan.
- Tightly roll up the crêpes with
  the sesame side facing out. Cut
  the rolls into thin slices.
- Wash and coarsely chop the
  parsley. Heat up the bouillon,
  season well and drop in the
  spirals. Garnish with parsley
  and serve.

Cream of Cucumber Soup

Ingredients for 4 servings:

2 cucumbers
1 leek
1 small onion
2 tbsp butter or unrefined coconut oil
2 cups (500 ml) vegetable stock
1 bunch of dill
1 bunch of pimpernel
 (or substitute parsley)
2 cups (500 ml) alfalfa sprouts
1 avocado
1 cup (250 g) buttermilk
1/2 cup (125 g) cream
salt
pepper, freshly ground
nutmeg, freshly grated

Preparation time: 30 min
Calories per serving: 330
7 g protein, 27 g fat,
11 g carbohydrate

- Wash the cucumber, cut it in half lengthwise then cut into thick slices. Wash and clean the leek and cut it into thick rings. Peel and chop the onion.
- Heat the butter or coconut oil in a saucepan and sauté the onion until translucent. Add the vegetables and sauté. Add stock and simmer for 10 minutes.
- Wash the dill and pimpernel and chop the sprouts. Set aside a little of the dill. Halve the avocado, remove the pit and spoon out the flesh.
- Purée the soup, herbs and avocado. Stir the buttermilk into the slightly cooled soup. Lightly whip the cream and fold it into the soup shortly before serving. Season with salt, some pepper and nutmeg. Serve sprinkled with dill.

Tip
To make the soup into a filling main course, add a soft-boiled egg to every serving. Serve with a fresh baguette.

Cold Summer Soup

Ingredients for 4 servings:

3 leeks
2 yellow peppers
1 lb (500 g) potatoes
1 1/4 lb (625 g) beefsteak
   tomatoes
1 clove of garlic
1/2 cup (100 g) short-grain
   brown rice
2 tbsp cold-pressed,
   extra-virgin olive oil
1 tbsp soy sauce
pepper, freshly ground
4 cups (1 l) tomato juice
   (lightly salted)
4 tbsp lemon juice
4 tbsp chopped chives
4 hard-boiled eggs
2/3 cup (150 g) crème fraîche
   (see page 32) or yogurt

Preparation time: 1 hr
Calories per serving: 520
18 g protein, 23 g fat,
56 g carbohydrate

- Wash the vegetables. Chop the leek into thick slices. Cut the peppers into diamond-shaped pieces, dice the peeled potatoes and chop the tomatoes into small pieces. Peel and chop the garlic.
- Sauté the rice in oil, add potatoes, peppers, soy sauce and pepper. Add the tomato juice.
- Bring to a boil, reduce the heat and let the soup simmer. After 20 minutes add the leek and tomatoes and cook for another 20 minutes.
- Season with lemon juice and leave to cool. Peel and finely chop the eggs. Serve the soup in bowls garnished with chives, eggs and crème fraîche or yogurt.

Cream of Radish Soup

Ingredients for 4 servings:

4 bunches of fresh radishes
1 clove of garlic
1 cup (250 g) buttermilk
1 1/4 cups (300 g) sour cream
2 tbsp neutral, unrefined organic
   salad oil
2/3 cup (150 g) cottage cheese
salt
pepper, freshly ground

Preparation time: 15 min
Calories per serving: 180
11 g protein, 10 g fat,
11 g carbohydrate

- Wash the radishes well. Chop them finely in a blender or food processor.
- Peel and mince the garlic. Stir it into the radishes. Add buttermilk, sour cream, oil and cottage cheese and blend.

- Season the soup well and chill, if desired. The soup may also be served with ice cubes. Hearty rye bread or wholewheat bread complete the presentation.

Tip

For a spicier soup, use daikon radish. This white, carrot-shaped vegetable helps speed up the breakdown of fat in the body and is an excellent source of vitamin C. Dill and green onions complement daikon.

Cold-pressed sunflower seed oil and wheat germ oil have a neutral taste. For a subtle, nutty flavor, substitute cold-pressed almond oil.

Noodles and Rice

Chinese Noodle Stir Fry

Ingredients for 4 servings:

1 lb (500 g) Chinese egg noodles
1/2 lb (250 g) small mushrooms
1 tbsp lemon juice
2 thin leeks
1/2 lb (250 g) carrots
salt
4 tbsp unrefined coconut oil or
  palm oil
2 cups bean sprouts
4 eggs

Preparation time: 30 min
Calories per serving: 570
25 g protein, 18 g fat,
79 g carbohydrate

- Add the noodles to a large
  pot of boiling water and
  bring to the boil again.
  Reduce the heat and simmer
  the noodles for 4–5 minutes.

- Clean and halve the
  mushrooms and drizzle
  lemon juice over top.
  Clean and slice the leek. Peel
  the carrots and cut them
  into narrow strips.
- Heat 3 tbsp oil in a large
  frying pan or a wok. Sauté
  the mushrooms, leek and
  carrots for 10 minutes,
  stirring constantly. Add the
  sprouts and sauté briefly.
  Season with soy sauce. Add
  the noodles and heat.
- Meanwhile, fry 4 eggs in the
  remaining oil and serve them
  on the noodles.

Tip
Fresh mushrooms add flavor to
any meal. Try using shiitake,
portobello or oyster
mushrooms in combination
with, or instead of, regular
mushrooms.

Vegetable Rolls

Ingredients for 4 servings:

1 1/2 cups (200 g) flour
2 small eggs
2 tsp lemon juice
1 lb (500 g) carrots
2 tbsp butter
2 tsp flour
pepper, freshly ground
1 pinch grated lemon peel
1–2 tbsp lemon juice
2 tsp tomato paste
2 tbsp crème fraîche
  (see page 32)
2/3 lb (300 g) small broccoli
  flowerets (or use larger ones,
  chopped)
salt
1–2 tbsp unrefined coconut oil or
  clarified butter

Preparation time: 1 1/2 hrs
Calories per serving: 560
12 g protein, 16 g fat,
45 g carbohydrate

- Prepare a dough with flour,
  eggs, salt and lemon juice;
  allow to rest for 15 minutes.
- Wash the carrots, cut into
  small pieces and sauté them in
  butter. Dust the carrot pieces
  with flour, season with salt,
  pepper, lemon peel and juice
  and cook over low heat for
  15 minutes. Blend. Stir in the
  cooled tomato paste and
  crème fraîche.
- Preheat oven to 325°F
  (160°C). Roll out four flat
  sections of dough to 8" x 10"
  (20 cm x 25 cm). Spread with
  the carrot paste, leaving a
  clean narrow border on the far
  edge. Sprinkle broccoli over
  the carrot. Roll the flat
  sections and fold in the ends.
- Sauté the rolls. Then place
  them close together in a
  roasting bag and seal. Bake
  on the middle rack for
  25 minutes. Serve with
  tomato sauce.

"Spaetzle" Variations

Ingredients for 4 servings:

1 cup (150 g) spelt flour
 (or substitute millet or
 wholewheat flour)
3/4 cup (100 g) unbleached
 white flour
3 eggs
1/2 tsp salt
1/3 cup (80 ml) milk
1/3 cup (80 ml) water
1 tsp butter

Preparation time: 30 min
Calories per serving: 310
13 g protein, 10 g fat,
42 g carbohydrate

Traditional German "spaetzle" are a cross between noodles and dumplings. They are delicious and simple to make. This technique, although unfamiliar to many North Americans, is rather efficient. Once you've prepared the first batch of spaetzle, you'll finish the rest surprisingly quickly.

- Mix both flours with the eggs. Add the salt and milk to form a very soft dough or stiff batter. It should be a loose dough, but not runny. Allow to rest for 15 minutes.
- Bring a large pot of salted water to a boil. Ladle some of the dough onto a small cutting board. Holding the board in one hand above the boiling water, angle it slightly downward. As the batter runs over the edge of the board, trim it off with a sharp knife, allowing it to drop into the water. Do not allow the water to boil too vigorously. Continue scraping bits of batter into the water with a swift motion.
- Stir occasionally to prevent spaetzle from sticking. When all the spaetzle are floating at the surface, remove them to a strainer using a slotted spoon. Load the next batch of batter onto the board.
- When all are done, gently reheat the drained spaetzle in a pan with a little butter.

Tip

Make these recipes dairy-free by substituting water for the milk. If you make spaetzle on a regular basis, invest in a "spaetzle grater." This tool is available from some specialty European outlets.

Variations

Red spaetzle:
Purée 1/2 lb (250 g) cooked beets and mix into the dough.

Green spaetzle:
Wash, blanch and squeeze the moisture out of 1 lb (500 g) spinach. Purée, and blend into the dough.

Yellow-orange spaetzle:
Scrub 1/2 lb (250 g) carrots and cut them into pieces. Chop as finely as possible in a food processor or blender and add to the spaetzle dough.

Classic cheese spaetzle:
In one part of Germany freshly cooked spaetzle are prepared with fried onions and grated cheese. Yet another variation is cheese spaetzle with leek. Clean three leeks and slice into rings. Sauté in 1 tbsp butter, season with salt, nutmeg and pepper. Grate 1/3 lb (150 g) Swiss cheese. Cover each serving of spaetzle with layers of cheese and leek, ending with leek. If the spaetzle have been prepared beforehand, bake for 25 minutes at 375°F (190°C).

Green Noodles

Ingredients for 4 servings:

1 lime
1/2 lb (250 g) goat's cheese
  or Feta
1 lb (500 g) spinach fettuccine
salt
1 2/3 lb (800 g) small zucchini
1 thick bunch of mixed herbs
  (e.g., basil, marjoram, dill,
  parsley)
2 tbsp cold-pressed,
  extra-virgin olive oil
pepper, freshly ground
nutmeg, freshly grated

Preparation time: 30 min
Calories per serving: 600
26 g protein, 23 g fat,
76 g carbohydrate

- Grate the lime peel and juice
  the lime. Cut the cheese into
  small pieces. Marinate cheese
  in the lime peel and juice.

- Cook the noodles *al dente* in
  salted water according to
  directions and drain well.
- Wash the zucchini. Slice
  them lengthwise into thin
  strips using a vegetable
  peeler. Wash and finely chop
  the herbs.
- Heat the olive oil in a large
  saucepan. Stir in the
  zucchini strips. Season
  them with salt, pepper and
  nutmeg. Add the noodles and
  cheese, mix well and heat.
  Add the herbs and season
  to taste.

Tip
Spinach is a rich source of
calcium and iron. You can add
1/4 lb (100 g) fresh, steamed
spinach to this dish for an
extra boost of energy.

Pink Thyme Noodles

Ingredients for 4 servings:

1/3 lb (150 g) peeled, cooked
  beets
2 cups (300 g) flour
1 egg
1 tsp unrefined, organic
  cooking oil
1/2 tsp dried thyme
salt
flour for rolling out the dough
butter or cold-pressed organic
  pumpkin seed or flax oil

Preparation time: 1 hr
Calories per serving: 300
10 g protein, 3 g fat,
57 g carbohydrate

- Purée the beets. Mix flour
  with the egg, beets, oil,
  thyme and 1/2 tsp salt to
  form a smooth dough. Leave
  the dough wrapped in a
  damp cloth for 30 minutes.

- Divide the dough into
  medium-sized balls and roll
  them through a pasta roller
  so that you have fettucine
  strips.
- Bring salted water to a boil
  in a saucepan. Add the
  noodles to the boiling water
  and watch that they don't
  stick together. Cook for
  6–8 minutes. Add butter,
  pumpkin seed oil or flax oil
  to the drained noodles
  before serving. Serve with
  crumbled Feta.

Tip
You can also use this dough for
filled pasta pockets. Use
Creamy Nut Dip or Salsa
Verde (page 77) as a filling, or
use the filling from Giant
Stuffed Mushrooms
(page 137). Brush the edges
of the pockets with egg white
so they stick together.

Noodle-Vegetable Gratin

Ingredients for 4 servings:

1 lb (500 g) eggplant
1 lb (500 g) red and yellow peppers
salt, freshly ground pepper
3 tbsp cold-pressed, extra-virgin
 olive oil
1/2 lb (250 g) noodles of your choice
1 cup (200 g) quark (see page 32)
2 eggs
2/3 cup cream
1 cup (200 g) sour cream
2/3 cup (150 g) sheep's cheese
2 tbsp herbes de Provence in oil
 (or substitute 1 tbsp dried herbs
 stirred in 1 tbsp oil)
2 tbsp bread crumbs
unrefined coconut oil or butter for the
baking sheet and dish

Preparation time: 1 1/4 hrs
Calories per serving: 600
24 g protein, 30 g fat,
58 g carbohydrate

- Preheat the broiler. Wash the
  vegetables. Slice the eggplant,
  halve the peppers and clean out
  the insides.
- Place the vegetables on an oiled
  baking sheet, the peppers with
  their cut surfaces down. Salt them,
  sprinkle with oil, then broil.
- Turn the eggplant over after
  2 minutes or when they have
  turned golden. Broil the peppers
  until golden, remove everything
  from the broiler and reduce heat
  to 375°F (190°C). Cook the
  noodles according to the package
  directions.
- Peel and cut the peppers into
  strips.
- Mix the quark with eggs, cream
  and sour cream. Mix cheese and
  herbs into the oil and season the
  mixture with salt and pepper.
  Blend until creamy.
- Spread half of the noodles, quark
  mixture and vegetables in a
  casserole dish. Repeat this so
  that there are 2 layers.
- Scatter bread crumbs over the
  top layer of vegetables and
  drizzle the remaining oil over
  top. Bake on the middle rack for
  25 minutes.

Noodle Nests au Gratin

Ingredients for 4 servings:

2/3 lb (300 g) fettuccine
salt
1 tbsp cold-pressed, extra-virgin olive oil
1/3 lb (150 g) Mozzarella cheese
1 tbsp butter

Preparation time: 40 min
Calories per serving: 400
17 g protein, 13 g fat,
53 g carbohydrate

- Cook the noodles in boiling water until *al dente*.
- Cut the Mozzarella into small pieces. Preheat the oven to 375°F (190°C). Grease a baking sheet.
- Shape eight noodle nests. Place the filling in the center of each nest and spread Mozzarella over it. Bake on the middle rack for 8 minutes.

Tomato filling:

Cut 4 tomatoes in half horizontally, remove the juice and seeds. Beat 2 eggs with 4 tbsp milk, salt, pepper and 4 tbsp finely chopped fresh basil. Place tomato halves on the nests and add the beaten egg mixture.

Zucchini filling:

Roast 3 tbsp sunflower seeds in 1 tbsp oil. Sauté 1 lb (500 g) zucchini strips briefly with the seeds, add salt and pepper and fill the nests. Top with the Mozzarella.

Mushroom filling:

Sauté 1/2 lb (250 g) small mushrooms in 1 tsp butter with 2 sliced green onions. Add 1 tsp lemon juice, salt and pepper and fill the nests. Top with the Mozzarella.

Each recipe should fill 8 noodle nests.

Creamed Spinach Lasagna

Ingredients for 4 servings:

2 2/3 cups (600 g) cooked, chopped spinach (or substitute frozen creamed spinach)
1–2 cloves of garlic
1 1/3 cups (275 g) quark (see page 32)
1/2 cup (100 g) cream
2/3 cup (100 g) Parmesan cheese, freshly grated
3 eggs
salt
pepper, freshly ground
nutmeg, freshly grated
1/2 lb (250 g) lasagna noodles (do not precook)
2 tbsp butter

Preparation time: 1 hr
Calories per serving: 570
36 g protein, 30 g fat,
44 g carbohydrate

- Drain the spinach. If using frozen spinach, thaw it first. Peel and mince the garlic. Blend the quark with the cream, garlic, 1/2 cup Parmesan cheese and the eggs until smooth. Season well with salt, pepper and nutmeg.
- Preheat oven to 375°F (190°C). Grease a lasagna pan with butter.
- Spread a few spoonfuls of spinach in the pan and cover with a layer of noodles. Thinly cover the noodles with the quark mix. Layer the remaining spinach, noodles and quark until all ingredients have been used. End with a layer of spinach.
- Spread the remaining Parmesan cheese over the spinach and drizzle butter over top. Bake for 30 minutes on the middle rack.

Saffron-Orange Risotto with Pea Pods

Ingredients for 4 servings:

3 oranges
2/3 lb (300 g) snowpeas
1 onion
2 tbsp butter
1 1/3 cups (275 g) short-grain rice
3 1/4 cups (750 ml) vegetable
 stock
1 pinch saffron
salt
pepper, freshly ground

Preparation time: 45 min
Calories per serving: 400
7 g protein, 8 g fat,
64 g carbohydrate

- Peel and section the orange and extract a little bit of juice. Wash the peas. Peel and finely chop the onion.
- Heat the butter. Sauté the onion until translucent. Add rice.

- Add 1 cup of stock. Boil off the liquid, stirring continuously. Dissolve the saffron in a little hot water and add it to the orange juice.
- When the liquid is almost entirely evaporated, add more stock mixed with the saffron and orange juice and continue to simmer. There should always be just enough liquid in the saucepan to cover the rice. Add the peas after 20 minutes and cook for 2 minutes.
- Add oranges to the rice and allow them to heat up.
- The rice should be cooked but still firm. Season the risotto with salt and pepper.

Tomato Risotto

Ingredients for 4 servings:

1 onion
1 lb (500 g) roma tomatoes
1 bunch of fresh basil
2 tbsp cold-pressed, extra-virgin
 olive oil
1 1/3 cups (275 g) short-grain rice
1 cup (200 ml) tomato juice
2 tsp vegetable stock
salt
pepper, freshly ground

Preparation time: 40 min
Calories per serving: 310
7 g protein, 6 g fat,
58 g carbohydrate

- Peel and finely chop the onion. Blanch the tomatoes. Remove skins and seeds. Chop coarsely.
- Wash and finely chop the basil.

- Heat the oil in a saucepan. Sauté the onion until translucent. Add the rice and heat, stirring continuously, until it is light and translucent.
- Pour in half of the tomato juice, followed by the vegetable stock, and continue to stir.
- When the liquid has almost evaporated, add more tomato juice or water and allow it to simmer, keeping the rice just covered.
- Stir in the tomatoes after 20 minutes and let them heat up.
- Season with basil, salt and pepper.

Tip
Use Arborio rice for an authentic risotto. The rice's distinctive flavor, texture and aroma make a creamy and delicious rice dish.

Coconut-Rice Ring

Ingredients for 4 servings:

1 cup (250 ml) milk
3/4 cup (175 g) grated coconut
1 cup (200 g) brown rice
1 cup (250 ml) vegetable stock
unrefined coconut oil or butter
for the mold

Preparation time: 35 min
Calories per serving: 250
6 g protein, 7 g fat,
53 g carbohydrate

- Bring milk to a boil with the coconut, remove from heat and cool for a few minutes. Strain the milk through a cheesecloth.
- Top up the coconut milk to 1 3/4 cups (400 ml) with the vegetable stock.
- Simmer the rice in a pot with the stock and coconut milk for 20 minutes.

- Grease a ring mold of 6 cups (1.5 l capacity). Place the cooked rice in the mold and press down well.
- Leave the rice to sit for 2–3 minutes before unmolding.
- Serve with sweet and sour vegetables (next recipe).

Tip
If you use canned coconut milk, delete the first step.

Variations
Carrot-Rice Ring:
Cook 1 cup (200 g) rice with 1 cup (250 ml) vegetable stock and 1 cup (250 ml) carrot juice. Sauté 1 cup (200 g) grated carrots in 1–2 tsp butter and mix into the rice. Season with salt and pepper.

Herbed Rice Ring:
Cook 1 cup (200 g) rice in vegetable stock or salted water. Mix in finely chopped herbs.

Sweet and Sour Vegetables

Ingredients for 4 servings:

1 walnut-sized piece of ginger
2/3 lb (300 g) small mushrooms
2/3 lb (300 g) Chinese cabbage
2 green onions
4–5 tbsp unrefined coconut oil
2/3 cup (150 g) cashews
salt
2/3 cup (150 g) canned baby
  corncobs
1 cup bean sprouts
1/2 cup (125 ml) vegetable stock
2 tbsp natural ketchup
1 tsp sugar
soy sauce
1 tsp cornstarch

Preparation time: 30 min
Calories per serving: 290
8 g protein, 21 g fat,
17 g carbohydrate

- Peel and mince the ginger. Wash and clean the vegetables. Quarter the mushrooms, cut the Chinese cabbage into thin strips and slice the green onions.
- Heat the oil in a frying pan and roast the cashews, adding salt to taste.
- Add the ginger, mushrooms and cabbage and sauté them for 4 minutes. Then add the corncobs.
- Blend the stock with ketchup, soy sauce and cornstarch; then add this mix to the vegetables and bring to a strong boil. Add the sprouts and green onions and stir for 1 minute. Season the vegetables to taste.

Tip
True Chinese cabbage is called *sui choy*. It has tall, slender stalks with slightly flared leaves. Remember that Chinese cabbage cooks more quickly than regular cabbage.

Creole Rice

Ingredients for 4 servings:

3 tbsp cold-pressed, extra-virgin
 olive oil
1 cup (200 g) brown rice
 (or substitute white rice)
1 3/4 cups (400 ml) vegetable stock
1/2 tsp pepper, freshly ground
1 lb (500 g) firm apricots
1 bunch of green onions
1/3 cup (50 g) each of green and
 black olives
soy sauce
cinnamon
1/2 cup (75 g) cashews

Preparation time: 1 hr
Calories per serving: 450
8 g protein, 21 g fat,
54 g carbohydrate

- Heat 1 tbsp oil and sauté the
 rice. Add the stock and pepper,
 bring to a boil and simmer for
 45 minutes (adjust cooking time
 if substituting white rice).
- Wash, halve and pit the apricots.
 Cut the fruit into segments.
- Preheat the oven to 450°F
 (230°C). Oil a baking sheet.
- Wash and clean the green onions
 and chop them into fine rings.
- Pit and thinly slice the olives.
- Season the rice with soy sauce
 and a little cinnamon. Mix it
 with apricots, onions, olives and
 cashews and arrange on a baking
 sheet. Drizzle the remaining oil
 over the rice and bake on the
 middle rack for 8 minutes.

Tip
The rice can be prepared ahead of
time. You can vary this recipe with
peeled tomato segments, zucchini
slices, thyme, capers, pine nuts and
onions.

Fried Rice

Ingredients for 4 servings:

1 1/3 cup (275 g) basmati rice
 or long-grain white rice
salt
1/2 lb (250 g) asparagus
1 tsp butter
pepper, freshly ground
nutmeg, freshly grated
1/2 lb (250 g) Swiss chard
1 green onion
1 bunch of parsley
2 tbsp unrefined coconut oil
 or clarified butter
1 pinch grated lemon peel

Preparation time: 45 min
Calories per serving: 310
8 g protein, 7 g fat,
52 g carbohydrate

- Heat the rice in a saucepan,
 add 1 1/4 cups (550 ml)
 salted water, bring to a boil
 and simmer over a low heat
 for 20 minutes.

- Wash the asparagus and cut
 into sections. Place the
 asparagus in a little salted
 water with the butter and a
 pinch each of pepper and
 nutmeg, and cook for
 10 minutes.
- Wash the Swiss chard and
 cut it into thin strips.
 Wash the green onion and
 chop it into rings. Wash and
 coarsely chop the parsley.
- Heat the coconut oil in a
 wok or a large frying pan
 with a high rim. Add the
 Swiss chard and asparagus
 and sauté for 2 minutes,
 stirring continuously. Add
 the rice and green onions.
- Just before serving, garnish
 the rice with the parsley.
 Season with salt, pepper and
 lemon peel.

Tip
Try using day-old rice for a
drier, more flavorful dish.

Cheesy Rice Fritters

Ingredients for 4 servings:

1 cup (200 g) long-grain white
 rice (adjust cooking time if
 substituting brown rice)
salt
1 bunch of green onions
3 eggs
1/3 cup (75 g) flour
1 cup (150 g) grated cheese
 (e.g., Emmenthal)
pepper, freshly ground
paprika
unrefined coconut oil or clarified
 butter for frying

Preparation time: 45 min
Calories per serving: 930
41 g protein, 41 g fat,
88 g carbohydrate

- Bring the rice to a boil in
 2 cups (500 ml) salted
 water. Cover the rice and
 simmer for 20 minutes.
 When the rice is cooked,
 cool it slightly, uncovered.
- Wash and finely slice the
 green onions.
- Mix the onions, eggs, flour
 and cheese into the rice and
 season with the spices.
- Heat the oil or clarified
 butter in a frying pan. Cook
 the fritters until crisp and
 golden on both sides.

Tip
Vary this basic recipe by adding
grated carrots, cauliflower or
broccoli, sprouts or any other
leftover vegetables. Children
especially like a sweet variation
made with coarsely grated
apple (leave out cheese and
spices).

Grains and Pulses

Polenta-Mushroom Slices

Ingredients for 4 servings:

1 1/2 cups (250 g) cornmeal
3 1/4 cups (750 ml) vegetable stock
3 tbsp butter
1 lb (500 g) mushrooms
1 onion
salt
pepper, freshly ground
nutmeg, freshly grated
2 tbsp chopped parsley
unrefined coconut oil for frying

Preparation time: 4 hrs (including 3 hrs for the polenta to set)
Calories per serving: 380
6 g protein, 18 g fat,
48 g carbohydrate

- To make the polenta, place the cornmeal in a saucepan with the vegetable stock and half of the butter and bring to a boil while stirring. Simmer for 15 minutes over low heat, stirring occasionally.
- Clean and slice the mushrooms. Peel and finely chop the onion. Heat the remaining butter and sauté the onion and mushrooms for 5 minutes or until cooked. Add salt and pepper.
- Stir cooked mushroom mix into the polenta. Add parsley.
- Spread the polenta about 1" (2.5 cm) thick on a greased baking sheet and let it set for 3 hours.
- Slice the polenta into strips and sauté on both sides in hot coconut oil until crisp. Serve with Tomato Sauce (page 72), if desired.

Tip
Cornmeal is an excellent source of carbohydrates.

Carrot Star

Ingredients for 4 servings:

1 lb (500 g) carrots
1 clove of garlic
2 tbsp butter
salt, freshly ground pepper
2 cups (500 ml) vegetable stock
1 cup (250 ml) milk
1 1/4 cups (250 g) coarse cornmeal or corn grits
1/2 cup (100 g) sour cream
1 cup (150 g) grated firm cheese (e.g., white Cheddar or Emmenthal)
oil or butter for the baking sheet

Preparation time: 1 hr
Calories per serving: 520
22 g protein, 23 g fat,
54 g carbohydrate

- Scrub the carrots and slice in half from end to end. Peel and mince the garlic. Melt butter in a frying pan and sauté the carrots with salt and pepper. Add 2 tsp of vegetable stock. Add the garlic and simmer with the lid on for 10 minutes.
- Remove carrots from the saucepan. Add the remaining stock and boil with the milk.
- Add cornmeal to the liquid. Cook for 5 minutes, stirring until thick. Remove from the heat and allow the mixture to cool for 15 minutes.
- Heat the oven to 375°F (190°C). Grease a large, deep pie plate or flan pan.
- Fold the sour cream into the cornmeal mixture, season with salt and pepper. Spread the mixture evenly in the pie plate.
- Arrange the carrots in a star shape on the polenta and sprinkle with cheese. Bake on the middle rack for 12 minutes or until the cheese has melted.

Spelt Patties with Cheese Sauce

Ingredients for 4 servings:

1 onion
1 clove of garlic
1/3 lb (150 g) zucchini
1 tbsp butter
1 cup (200 g) coarsely ground spelt
1 2/3 cups (375 ml) vegetable stock
1 bunch of mixed herbs
1 egg
1 cup (225 g) herbed cream cheese
salt
pepper, freshly ground
unrefined coconut oil, coconut butter
 or clarified butter for frying

Preparation time: 30 min
Calories per serving: 380
15 g protein, 17 g fat,
23 g carbohydrate

- Mince the onion and garlic.
  Wash and grate the zucchini.
- Heat the butter, then sauté the
  onion and garlic until
  translucent. Add the zucchini
  and spelt and sauté these briefly.
  Then add 1 cup (250 ml) stock
  and bring to a boil. Cover and
  simmer for 3 minutes. Allow the
  mixture to cool.
- Meanwhile, wash and finely chop
  the herbs.
- Add the egg, 1/3 cup (75 g)
  cream cheese and the herbs to
  the spelt. Mix together and
  season with salt and pepper.
- Using damp hands, shape
  8 patties. Heat the coconut oil,
  fry the patties briefly, place a lid
  on the frying pan and bake for
  8–10 minutes or until cooked,
  turning once during cooking.
  Remove the patties and keep
  warm.
- Add the remaining stock to the
  frying pan and dissolve the rest
  of the cream cheese in it. Season
  with salt and pepper. Serve with
  the patties.

Tip
The patties can also be served with
salad or vegetables instead of the
sauce.

Spelt Dumplings

Ingredients for 4 servings:

1 1/4 cups (250 g) coarsely ground
  spelt
1 cup (250 ml) vegetable stock
1 cup (250 ml) milk
1/4 cup (50 g) Parmesan cheese,
  freshly grated
salt
pepper, freshly ground
3 tbsp butter

Preparation time: 30 min
Calories per serving: 330
12 g protein, 12 g fat,
25 g carbohydrate

- Bring the spelt to a boil in
  the stock and milk. Stir in
  cheese, salt and pepper, cook
  for 15 minutes or until thick.
- Shape dumplings using two
  spoons (see technique,
  page 84).
- Melt the butter and drizzle
  over the dumplings.

Spelt Quiche

Ingredients for 4 servings:

1 1/4 cups (250 g) spelt
1 onion
1 clove of garlic
1 tsp butter
2 cups (500 ml) vegetable stock
1/2 lb (250 g) carrots
1/4 lb (125 g) edible-pod peas
  (e.g., snowpeas, sugar-snap peas)
1/2 lb (250 g) asparagus
salt, freshly ground pepper
3 eggs
1/2 cup (120 g) herbed
  cream cheese
1/2 cup (100 g) sour cream
1 bunch of fresh basil
1–2 tbsp cold-pressed,
  extra-virgin olive oil
unrefined coconut oil or butter
  to grease the pan

Preparation time: 2 hrs
(+ 12 hrs soaking time)
Calories per serving: 450
18 g protein, 20 g fat,
47 g carbohydrate

- Soak the spelt in water
  overnight.
- The next day, mince the
  onion and garlic and sauté in
  melted butter. Add the spelt,
  pour in the stock and
  simmer the mixture for
  1 1/4 hours in a covered
  saucepan. Remove from the
  heat and cool.
- Scrub the carrots. Cut into
  bite-sized pieces. Wash the
  peas. Clean and prepare the
  asparagus and cut them into
  sections.
- Place the carrots and
  asparagus in a large, flat
  saucepan. Add a little salted
  water and cook for
  15 minutes. Add the peas
  during the last 5 minutes.
  Remove vegetables and drain.
- Preheat the oven to 375°F
  (190°C). Grease a large pie
  plate or flan pan.
- Separate the eggs. Stir the
  egg yolks into the spelt,

season with a little salt and
pepper then pour into the
pie plate.
- Beat the egg whites until
  stiff, and combine them with
  the cream cheese and sour
  cream. Season the mixture
  with salt and pepper.
- Spread the egg mix over the
  spelt. Scatter the vegetables
  decoratively over the top and
  press in gently. Coarsely
  chop the basil and sprinkle it
  over the quiche.
- Bake the quiche on the
  middle rack for 20 minutes.
  Halfway through the cooking
  drizzle olive oil over the
  vegetables.

Crispy Moons with Tomato Sauce

Ingredients for 2 servings:

1 1/2 cups (350 ml) milk
3/4 cup (150 g) buckwheat groats
1/4 cup (25 g) grated cheese
 (e.g., Emmenthal)
1 lb (500 g) tomatoes
1 bunch of chives
butter for frying
salt
pepper, freshly ground

Preparation time: 50 min
Calories per serving: 520
20 g protein, 17 g fat,
72 g carbohydrate

- Bring 1 1/4 cups (300 ml) milk to a boil. Add the groats and return to a boil. When the mixture thickens (after 2 minutes), stir in the cheese.
- Using a wet knife, spread the mixture out on a cutting board (to about 1/3 " (1.5 cm) thick) and allow it to cool completely.
- Blanch the tomatoes. Remove the skins and seeds. Purée the tomato flesh with the rest of the milk.
- Wash and chop the chives. Using the rim of an overturned glass, cut moon shapes from the buckwheat.
- Melt the butter and fry the moons over low heat until they are golden.
- Heat the tomato-milk purée, season with salt and pepper and stir in the chopped chives. Serve with the moons.

Tip

Buckwheat seeds are called groats. When coarsely ground, they are called grits; when finely ground, they become buckwheat flour.

Millet Dumplings with Peppers

Ingredients for 4 servings:

1 1/4 cups (250 g) millet
3 eggs
1 3/4 cups (400 g) quark
 (see page 32)
salt
nutmeg, freshly grated
1 tbsp Parmesan cheese,
 freshly grated
3 red peppers
1 onion
2 tbsp butter
1/2 cup (125 ml) vegetable stock
1/4 cup (50 g) crème fraîche
 (see page 32)

Preparation time: 1 1/2 hrs
Calories per serving: 550
27 g protein, 25 g fat,
52 g carbohydrate

- Grind the millet to a flour. Separate the eggs. Mix the egg yolks with millet, quark, salt, nutmeg and Parmesan cheese and set aside.
- Preheat the oven to 375°F (190°C). Fill a deep cake pan with salted water, place on the middle rack of the oven and allow to heat.
- Wash the peppers and cut them into thin strips. Peel the onion and cut into pieces.
- Sauté the onion and pepper in melted butter, add stock and spices and cook for 5 minutes. Season with crème fraîche and salt.
- Beat the egg whites until stiff then fold into the millet dough. Shape dumplings using two spoons (see page 84). Place dumplings into the water in the cake pan. Let them bake for 20 minutes, turning them after 10 minutes.
- Drain the dumplings and arrange them on the peppers.

Millet Pudding with Chive Sauce

Ingredients for 4 servings:

1 tbsp cold-pressed, extra-virgin olive oil
1 1/4 cups (250 g) millet
1 3/4 cups (400 ml) vegetable stock
1 cup (200 g) quark (see page 32)
salt
pepper, freshly ground
paprika
2 small red peppers
1 green pepper
1 small leek
4 eggs
2/3 cup (150 g) cream cheese
1 cup (250 g) natural yogurt
1 small bunch of chives
butter, millet and bread crumbs
 for the pan

Preparation time: 2 hrs
(includes 1 hr baking time)
Calories per serving: 550
30 g protein, 23 g fat,
53 g carbohydrate

- Heat the oil and lightly sauté the millet. Add the stock and bring the mixture to a boil.
- Fold in the quark, season the mixture well and cook for 20 minutes over low heat. Cool.
- Wash and chop the peppers into small pieces. Wash and thinly slice the leek. Preheat the oven to 375°F (190°C). Grease a tube pan and dust with the millet and bread crumbs.
- Separate the eggs. Fold the egg yolks and the vegetables into the millet mixture. Beat the egg whites until stiff, fold into the mixture. Place batter in the pan and bake on the middle rack for 55 minutes.
- Blend the cream cheese and yogurt well. Wash the chives and cut them into short sections. Stir them into the yogurt sauce. Season with salt and pepper.
- Remove the tube pan from the oven; allow to cool for a few minutes before unmolding.

Bulgur Pilaf

Ingredients for 4 servings:

1 onion
2 tbsp clarified butter
1 cup (200 g) bulgur
2 cups (500 ml) vegetable stock
1 cup (150 g) dried apricots
1 bunch of parsley
2–3 sprigs of fresh mint
2 tbsp slivered or flaked almonds
salt
pepper, freshly ground
ginger powder

Preparation time: 20 min
Calories per serving: 360
4 g protein, 8 g fat,
23 g carbohydrate

• Peel and mince the onion. Heat the clarified butter in a heavy saucepan or casserole dish and sauté the onion until translucent. Add the bulgur and stir constantly.

Add the stock and simmer, with the lid, on for 5 minutes.
• Wash the apricots, pat them dry and cut into thin strips. Wash and chop the parsley and mint.
• Mix the apricots and almonds into the bulgur and cook for another 5 minutes. The liquid should be entirely absorbed. Season the bulgur with salt, pepper and ginger, stir in the parsley and mint. This pilaf goes well with any type of vegetable, whether barbecued, stuffed or stir fried.

Tip
Any grain can be used to make a pilaf. Sauté the grain until golden, add the liquid and simmer, covered, until cooked.

Pan-fried Bulgur

Ingredients for 4 servings:

1 1/2 cups (350 ml) vegetable stock
3/4 cup (175 g) bulgur
2/3 lb (300 g) broccoli
salt
4 celery stalks
1/3 lb (150 g) carrots
3 tbsp unrefined, organic sesame oil
2/3 cup (100 g) unsalted peanuts
pepper, freshly ground
ground lemon grass to taste (available at Asian grocery stores)
soy sauce

Preparation time: 40 min
Calories per serving: 380
10 g protein, 19 g fat,
8 g carbohydrate

• Bring the stock to a boil, add the bulgur, turn off the heat and allow to cool for

30 minutes. The bulgur will absorb the liquid.
• Wash the broccoli, cut it into small flowerets and blanch for 3 minutes in boiling salted water. Wash the celery and carrots and cut into thin slices.
• Dry roast the peanuts for a short time. Heat the oil in a large frying pan, then sauté the vegetables and peanuts in the oil for 5 minutes, stirring constantly.
• Add the bulgur and let it heat up. Season with salt, pepper, lemon grass and a little soy sauce.

Tip
This recipe can be varied with seasonal vegetables.

Couscous with Ratatouille

Ingredients for 4 servings:

1 large eggplant
1 lb (500 g) zucchini
1 lb (500 g) tomatoes
1 onion
1–2 cloves of garlic
4–5 tbsp cold-pressed,
  extra-virgin olive oil
salt
white pepper, freshly ground
1 1/2 cups (300 g) couscous
2 cups (500 ml) tomato juice
1 1/3 cups (300 g) sour cream

Preparation time: 35 min
Calories per serving: 500
16 g protein, 17 g fat,
71 g carbohydrate

- Wash the vegetables. Blanch the tomatoes and remove their skins and seeds. Cut the vegetables into bite-sized pieces. Peel and mince the onion and garlic.
- Heat the oil, sauté the onion and eggplant pieces until golden, add the zucchini and season with garlic, salt and pepper.
- Add the tomato juice with 2 cups (500 ml) water and the couscous. Simmer for 20 minutes. Add the tomato pieces 5 minutes before the end of the cooking time. If necessary, add more liquid. Serve with the sour cream.

Tip
The vegetables can also be prepared without the couscous. Season with mixed dried herbs. Serve the couscous separately or replace it with polenta or nutritious bread.

Quinoa Ring with Wild Herb Sauce

Ingredients for 4 servings

1 1/4 cups (250 g) quinoa
1 3/4 cups (400 ml) vegetable stock
1 lb (500 g) carrots
2 eggs
1 cup (200 g) grated Gouda cheese
salt, freshly ground pepper
nutmeg, freshly grated
unrefined coconut oil or butter to
 grease the cake mold

For the sauce:
2 handfuls nettle tips or baby leaf
 spinach
1 handful dandelion greens
1 handful sorrel
1 onion
1 tsp butter
2/3 cup (150 ml) vegetable stock
1/2 cup (100 g) crème fraîche
 (see page 32)
1 tbsp finely ground millet flour
2 tbsp lemon juice

Preparation time: 1 hr
Calories per serving: 520
19 g protein, 26 g fat,
54 g carbohydrate

- Heat the quinoa in a saucepan.
 add the stock and simmer for
 15 minutes.
- Wash the carrots, chop into small
 pieces and add to the quinoa
 after 5 minutes of simmering.
- Preheat the oven to 375°F
 (190°C). Grease a tube pan
 (6-cup capacity (1.5 l)).
- Separate the eggs. Stir egg yolks
 and cheese into the cooled quinoa.
- Beat egg whites until stiff and
 fold in. Season the mixture and
 place in the pan.
- Bake the quinoa ring on the
 middle rack for 25 minutes.
- To prepare the sauce: wash and
 finely chop herbs. Peel and mince
 the onion and sauté it in the
 butter. Add the stock, crème
 fraîche and herbs, stir well and
 bring to a boil. Add the flour
 then let the sauce simmer. Season
 with lemon juice and spices.
 Serve with the quinoa ring.

Amaranth-Mushroom Fry

Ingredients for 2 servings:

3/4 cup (150 g) amaranth
1 1/2 cups (350 ml) vegetable
 stock
1 lb (500 g) mushrooms
1/2 lb (250 g) tomatoes
2 tbsp butter or unrefined coconut
 oil for frying
salt
pepper, freshly ground
2 tbsp lemon juice
2 tbsp chopped parsley
1/4 cup (50 g) sour cream

Preparation time: 30 min
Calories per serving: 500
17 g protein, 20 g fat,
62 g carbohydrate

- Heat the dry amaranth in a
 saucepan, add the stock and
 simmer for 10–15 minutes.
 Remove from heat, cover and
 allow to cool.

- Briefly wash, clean and
 quarter the mushrooms.
 Blanch the tomatoes for
 1 minute, remove the skins
 and cut them into segments.
- Heat the butter in a frying
 pan, sauté the mushrooms
 until golden then season
 with salt, pepper and
 lemon juice.
- Add amaranth to the
 mushrooms and sauté them
 together. Add the parsley and
 tomatoes at the last minute.
- Serve with sour cream.

Variation
Amaranth has a sweet, nutty
flavor. For a slightly milder
taste, substitute barley, millet
or quinoa. For a heartier dish,
try wild rice on its own or in
combination with long-grain
brown rice.

Quinoa "Tortilla"

Ingredients for 4 servings:

3/4 cup (150 g) quinoa
1 cup (250 ml) sauerkraut juice
 (from the health food store)
1 red pepper
3–4 green onions
2–3 boiled potatoes (skins left on)
3 eggs
4 tbsp cream
salt
pepper, freshly ground
paprika
1 tbsp clarified butter
1/3 lb (150 g) dry Ricotta cheese
2 frying pans

Preparation time: 40 min
Calories per serving: 550
22 g protein, 29 g fat,
46 g carbohydrate

- Bring the quinoa to a boil
 in the sauerkraut juice then
 simmer for 20 minutes.

- Meanwhile, clean the
 vegetables. Chop the pepper
 into small pieces and slice the
 onion into rings. Peel and
 slice the potatoes.
- Stir the eggs and cream into
 the cooled quinoa to form a
 thick batter and season with
 salt, pepper and paprika.
- Heat half the clarified butter
 in a large frying pan, add
 half of the potatoes and
 distribute half of the quinoa
 mixture over them. Scatter
 half of the onions and
 peppers over top.
- Crumble the cheese and
 scatter half of it over the
 quinoa. Cook covered for
 20 minutes or until the top
 layer is done. Keep warm.
 Bake the second "tortilla"
 in the same way in a second
 frying pan.

Red Lentil-stuffed Peppers

Ingredients for 4 servings:

8 small or 4 large red peppers
1 tbsp butter
1 cup (200 g) red lentils
1 cup (200 g) fresh or frozen corn
2–3 green onions
1 1/4 cups (250 g) grated cheese
  (e.g., Emmenthal)
1 tsp turmeric
1 tsp paprika
1 3/4 cups (400 ml) vegetable
  stock
1/2 cup (125 g) cream
3 tsp millet flour
2 tbsp nutritional yeast

Preparation time: 1 hr
Calories per serving: 620
39 g protein, 28 g fat,
55 g carbohydrate

- Wash the peppers, cut out
  their lids, clean out the
  interiors and pat dry with a

paper towel. Heat the butter
and sauté the peppers,
turning them often. Remove
them from the pan.
- Mix the corn and lentils.
- Wash the green onions, cut
  into rings and fold into the
  corn-lentil mix with 1 cup
  (150 g) of the cheese,
  turmeric and paprika.
- Fill peppers with the mix
  and distribute the remaining
  cheese over top. Replace
  the lids and place in the
  saucepan for cooking.
  Add the stock and cook for
  40 minutes over low heat.
- Remove the vegetables, add
  cream to the sauce, add the
  millet flour for thickening
  and season with the yeast.

Tip
Serve with rice or boiled
potatoes. Stuffed peppers are
a great party favorite.

Dal

Ingredients for 4 servings:

1 1/4 cups (250 g) brown lentils
3 onions
2 cloves of garlic
1 piece fresh ginger, walnut-sized
3 tbsp clarified butter
1 tsp turmeric
1 tsp cumin
salt
pepper, freshly ground
1/2 bunch of cilantro
1–2 tbsp lemon juice

Preparation time: 1 hr
Calories per serving: 310
16 g protein, 10 g fat,
38 g carbohydrate

- Rinse lentils in a sieve under
  cold running water.
- Peel and mince one onion
  and the garlic. Peel and finely
  grate the ginger.

- Heat 1 tbsp clarified butter
  in a saucepan, sauté the
  onion, garlic and ginger. Add
  the spices and lentils. Add
  2 cups (500 ml) water and
  1 tsp salt. Cook covered for
  30 minutes.
- Meanwhile, peel the
  remaining 2 onions, halve
  and slice them. Wash the
  cilantro and remove leaves.
- When the lentils are cooked,
  season with salt, pepper and
  lemon juice then stir in half
  of the cilantro leaves.
- Sauté the onions in the
  remaining butter until
  golden. Arrange the dal in a
  bowl with onions and
  cilantro.

Variation
Make a dish combining rice
and lentils. Use 3/4 cup
(150 g) yellow lentils and
1/2 cup (100 g) basmati rice in
place of the brown lentils.

Spicy Baked Lentils

Ingredients for 4 servings:

1 cup (150 g) wholewheat flour
4 tbsp cold-pressed, extra-virgin olive oil
2 red peppers
2 red chili peppers
2 cloves of garlic
2 onions
1 lb (500 g) potatoes
1 1/2 cups (300 g) lentils
2 cups (500 ml) vegetable stock
1 sprig of thyme
1 tsp curry powder
3 tbsp tomato paste
1 tbsp unrefined, organic sesame
 or olive oil
1/4 cup (30 g) sunflower seeds
salt

Preparation time: 2 1/2 hrs
Calories per serving: 620
29 g protein, 16 g fat,
89 g carbohydrate

- Add 1 tsp salt to the flour.
  Stir in 6 tbsp water and then
  knead in the olive oil. Add
  enough water to form a flexible
  dough. Refrigerate it for
  1 hour.
- Preheat the oven to 325°F
  (160°C).
- Wash the peppers and the chilis,
  remove the interiors (use caution
  with the chili peppers) and chop
  finely.
- Peel and cut the potatoes into
  small pieces.
- Mix all the vegetables with the
  lentils, vegetable stock, some salt,
  thyme, curry powder and tomato
  paste and place them in a large
  cake pan or stoneware baking
  dish. Roll the dough out over
  top and press down all around.
  Drizzle sesame oil over the
  dough and sprinkle with
  sunflower seeds. Bake for
  65 minutes on the middle rack.

Chili sans carne

Ingredients for 4 servings:

1 1/4 cups (250 g) kidney beans
2 red peppers
salt
1 lb (500 g) tomatoes
2 onions
1 cup (150 g) black olives
1 bunch of fresh basil
2 tbsp clarified butter
2 tbsp chili paste
1/2 cup (100 ml) tomato juice
cayenne pepper

Preparation time: 50 min
(+ overnight soaking time)
Calories per serving: 880
43 g protein, 22 g fat,
120 g carbohydrate

- Soak kidney beans overnight in 3 1/4 cups (750 ml) water.
- Drain and add 3 1/4 cups (750 ml) of fresh water.

Simmer the beans for 45 minutes and drain.
- Meanwhile, broil the peppers on a baking sheet directly under the element. Roast them on all sides. Remove from the oven, salt them all over and cover with a damp cloth. Remove skins while the peppers are still warm; remove seeds and stalks. Reserve the juice and cut the peppers into large pieces.
- Blanch the tomatoes, remove their skins and seeds and cut into large pieces. Peel the onions and slice into thin rings. Pit the olives, wash the basil and remove their stems. Blend the olives and basil together.
- Heat the clarified butter and sauté the onions until translucent. Add the chili paste and cook briefly.

- Add the tomatoes, peppers, beans and olives, tomato and pepper juices and simmer for another 10 minutes. Season with salt and cayenne pepper.

Variations

For variety, use black beans or garbanzo beans (chickpeas), or use grains like bulgur or spelt. Try tofu or tempeh with the vegetables as additional or alternative sources of protein. Tofu is also rich in calcium and essential fatty acids which promote brain development. For a colorful, vegetable chili, stir in chopped carrots, corn, small amounts of zucchini and green pepper. Add some fresh chopped chilies for extra heat.

Tip

As beans soak, gases from them escape into the water. After soaking, always rinse and cook beans with fresh water. This goes for canned beans as well.

To prepare a Mexican meal, make the Avocado Dip (page 74) as an appetizer. Eliminate the basil and use lime juice instead of lemon juice and call it "guacamole." Serve with tortilla chips and Tomato-Yogurt Salad (page 64), tostada shells or crisp corn bread. Pineapple with coconut or lime ice cream is best as a dessert. Or, serve the pineapple with coconut cream (made by adding grated coconut to whipped cream).

Beans and Tomatoes with Cheese Crust

Ingredients for 4 servings:

1 cup (200 g) fresh or frozen
  broad beans
1 cup (250 ml) vegetable stock
1 tsp cold-pressed, extra-virgin
  olive oil
1 pinch of dried thyme
salt
pepper, freshly ground
1 lb (500 g) firm tomatoes
1/3 cup (100 g) cream
2 cups (150 g) grated cheese
  (e.g., Emmenthal)
1/3 cup (25 g) fresh bread crumbs
2 tbsp butter
unrefined coconut oil or butter to
  grease the dish

Preparation time: 40 min
Calories per serving: 450
26 g protein, 24 g fat,
32 g carbohydrate

- Heat the oil, stir the beans into it, add the stock and boil uncovered for 15 minutes or until the liquid has evaporated.
- Blanch the tomatoes, wait for a minute, remove the skins and cut into quarters.
- Grease a casserole dish. Preheat the oven to 400°F (200°C).
- Layer the tomatoes and beans in the dish. Cover the layers with cream. Mix the cheese with the bread crumbs, scatter them over the top and drizzle with butter.
- Bake for 12 minutes on the middle rack. Roasted potatoes make a good accompaniment to this savory dish.

Tip
If possible, use flageolet beans in this recipe. These long, slender beans are used extensively in French cooking. They taste best when fresh, but they are also available in tins or jars. When picking fresh beans, look for soft, thick green beans rather than the more intense-tasting brown beans. If you use canned flageolet beans in this recipe, cook them for 20 minutes; fresh beans will need slightly less cooking time.

Variations
Fresh broad beans make a good side dish. Sauté chopped onion and garlic in butter, add the beans and vegetable stock. After 15–20 minutes let the liquid boil down and serve the beans sprinkled with chopped parsley. Or, blend them with sour cream and serve as a purée.

Vary the type of cheese for different flavors and textures. Cheeses can be classified according to their water content. The hardest cheeses contain less than 57% water and the softest cheeses contain more than 73% water.

- Hard cheeses, such as Parmesan, Romano and Asiago, have a robust flavor.
- Semi-hard or firm cheeses, such as Cheddar, Gouda, Edam and Emmenthal, taste milder and are suitable for sandwiches, salads and cooking.
- Semi-soft cheeses, such as Feta, Monterey Jack and Mozzarella, vary greatly in taste.
- Examples of soft cheeses are Camembert, Brie and Roquefort.

Chickpea-Spinach-Herbed Cheese Medley

Ingredients for 4 servings:

1 1/4 cups (250 g) chickpeas
dried thyme
salt
1 onion
1 clove of garlic
1 1/2 lb (750 g) fresh spinach
1 1/2–2 tbsp unrefined coconut oil
1/4 cup (50 g) oat flakes
1/2 cup (120 g) herbed cream cheese
nutmeg, freshly grated
pepper, freshly ground
soy sauce

Preparation time: 2 1/4 hrs
(+12 hrs soaking time)
Calories per serving: 380
21 g protein, 15 g fat,
43 g carbohydrate

- Soak the chickpeas overnight.
- The next day, drain the chickpeas and cook them in 2 cups (500 ml) of fresh water and 1 tsp thyme for 1 3/4 hours. Drain when done.
- Peel and mince the onion and garlic.
- Wash the spinach, tear into bite-sized pieces and remove any hard stems. Cook briefly in boiling water and drain well.
- Heat the coconut oil in a large frying pan or a wok and sauté the onion and garlic with the chickpeas and oats.
- Add the spinach and cream cheese and heat gently. Season with nutmeg, pepper, salt and soy sauce.

Fresh Mint Peas

Ingredients for 4 servings:

2 cups (400 g) dried green peas
1 bunch of mixed herbs
1 tsp salt
1 bunch of fresh mint
2 sprigs of lemon balm
1 bunch of green onions
2 tbsp butter

Preparation time: 1 1/2 hrs
(+12 hrs soaking time)
Calories per serving: 140
6 g protein, 7 g fat,
12 g carbohydrate

- Wash the peas and soak them overnight in 3 1/4 cups (750 ml) cold water. Wash and finely cut the herbs.
- Add the herbs and salt to the undrained peas and simmer for 45 minutes or until cooked. (Cooking time may be longer for older peas.)
- Wash and finely chop the mint and lemon balm. Wash and clean the green onions and chop them into fine rings.
- Heat the butter and sauté the green onions briefly. Add the peas, mint and lemon balm, and heat.

Tip

This recipe tastes delicious with fresh peas. Sauté them with the green onions and they should cook in 8–10 minutes. Peppermint has stronger healing properties than either spearmint or wintermint. Use fresh peppermint to boost your energy and help relieve digestive ailments.

Curried Chickpea Fritters

Ingredients for 4 servings:

2 cups (400 g) chickpeas
2 tsp powdered vegetable broth
1 onion
1 clove of garlic
1 tbsp butter
2 stalks of lemon thyme
1 small bunch of salad greens
3 eggs
chili powder
curry powder
nutritional yeast
salt
lemon juice
unrefined coconut oil for frying

Preparation time: 1 1/2 hrs
(+ 12 hrs soaking time)
Calories per serving: 450
27 g protein, 14 g fat,
52 g carbohydrate

- Soak the chickpeas in 3 1/4 cups (750 ml) water overnight. The next day drain the water and add 5 1/4 cups (1.25 l) of fresh water. Add the powdered vegetable broth. Cook the chickpeas in the broth for just 1 hour.
- Peel and mince the onion and garlic. Sauté in butter until translucent.
- Wash the herbs and remove stems.
- Blend the chickpeas with the herbs and eggs. Add the onion and garlic and season to taste with spices and salt.
- Using two spoons, pass the mixture back and forth to shape the fritters (see technique, page 84).
- Heat about 1/2" (1 cm) coconut oil in a frying pan. Fry fritters over medium heat for 5 minutes, turning them several times. Drain them on paper towels. Drizzle with lemon juice. Serve with Pear-Mustard Dip or Hot Pepper Dip (recipes on page 74).

Vegetables and Mushrooms

Stuffed Swiss Chard Rolls

Ingredients for 4 servings:

2 lb (1 kg) Swiss chard
salt, freshly ground pepper
1 onion
2 tbsp butter
1 bunch of chives
1 cup (250 g) quark (see page 32)
2 small eggs
3/4–1 cup (150 g) grated cheese
nutmeg, freshly grated
1/2 cup (100 ml) vegetable stock

Preparation time: 45 min
Calories per serving: 310
28 g protein, 18 g fat,
6 g carbohydrate

- Wash the Swiss chard and
  remove tough stems. Blanch
  the leaves in salted water,
  rinse in cold water and drain.
  Slice the leaf ribs so they lie
  flat. Chop the remaining
  stems into small pieces.

- Peel and dice the onion.
  Sauté the onion and the
  chard stems in half of the
  butter for 5 minutes. Allow
  to cool.
- Wash and chop the chives.
  Mix the cooled chard stems
  with the quark, eggs, cheese
  and chives and season to
  taste.
- Place the chard leaves on a
  work surface (with small
  leaves lay two together),
  divide the quark stuffing
  among them, roll them up
  and fold in the ends.
- Melt the remaining butter in
  a large, flat saucepan. Add
  the rolls, pour in the stock
  and cook covered for
  20 minutes.

Tip
Chard is a member of the beet
family, but is nutritionally
similar to spinach.

Swiss Chard with Cheesy Mashed Potatoes

Ingredients for 4 servings:

2 lb (1 kg) potatoes for mashing
3 1/3 lb (1.6 kg) Swiss chard
2 onions
1 clove of garlic
3 tbsp butter
2 cups (500 ml) milk
salt, freshly ground pepper
nutmeg, freshly grated
1/2 cup (100 g) crème fraîche
 (see page 32)
1 tbsp chopped almonds
1 tbsp cold-pressed,
 extra-virgin olive oil
1 pinch of thyme
1 cup (150 g) grated Cheddar
1/2 cup (100 g) Ricotta cheese or
 quark (see page 32)

Preparation time: 45 min
Calories per serving: 670
20 g protein, 29 g fat,
51 g carbohydrate

- Wash the potatoes and cook
  in a little water. Wash the
  Swiss chard, separate leaves
  from the stalks. Chop the
  stalks into short pieces and
  cut the leaves into strips.
- Peel and chop the onions and
  garlic into small pieces.
  Sauté the onion and Swiss
  chard stalks in 1 tbsp
  butter. Add 1/2 cup
  (125 ml) milk, season and
  cook for 20 minutes then
  add the crème fraîche.
- Sauté the almonds in oil,
  add the chard leaves, garlic,
  salt and pepper, stirring
  continuously. Season with
  the thyme.
- Heat the remaining milk.
  Peel and mash the potatoes
  and beat them with the milk,
  grated cheese, butter and the
  Ricotta until the potatoes
  are light and fluffy. Serve
  with both chard dishes.

Herbed Asparagus Quiche

Ingredients for 2 servings:

2 lb (1 kg) asparagus
1 tsp lemon juice
salt
nutmeg, freshly grated
1 pinch sugar
1 bunch of mixed herbs
1/2 cup (100 g) mild, soft cheese
2/3 cup (150 g) sour cream
3 eggs
1 tsp cornstarch

Preparation time: 40 min
Calories per serving: 380
24 g protein, 22 g fat,
18 g carbohydrate

- Clean and prepare the asparagus. Mix the lemon juice with salt, nutmeg and sugar.
- Place the asparagus with the lemon juice mixture in a flat saucepan and add just enough water to cover. Simmer for 10 minutes.
- Wash, clean and finely chop the herbs.
- Break up the cheese with a fork and place it in a blender with the sour cream and eggs. Blend until frothy. Fold in the cornstarch, herbs, salt and nutmeg.
- Drain all but a small amount of the liquid from the asparagus. Pour the cream mixture over the asparagus and cook covered for 10 minutes over medium heat.

Tip
Serve the quiche topped with dry roasted, slivered almonds or use pine nuts for a richer flavor.

Asparagus with Roast Mushrooms

Ingredients for 2 servings:

2 lb (1 kg) asparagus
2 tbsp butter
1 large pinch each salt, nutmeg and sugar
1 tsp lemon juice
2/3 lb (300 g) mushrooms
2 tbsp chopped hazelnuts
2 tsp sesame seeds (or substitute sunflower seeds)
pepper, freshly ground
1 bunch each of parsley and chives

Preparation time: 45 min
Calories per serving: 720
36 g protein, 44 g fat,
36 g carbohydrate

- Wash and trim the ends of the asparagus. Lay them as flat as possible in a saucepan, adding just enough water to cover. Add 1/3 of the butter, herbs and a little lemon juice. Bring the asparagus to a boil, then simmer for 15 minutes.
- Wash, clean and thinly slice the mushrooms.
- Heat the remaining butter in a frying pan, roast the nuts and sesame seeds, add mushrooms and fry for 5 minutes, stirring continuously. Season with salt and pepper.
- Wash and finely chop the parsley and chives. Mix half of the herbs into the mushrooms and season with salt, pepper and lemon juice.
- Remove asparagus from the liquid, scatter with the roasted mushrooms and garnish with remaining herbs. Serve with small, buttered potatoes.

Steamed Vegetables with Parsley Sauce

Ingredients for 4 servings:

1 lb (500 g) asparagus
1 lb (500 g) snowpeas or
  sugar-snap peas
1 lb (500 g) carrots
2 lb (1 kg) new potatoes
salt

For the sauce:
1 cup (250 ml) vegetable stock
1 tsp millet flour (or substitute
  wheat flour)
1 tbsp lemon juice
1 cup (200 ml) cereal cream
  (a light cream with only 10% fat)
2 bunches of parsley
3 eggs
white pepper, freshly ground

Preparation time: 50 min
Calories per serving: 450
14 g protein, 19 g fat,
41 g carbohydrate

- Wash the vegetables and quarter the carrots lengthwise. Steam them for 20 minutes.
- Cook the potatoes in a little salted water with skins left on.
- For the sauce, whisk together the stock and millet flour over medium heat and then simmer for 2 minutes.
- Stir cream and lemon juice into the stock. Wash and finely chop the parsley.
- Separate the eggs. Beat the egg whites until stiff. Stir the yolks into the sauce and heat to just below the boiling point, stirring constantly.
- While stirring, pour the hot sauce into the egg whites. Fold in the parsley and season with salt and pepper. Serve the sauce with the vegetables immediately.

Stuffed Kohlrabi with Green Sauce

Ingredients for 4 servings:

8 kohlrabi
salt
1 cup (250 ml) milk
1/2 cup (100 g) coarse cornmeal
  or corn grits
2 tbsp crème fraîche (see page 32)
1 1/2–2 cups (200 g) grated
  Emmenthal
pepper, freshly ground
2 green onions
2 tbsp butter
1/3 cup (100 g) cream
1/2 cup (125 ml) vegetable stock
nutmeg, freshly grated

Preparation time: 50 min
Calories per serving: 550
30 g protein, 32 g fat,
37 g carbohydrate

- Break off the kohlrabi leaves and set them aside.
- Peel and hollow out the kohlrabi, making sure the bottoms are flat. Cook in salted water for 15 minutes.
- Bring the milk to a boil, add the cornmeal and cook for 5 minutes. Reduce the heat.
- Fold the crème fraîche and the grated cheese into the cornmeal and add salt and pepper. Fill the kohlrabi.
- Clean and thinly slice the onions. Cut the stalks from the kohlrabi leaves. Thinly slice the leaves and sauté in butter with the kohlrabi flesh and the onions.
- Sauté the stuffed kohlrabi for 15 minutes over low heat. Keep warm. Blend the vegetables with cream and stock, season with spices and serve with the kohlrabi.

123

Asian Vegetable Stir Fry

Ingredients for 4 servings:

1 cup (200 g) basmati rice
salt, freshly ground pepper
1/4 cup (20 g) dried mushrooms
1/4 lb (125 g) bean sprouts
1/3 lb (150 g) carrots
2–3 green onions
1/4 lb (125 g) snowpeas or
  sugar-snap peas
1/2 lb (250 g) Chinese cabbage
1 cup (150 g) canned bamboo
  shoots (optional)
1 piece of ginger, walnut-sized
8 canned water chestnuts
2–3 tbsp unrefined sesame
  or coconut oil
1/4 cup (50 g) cashews
4–5 tbsp natural sweet and sour
  sauce (or substitute 4 tbsp
  natural ketchup mixed with
  1 tsp sugar)
1 tsp tapioca starch
2–3 tbsp rice wine or dry sherry
soy sauce

Preparation time: 1 hr
Calories per serving: 450
10 g protein, 15 g fat,
66 g carbohydrate

- Bring the rice to a boil in
  1 3/4 cups (400 ml) water
  and salt. Simmer over low
  heat for about 25 minutes.
- As cooking time is different
  for each vegetable, they must
  be cut into proper sizes and
  added in an order so that
  they are ready at the same
  time. This is the cornerstone
  of a successful stir fry.
- Soak the dried mushrooms
  in warm water for
  15 minutes then drain. Slice
  into fine strips. Wash the
  bean sprouts and drain well.
  Scrub the carrots and cut
  them into matchstick-sized
  strips. Wash the green
  onions and chop into rings.
  Wash the peas, remove fibers

and chop diagonally into
sections.
- Wash the Chinese cabbage
  and cut diagonally into
  1" (2.5 cm) strips. Drain
  the bamboo shoots, reserving
  the liquid, and cut the
  shoots into strips. Peel and
  mince the ginger. Drain the
  water chestnuts.
- In a small saucepan, combine
  the sweet and sour sauce and
  1/4 cup (100 ml) of liquid
  from the bamboo shoots or
  water chestnuts. Bring to a
  simmer.
- Mix the tapioca starch with
  rice wine and thicken the
  sweet and sour sauce with it.
- Heat the sesame oil in a
  wok. Stir fry the vegetables,
  adding them in the following
  order: mushrooms, carrots,
  bamboo shoots, green
  onions, Chinese cabbage,
  peas, ginger and cashews.

Stir fry for 3 minutes.
- Add the sweet and sour
  sauce, water chestnuts and
  bean sprouts to the
  vegetables. Cover and let
  simmer for 2 minutes.
  Season with soy sauce and
  pepper. Serve with rice.

Tip

Let your guests get involved
with this recipe. Wash
vegetables ahead of time and
let them do the preparation:
thus the actual cooking time is
very short. For a spicier stir fry,
add 1 clove of garlic and
substitute black bean paste for
the sweet and sour sauce.
Sprinkle the stir fry with
sesame seeds before serving.
When using dried mushrooms,
look for the ones with thick
caps—they are the most juicy
and flavorful when cooked.

Garden Vegetables au Gratin

Ingredients for 4 servings:

1 lb (500 g) fresh green beans
1 3/4 lb (800 g) carrots
1 lb (500 g) potatoes
1 tbsp butter
1–2 cups (200 g) grated cheese
salt
pepper, freshly ground
2 cups (500 ml) milk
1 cup (250 g) cream

Preparation time: 1 1/2 hrs
Calories per serving: 670
30 g protein, 41 g fat,
46 g carbohydrate

- Wash the vegetables. Cut the ends off the beans and remove any stringy fibers. Peel and thinly slice the carrots and potatoes.
- Preheat the oven to 375°F (190°C).

- Grease a large baking pan (10" x 12" (25 x 30 cm)) with butter. Add alternating layers of potatoes, carrots and beans, scattering the cheese over each layer.
- Whisk the milk and cream together with the spices and pour over the gratin. Bake for 65 minutes on the middle rack.

Tip
This recipe is ideal for a large number of guests. It can be prepared in a deep baking dish to serve 10–12 people. Simply triple the recipe. Also try a variation using dill, tarragon or fennel seeds. Any of these herbs will help to relieve digestive ailments.

Peas and Beans

Ingredients for 4 servings:

3/4 lb (375 g) green beans
1 lb (500 g) fresh shelling peas
3/4 lb (375 g) edible-pod peas
1 sprig of savory
1 onion
1 tbsp cold-pressed, extra-virgin olive oil
1/2 cup (125 ml) vegetable stock
2 tbsp herbed crème fraîche (see page 32)
seasoning salt
1 tbsp green peppercorns, freshly ground (or substitute black peppercorns)

Preparation time: 45 min
Calories per serving: 200
8 g protein, 6 g fat,
17 g carbohydrate

- Wash the vegetables and savory. Shell the peas. Peel and thinly slice the onion.

- Heat the olive oil and sauté the onions until translucent. Add the beans and shelled peas and sauté briefly. Add the vegetable stock and the savory. Cover and cook for 15 minutes.
- After 10 minutes add the pea pods. When all are cooked, the liquid should be fully absorbed by the vegetables. (If not, remove the lid and allow the liquid to evaporate.)
- Remove the savory and stir crème fraîche into the vegetables. Season with seasoning salt and pepper. Serve with potatoes.

Tip
Vegans can leave out the crème fraîche. Substitute 1/2 clove of crushed garlic and sauté with the onion.

Cabbage and Potatoes with Cheese Sauce

Ingredients for 4 servings:

2 lb (1 kg) potatoes
salt
1 cabbage (2 lb (1 kg))
1 bunch each parsley, dill, basil
 and marjoram
1 cup (200 g) sour cream
1/3 cup (100 g) cream cheese
1/2 cup (100 g) dry Ricotta
 (or try soft Feta for a stronger flavor)
1 tsp cornstarch
1/2 cup (125 ml) milk
pepper, freshly ground
nutmeg, fresh ground

Preparation time: 1 hr
Calories per serving: 430
30 g protein, 14 g fat,
58 g carbohydrate

- Wash the potatoes and place them in a saucepan with a little salted water. Wash and quarter the cabbage and place on top of the potatoes. Simmer for 45 minutes over medium heat.
- Wash the herbs and blend them with the sour cream and cheeses.
- Mix the cornstarch with a little milk. Bring the remaining milk to a boil, then stir in the cornstarch-milk mixture and herbs, and simmer for 2 minutes. Season with pepper and nutmeg.
- Arrange the cabbage quarters and potatoes on a plate and pour the cheese sauce over them.

Tip

This meal is rich in protein and roughage but low in fat. The recipe will be more filling if the cooked potatoes are sautéed with 1/3 cup (80 g) sunflower seeds in 4 tbsp unrefined extra-virgin olive oil. Or, dot the cabbage and potatoes with butter and sprinkle roasted sesame seeds over them then broil briefly.

Deep-fried Broccoli

Ingredients for 4 servings:

3/4 cup (120 g) wholewheat flour
salt
3 eggs
2/3 cup (150 g) yogurt
1 tsp cumin
pepper, freshly ground
1 1/3 lb (650 g) broccoli
about 1 1/4 cups (300 ml)
  unrefined coconut oil for frying
lemon slices

Preparation time: 45 min
Calories per serving: 450
14 g protein, 35 g fat,
22 g carbohydrate

- Mix flour with a little salt, eggs, yogurt and spices to form a thick batter. Allow to rest for 15 minutes.
- Meanwhile, wash and dry the broccoli. Cut the heads into flowerets and the peeled stalks into bite-sized pieces.
- Heat the oil to 335–375°F (170–190°C). Dip the vegetable pieces into the batter then fry them in the oil, until they become golden.
- Drain briefly on paper towels and serve hot with lemon, herbed quark or Pear-Mustard Dip (page 74).

Tip

The oil is hot enough when a drop of batter will rise to the surface and sizzle. Clarified butter can be substituted for the deep frying. Although it is not recommended that you deep fry often, these two fats are the safest to use. Place the cooled fat in a container and dispose in the garbage.

Broiled Cauliflower

Ingredients for 4 servings:

1 large cauliflower
salt
1 cup (80 g) wholewheat bread
  crumbs
1/3 cup (50 g) ground hazelnuts
3 tbsp butter
1 bunch of parsley
1 1/2 cups (350 g) sour cream
1 cup (150 g) grated Gouda
pepper, freshly ground
unrefined coconut oil or butter
  for the baking sheet

Preparation time: 50 min
Calories per serving: 480
19 g protein, 33 g fat,
27 g carbohydrate

- Wash the cauliflower. Cut an X into the bottom of the stalk. Bring salted water to a boil in a large saucepan and cook the cauliflower for 15 minutes.
- Meanwhile, roast the bread crumbs and nuts in the butter and let cool. Wash and mince the parsley.
- Mix the sour cream, cheese and bread crumbs and season with salt and pepper.
- Cut the cauliflower into thick slices, lay out on an oiled baking sheet and top with the cheese mixture.
- Broil for 5 minutes or until golden. Or you can bake the cauliflower for 12 minutes at 400°F (205°C) in a preheated oven on the highest rack.

Tip

Cauliflower is an excellent source of vitamin C and a good source of potassium. Substitute broccoli if cauliflower is unavailable.

Baked Tomatoes with Pasta Salad

Ingredients for 4 servings:

8 large tomatoes
1/4 lb (125 g) mild blue cheese
1/4 cup (20 g) quick-cooking oats
1/2 cup (125 ml) milk
1/4 cup (30 g) ground hazelnuts
2 eggs
salt
pepper, freshly ground
nutmeg, freshly grated
1 clove of garlic
3 tbsp cream
1 tbsp basil
3 1/2 cups (500 g) cooked
  shell noodles

Preparation time: 35 min
Calories per serving: 710
31 g protein, 23 g fat,
100 g carbohydrate

- Preheat oven to 375°F (190°C). Wash the tomatoes. Cut a lid in each tomato, scoop out the inner flesh and set it aside.
- Cut the cheese into small pieces. Cook the oats in the milk for 2 minutes. Fold in the nuts and cheese and allow the cheese to melt before removing the oats from the heat.
- Separate the eggs, fold the yolks into the oats mixture and season. Beat egg whites until stiff, fold in, then spoon the mixture into the tomatoes.
- Bake for 15–20 minutes on the middle rack. Meanwhile, blend the tomato flesh with the crushed garlic, cream and chopped basil. Mix the cold noodles with this sauce. Serve as a side dish to the tomatoes.

Tomato Lasagna

Ingredients for 6 servings:

2 lb (1 kg) beefsteak tomatoes
3 tbsp butter
1/2 cup (60 g) flour
1 3/4 cups (400 ml) milk
1/2 cup (100 g) cream
1 cup (200 ml) dry white wine
  (or substitute vegetable stock)
3/4 cup (100 g) Parmesan cheese,
  freshly grated
salt
nutmeg, freshly grated
white pepper, freshly ground
2/3 lb (300 g) Mozzarella cheese
1 bunch of fresh basil
enough precooked lasagna
  noodles to fill your pan
unrefined coconut oil
  or butter to grease the pan

Preparation time: 50 min
Calories per serving: 600
28 g protein, 28 g fat,
53 g carbohydrate

- Wash the tomatoes, blanch them, remove skins and slice.
- Melt the butter, add flour and sauté briefly, then add milk, cream and wine one at a time, stirring constantly.
- Simmer the sauce for 3 minutes, season with Parmesan cheese, salt, nutmeg and pepper.
- Cut the Mozzarella into small pieces. Wash the basil and cut the leaves into fine strips.
- Preheat the oven to 375°F (190°C). Grease a lasagna pan. Place sauce in the bottom of the pan, cover with tomato slices, Mozzarella and basil. Add a layer of noodles then the sauce. Keep adding layers, ending with tomatoes and the Mozzarella. Bake for 35 minutes on the middle rack.

Broiled Mediterranean Vegetables

Ingredients for 4 servings:

3/4 cup (150 g) amaranth
3/4 cup (150 g) quinoa
  (or substitute rice cooked
  for 20 minutes)
4 tbsp lemon juice
1 pinch saffron
salt, freshly ground pepper
1 medium eggplant
1 lb (500 g) small zucchini
1 1/4 lb (625 g) tomatoes
1 sprig of thyme
5 tbsp cold-pressed,
  extra-virgin olive oil
1/2 lb (250 g) sliced Raclette
  cheese
unrefined coconut oil or butter
  for the baking sheet

Preparation time: 30 min
Calories per serving: 690
30 g protein, 34 g fat,
61 g carbohydrate

- Bring the amaranth and
  quinoa to a boil in 2 cups
  (500 ml) water with lemon
  juice, saffron and a little salt.
  Simmer for 10–15 minutes
  until cooked.
- Preheat the broiler. Wash the
  vegetables, cut the eggplant
  and zucchini lengthwise into
  thin slices. Halve the
  tomatoes. Wash the thyme
  and separate the leaves.
- Lay the vegetables cut sides
  down on a greased baking
  sheet, brush with olive oil,
  season with salt, pepper and
  thyme.
- Broil vegetables on both
  sides for 5 minutes. Cover
  with Raclette cheese and
  broil again until the cheese
  melts. Serve with the
  amaranth-quinoa mix.

Mediterranean Medley

Ingredients for 4 servings:

2 small eggplants
1 1/3 lb (650 g) small zucchini
salt
2 onions
3 tbsp cold-pressed,
  extra-virgin olive oil
pepper, freshly ground
1 clove of garlic
2/3 cup (150 ml) tomato juice
2/3 cup (150 ml) dry red wine
  (or substitute vegetable stock)
1 bunch of fresh basil
3/4 cup (100 g) black olives
1/2 cup (100 g) Feta cheese

Preparation time: 30 min
Calories per serving: 290
8 g protein, 20 g fat,
13 g carbohydrate

- Wash the vegetables. Cut the
  eggplants into bite-sized
  cubes, slice the zucchini.
- Sprinkle salt over the
  eggplant and allow to
  "perspire" for about
  10 minutes. Rub the
  eggplants dry with a paper
  towel.
- Peel the onions and slice into
  rings.
- Heat the oil in a large frying
  pan. Add the onion and
  eggplants and sauté for
  about 2 minutes while
  stirring. Add the zucchini
  slices and sauté for another
  5 minutes.
- Season the vegetables with
  pepper and crushed garlic.
  Add the tomato juice and
  wine and briefly bring to a
  boil. Wash the basil and add
  the leaves to the vegetables.
  Season to taste. Serve
  sprinkled with olives and
  crumbled cheese and rice or
  a baguette on the side.

Stuffed Cucumbers in Tomato Sauce

Ingredients for 4 servings:

1 onion
4 tsp butter
1 cup (200 g) spelt grits or
  coarsely ground spelt
1 1/4 cups (300 ml)
  vegetable stock
1/3 cup (80 g) Feta
pepper, freshly ground
nutmeg, freshly grated
1 egg
4 small cucumbers
  (or 2 long English cucumbers)
2 cups (500 g) strained tomatoes
  (or substitute puréed tomatoes)
1 bunch of fresh basil
1/3 cup (80 g) crème fraîche
  (see page 32)
salt

Preparation time: 50 min
Calories per serving: 330
13 g protein, 12 g fat,
27 g carbohydrate

- Peel and mince the onion. Sauté in butter. Add the spelt and stock, boil for 5 minutes or until thick, stirring occasionally. Remove from heat and cover.
- Crumble the Feta into the spelt with pepper, nutmeg and egg.
- Wash and halve the cucumbers (cut long cucumbers into 4 pieces) and remove the ends. Hollow the centers with an apple corer and then fill with the spelt mix.
- Stand the stuffed cucumbers in a saucepan with the puréed tomato and cook for 20 minutes. Remove the cucumbers.
- Let the sauce cook down a little. Wash and cut the basil into strips, fold them into the sauce with the crème fraîche and season. Serve the remaining spelt grits on the side.

Vegetable Kabobs

Ingredients for 8 kabobs:

1/2 bunch of mixed herbs
  (e.g., parsley, chives, basil,
  thyme, rosemary)
6 tbsp cold-pressed, extra-virgin
  olive oil (or substitute cold-
  pressed unrefined almond oil)
salt
pepper, freshly ground
1 clove of garlic, crushed
1 small eggplant
1 yellow pepper
2/3 lb (300 g) zucchini
16 small mushrooms

Preparation time: 2 hrs
(includes 30 min assembly time)
Calories per skewer: 83
2 g protein, 7 g fat,
3 g carbohydrate

- Wash and finely chop the herbs. Make a marinade with the oil, salt, pepper, herbs and garlic.
- Wash the eggplant and cut it into bite-sized cubes. Wash and quarter the pepper. Clean out the interior and cut the quarters into squares. Wash, clean and thickly slice the zucchini. Wash and clean the mushrooms.
- Place vegetables in the marinade and refrigerate for 1 1/2 hours. Preheat the broiler. Arrange the vegetables on skewers and place on a baking sheet. Turn the kabobs 2–3 times while they are cooking.

Tip
Kabobs can be cooked over the barbecue for a tasty summer meal. Reserve some of the marinade to baste the vegetables as they cook. Firm marinated tofu blocks and cherry tomatoes also make excellent additions.

Zucchini Vegetables

Ingredients for 4 servings:

3 1/3 lb (1.5 kg) small zucchini
2 red peppers
1 bunch of green onions
1 bunch of carrots
1 lb (500 g) green beans
2 tbsp cold-pressed,
  extra-virgin olive oil
1/2 cup (125 ml) vegetable stock
1 bunch of parsley
1 bunch of tarragon
2 tbsp capers
2 tbsp lemon juice
salt
pepper, freshly ground

Preparation time: 35 min
Calories per serving: 190
11 g protein, 6 g fat,
20 g carbohydrate

- Wash the zucchini, cut them
  in half lengthwise and slice.

- Wash and halve the peppers
  and remove the stalks,
  interior and seeds. Chop the
  peppers into small pieces.
  Wash and chop the onions.
  Scrub the carrots clean and
  cut the larger ones in half.
  Cut the ends off the beans
  and remove any stringy
  fibers.
- Sauté the beans, carrots and
  peppers in oil, add stock and
  simmer for 10 minutes.
- Wash the herbs and remove
  the stems. When the
  vegetables are cooked, add
  the herb leaves, capers,
  lemon juice and season with
  salt and pepper.

Tip
Serve with rice and garlic
mayonnaise.

Fried Eggplant with Noodles

Ingredients for 4 servings:

1 large eggplant
salt
2 yellow peppers
1 onion
2 bunches of basil
1/2 lb (250 g) fettuccine noodles
2 tbsp cold-pressed,
  extra-virgin olive oil
pepper, freshly ground
paprika
1/3 cup (50 g) freshly grated
  Parmesan cheese

Preparation time: 30 min
Calories per serving: 330
15 g protein, 10 g fat,
50 g carbohydrate

- Wash the eggplant, quarter it
  lengthwise and slice.

- Salt the eggplant slices and
  allow to "perspire" for
  10 minutes. Wash, clean and
  slice the peppers into thin
  strips. Peel and mince the
  onion. Wash and finely chop
  the basil.
- Cook the noodles in salted
  water then drain and rinse in
  cold water. Keep them warm.
- Dry the eggplant slices with
  a paper towel. Heat oil in a
  large frying pan. Sauté the
  onion until translucent.
  Add the eggplant and sauté
  it. Add the peppers and sauté
  them. Season with basil and
  spices.
- Arrange the vegetables on
  the noodles and serve
  sprinkled with Parmesan
  cheese.

Variation
Add crushed tomatoes or
cooked tomato slices for an
Italian touch.

Creamed Pumpkin with Tortellini

Ingredients for 4 servings:

1/2 lb (250 g) vegetarian tortellini
salt
1 1/3 lb (650 g) pumpkin or
 squash
1/4 cup (30 g) hulled (green)
 pumpkin seeds
2 tbsp unrefined almond oil or
 cold-pressed, extra-virgin olive oil
1 cup (200 g) sour cream or
 extra-thick yogurt
pepper, freshly ground
ginger powder
a few drops of lemon juice
1/4 cup (40 g) currants

Preparation time: 45 min
Calories per serving: 380
13 g protein, 14 g fat,
50 g carbohydrate

- Cook the tortellini in boiling salted water for 15 minutes.
- Remove the pumpkin skin and cut the flesh into large pieces. Chop pumpkin seeds coarsely. Heat the oil in a skillet and sauté the pumpkin for 6–7 minutes. Add the sour cream or yogurt then purée the pumpkin mix.
- Season the mix with salt, pepper, ginger and lemon juice and add the currants.
- Add the tortellini to the sauce and heat again, but do not cook. Serve sprinkled with pumpkin seeds.

Tip

The pumpkin may be seasoned with sautéed sage leaves instead of ginger and currants. Roasted pine nuts also work well in this recipe.

Stuffed Zucchini

Ingredients for 4 servings:

1 cup (200 g) wild rice mixed
 with long-grain brown rice
salt
1 1/3 lb (650 g) small mushroom
 caps
1 small onion
1/2 bunch of fresh basil
2 tbsp cold-pressed,
 extra-virgin olive oil
pepper, freshly ground
a few drops of lemon juice
1 large zucchini
1/2 cup (100 g) Gorgonzola
1/2 cup (100 g) sour cream
1/2 cup (100 g) cream

Preparation time: 1 hr
Calories per serving: 450
18 g protein, 23 g fat,
42 g carbohydrate

- Bring the rice to a boil in 2 cups (500 ml) water and simmer for 40 minutes.
- Clean the mushrooms, leaving the heads whole. Peel and finely chop the onion. Wash and finely chop the basil leaves.
- Preheat the oven to 375°F (190°C). Heat the oil and sauté the onions until translucent. Add the mushrooms and sauté until all the liquid has steamed off. Season with salt, pepper, lemon juice and basil, then mix with the rice.
- Cut the zucchini lengthwise and scoop out the seeds. Fill the zucchini halves with the rice-mushroom mixture. Blend the Gorgonzola with the sour cream and cream. Pour the mixture over the zucchini halves and bake for 12 minutes on the middle rack.

Cabbage with Peppers

Ingredients for 4 servings:

1 small cabbage
2 red peppers
1 red chili pepper
4 tbsp clarified butter
1 tbsp chili powder
2 tbsp paprika
salt
pepper, freshly ground
1 cup (250 ml) apple juice
4 tbsp cream

Preparation time: 1 hr
Calories per serving: 210
4 g protein, 14 g fat,
19 g carbohydrate

- Wash the cabbage, cut it into quarters or eighths, remove the core and grate it into thin strips.
- Wash the peppers, clean out the inside and chop finely. Wash and mince the chili pepper.

- Heat the clarified butter and sauté the pepper and chili pepper. Season the peppers with the chili powder, paprika, salt and pepper. Add the cabbage and apple juice.
- Mix the peppers and cabbage and simmer for about 45 minutes. Add the cream. Serve with noodles or gnocchi.

Tip
Try using sauerkraut instead of cabbage. Add it to the warm peppers just before serving. Naturally fermented sauerkraut provides the body with healthy acid bacteria which aid in digestion. Sauerkraut is rich in potassium, zinc and energy-giving carbohydrates.

Pineapple-Cabbage Noodles

Ingredients for 4 servings:

2/3 lb (300 g) spinach fettuccini
salt
1 tsp unrefined, organic sunflower or safflower oil
1 cabbage
1 onion
2 tbsp butter
pepper, freshly ground
nutmeg, freshly grated
1/2 pineapple
3–4 tbsp cream

Preparation time: 40 min
Calories per serving: 480
14 g protein, 13 g fat,
78 g carbohydrate

- Cook the noodles in boiling salted water with the oil. Drain, rinse in cold water and drain again.

- Clean and wash the cabbage and cut into thin strips. Peel and finely chop the onion.
- Melt the butter in a heavy pot and sauté the onion until translucent. Add the cabbage and season with pepper and nutmeg. Cover and cook over medium heat for 20 minutes. If necessary, add some water.
- Meanwhile, peel the pineapple (cut off both ends, stand it upright and slice the skin from top to bottom). Remove the fibrous core, and cut into small pieces. Add pineapple pieces to the cabbage and cook for 5 minutes over low heat. Season with the cream and spices.
- Mix the noodles with the cabbage.

Belgian Endive with Orange Sauce

Ingredients for 2 servings:

1 lb (500 g) potatoes
4 Belgian endives
4 oranges
1/4 lb (125 g) blue cheese
2 tsp butter
salt
pepper, freshly ground
1/2 tsp cornstarch
2 sprigs of dill

Preparation time: 30 min
Calories per serving: 760
29 g protein, 25 g fat,
110 g carbohydrate

- Wash the potatoes thoroughly, then cook them in a little water.
- Meanwhile, wash the endive and cut out the bitter stalk.
- Squeeze the juice from 2 oranges. Peel the others and quarter them. Remove the white pith as thoroughly as possible and thinly slice the oranges.
- Remove the rind from the cheese. Cut the cheese into small pieces.
- Melt the butter, sauté the endive on all sides, add salt and pepper and simmer in the orange juice for about 10 minutes or until cooked.
- Remove the endives and set aside 1 tbsp of the cooking liquid to cool. Add cheese to the remaining liquid in the pan. Stir until the cheese melts. Dissolve cornstarch in the cooled liquid and add it to the cheese sauce. Allow the sauce to thicken, add the orange slices and heat gently.
- Peel the potatoes, arrange them on a plate with the endive and pour the orange juice over them. Sprinkle with dill tips.

Tofu Ragout with Chinese Cabbage

Ingredients for 4 servings:

1 lb (500 g) tofu
1 tbsp soy sauce
1 lb (500 g) Chinese cabbage
1 2/3 lb (800 g) tomatoes
1/4 cup (50 g) slivered almonds
2 tbsp unrefined, organic sesame oil
salt
white pepper, freshly ground
1 tbsp green peppercorns

Preparation time: 30 min
Calories per serving: 230
13 g protein, 12 g fat,
13 g carbohydrate

- Cut the tofu into small pieces and sprinkle with soy sauce.
- Remove the outer leaves from the Chinese cabbage, cut it in half and remove the thick central stalk. Cut the halves into strips, wash and drain them well.
- Blanch the tomatoes and leave for about 2 minutes. Remove the skins and seeds and cut into large pieces.
- Dry roast 1 tbsp slivered almonds until golden. Heat the oil and sauté the cabbage strips. Add the tomatoes, unroasted almonds, salt and pepper.
- When the cabbage has cooked, add the tofu and heat through for several minutes. Season with the green peppercorns.

Tip
Make an excellent marinade from 1 clove of garlic, 1 tsp freshly minced ginger, 6 tbsp unrefined, organic sesame oil, 3 tbsp soy sauce and lemon juice to taste. Drizzle some of the marinade over the cooked vegetables.

Red Cabbage with Millet Gratin

Ingredients for 4 servings:

1 cup (200 g) millet
2 1/2 cups (600 ml) vegetable stock
2 small onions
2 eggs
1/3 cup (80 g) quark (see page 32)
salt, freshly ground pepper
2 lb (1 kg) red cabbage
1 small sour apple
1 tbsp clarified butter
1 pinch powdered cloves
1/4 lb (125 g) blue cheese
1/3 cup (150 g) cream
1/2 cup (100 ml) milk
nutmeg, freshly grated
unrefined coconut oil or butter for the
  baking dish

Preparation time: 1 hr
Calories per serving: 480
22 g protein, 22 g fat,
51 g carbohydrate

- Heat the millet and cook for 20 minutes in 1 3/4 cups (400 ml) vegetable stock.
- Peel and mince the onions. Season the millet with half of the onion then turn off the heat and allow to finish cooking.
- Fold eggs, quark, salt and pepper into the millet.
- Wash, core and shred the cabbage. Peel, quarter and thinly slice the apple.
- Heat the clarified butter, sauté the remaining onion until translucent, add the cabbage and cook briefly. Add the remaining stock, apple, salt, powdered cloves and pepper and cook for about 20 minutes at medium heat.
- Preheat the oven to 325°F (160°C). Grease the baking dish. Blend the cheese with the cream and milk, season with salt, pepper and nutmeg. Place the cabbage in the dish. Make dumplings from the millet mixture and fill the cabbage. Pour the cheese mixture over top and bake for 18 minutes on the middle rack.

Oyster Mushroom Schnitzel with Herb Sauce

Ingredients for 2 servings:

2/3 lb (300 g) large oyster
 mushrooms
2 eggs
salt, freshly ground pepper
1/4 cup (50 g) finely chopped
 almonds
1/2 cup (50 g) bread crumbs
2 tbsp flour
2 tbsp unrefined coconut oil,
 coconut butter, or clarified butter
 for frying

Preparation time: 20 min
Calories per serving: 900
38 g protein, 42 g fat,
52 g carbohydrate

- Clean the mushrooms
 with a paper towel then
 remove the stems.
- Beat the eggs with some salt
 and pepper. Mix the almonds
 into the bread crumbs.
- Roll the mushrooms first in
 flour, then in egg and finally
 press them firmly into the
 bread crumb mix.
- Heat the oil and sauté the
 mushrooms over medium
 heat until golden. Drain the
 mushroom schnitzels briefly
 on paper towels.

Tip
This recipe can be also be used
for sautéed celery, beet or
fennel slices. A good side dish
is a dip of 1/3 cup (75 g)
kefir and 3 tbsp sour cream
seasoned with salt, pepper and
chopped herbs. Serve with
fresh wholegrain bread and a
sliced tomato.

Italian Medley

Ingredients for 4 servings:

1 3/4 lb (875 g) spinach
2 sprigs of oregano (or substitute
 1/2 tsp dried oregano)
1 lb (500 g) mushrooms
1 onion
2 cloves of garlic
salt
2 tbsp butter
1/4 cup (30 g) pine nuts
pepper, freshly ground
1/3 cup (40 g) Parmesan cheese,
 freshly grated

Preparation time: 30 min
Calories per serving: 200
13 g protein, 18 g fat,
4 g carbohydrate

- Wash and drain the spinach.
 Wash the oregano, remove
 the stems and crush the
 leaves in a mortar. Clean and
 thinly slice the mushrooms.
- Peel and mince the onion.
 Peel and coarsely chop the
 garlic, sprinkle with salt then
 crush with the flat side of a
 knife.
- Melt butter in a large frying
 pan. Briefly sauté the onion,
 garlic and pine nuts. Add the
 spinach, mushrooms and
 oregano. Sauté together until
 the spinach becomes limp
 (about 10 minutes), stirring
 continuously. Season with
 salt and pepper and sprinkle
 with Parmesan cheese.

Tip
This medley can be served over
rice or noodles, or used as a
stuffing for tomatoes, green
peppers or zucchini.

Mushroom Stew with Bread Dumplings

Ingredients for 2 servings:

3 bread rolls, day-old
1/2 cup (150 ml) milk
1 egg
nutmeg, freshly grated
1/2 bunch of parsley
1 onion
1 lb (500 g) mixed mushrooms
salt
2 tsp butter
pepper, freshly ground
1 tbsp lemon juice
1/2 cup (100 g) crème fraîche
(see page 32)

Preparation time: 35 min
Calories per serving: 570
19 g protein, 32 g fat,
45 g carbohydrate

- Slice the rolls very thinly. Warm the milk, beat in the egg and a pinch of nutmeg and pour the mixture over the rolls. Let the bread soak for 15 minutes.
- Wash and finely chop the parsley. Peel and mince the onion. Clean the mushrooms and, if desired, cut them into smaller pieces.
- Mix 1 tbsp parsley with the soaked bread. Make 8–10 dumplings from the dough.
- Cook the dumplings in boiling salted water for 15 minutes. Drain and keep them warm.
- Melt the butter and sauté the onion until translucent. Add mushrooms, salt and pepper. Cook for 5 minutes then season with lemon juice. Fold in the crème fraîche, add the remaining parsley and arrange the dumplings on top.

Giant Stuffed Mushrooms

Ingredients for 4 servings:

16 large mushrooms
3 tbsp lemon juice
3 tbsp unrefined, organic
 sesame or olive oil
salt
2 tbsp pumpkin seeds
2 tbsp sunflower seeds
2 tbsp sesame seeds
3 oz blue cheese
2 tbsp sour cream
1 sprig of thyme
coconut butter to grease the pan

Preparation time: 30 min
Calories per serving: 260
15 g protein, 20 g fat,
4 g carbohydrate

- Clean mushrooms with a paper towel and remove the stems (which can be used elsewhere).
- Mix the lemon juice, oil and a pinch of salt. Dip the mushrooms in this mixture.
- Chop the pumpkin and sunflower seeds and mix them with the sesame seeds. Crumble the cheese with a fork and stir it into the sour cream. Blend in the seeds.
- Wash the thyme and chop the leaves then fold them into the cheese mixture.
- Preheat the oven to 375°F (190°C). Grease a baking dish. Fill the mushroom caps with the cheese mixture. Sprinkle with the remaining lemon juice and place in the baking dish. Bake for 12 minutes on the middle rack or until golden. Cool slightly before serving.

Potatoes

Pan-fried Potatoes

Ingredients for 4 servings:

2 lb (1 kg) firm-fleshed potatoes
salt
white pepper, freshly ground
1 tbsp clarified butter
1 tbsp unrefined coconut
 or olive oil

Preparation time: 1 hr
Calories per serving: 230
5 g protein, 6 g fat,
39 g carbohydrate

- Wash the potatoes and steam
  them unpeeled until almost
  cooked. Rinse in cold water,
  drain, peel and grate coarsely.
- Season the grated potatoes
  with salt and pepper. Heat
  half of the clarified butter
  and oil in 2 large frying pans,
  then reduce the heat. Separate
  the potatoes into both pans,
  cover and fry for 10 minutes
  over medium heat.

- Flip the potatoes and fry on
  the other side uncovered for
  about 15 minutes.

Variation

Raw potatoes can also be used
for this recipe. In this case
reduce the heat and double the
cooking time. Or replace 1/3 of
the potatoes with finely grated
carrots, beets, zucchini, leek or
grated cabbage.

Tip

This dish comes from
Switzerland where it is called
rösti. Potatoes are a good
source of potassium, iron and
vitamin C, most of which are
found in, or directly under, the
skin. Whenever possible, steam
or boil potatoes with their
skins on to retain their
nutrients.

Crisp Baked Potatoes

Ingredients for 4 servings:

2 2/3 lb (1.2 kg) firm-fleshed
 potatoes
3 tbsp clarified butter
salt
3/4 cup (100 g) Parmesan cheese,
 freshly grated
1/4 cup (40 g) sesame seeds

Preparation time: 40 min
Calories per serving: 480
17 g protein, 24 g fat,
47 g carbohydrate

- Preheat oven to 375°F
  (190°C). Wash, peel and
  very thinly slice the potatoes.
  Melt the clarified butter and
  spread half on a baking
  sheet.
- Arrange the potato slices on
  the baking sheet in an
  overlapping pattern. Drizzle
  the remaining clarified butter
  over them and salt lightly.

Sprinkle Parmesan cheese
and sesame seeds over the
top. Bake on the middle rack
for 25 minutes or until
done.

Variation

French fries can also be cooked
on a baking sheet. Peel the
potatoes and cut them into
chips the thickness of a finger.
Blanch a few at a time in salted
boiling water, then remove and
drain on a paper towel.
Heat 1/2 cup (125 ml)
unrefined coconut oil in a
baking dish in a 400°F
(200°C) oven. Place the fries
in the dish and bake for
25 minutes, or until golden.

Tip

Peel potatoes just before
cooking. Never soak peeled
potatoes in water, as vitamins
B and C will be lost.

Stuffed Oven Potatoes

Ingredients for 4 servings:

4 large, firm-fleshed potatoes
1 tbsp butter
salt
1/3 cup (40 g) grated cheese

Preparation time: 1 1/2 hrs
Calories per serving: 290
11 g protein, 8 g fat,
41 g carbohydrate

- Preheat oven to 400°F (200°C). Wash the potatoes. Cut a lid in each potato and hollow out the flesh until medium-thick walls remain. Spread butter on the inside and salt lightly.
- Fill potatoes with the filling of your choice, replace the lid and wrap in aluminum foil (shiny side inward). Bake on the middle rack for 50 minutes.
- Open the foil, remove lids, sprinkle with cheese and bake for another 5 minutes.

Broccoli-Carrot Filling

Mix 1/2 lb (250 g) broccoli flowerets, 1/2 lb or 2 1/2 cups (250 g) grated carrot, 2 sliced green onions with 4 tbsp sour cream.

Sauerkraut Filling

Mix 1 cup (250 g) sauerkraut, 2/3 cup (150 g) Ricotta cheese, 1 green pepper and 1 onion. Chop the ingredients. Season with salt, pepper and paprika.

Leek-Apple Filling

Slice 1 leek into rings, mix with 1 sour apple cut into matchsticks, 2 tbsp chopped parsley, 1/2 cup (100 g) crème fraîche, 2 tbsp pumpkin seeds, salt, pepper and nutmeg.

Zucchini Filling

Stir 1/2 lb (250 g) zucchini, 2 diced tomatoes, 1/4 cup (50 g) minced green olives, salt, pepper, 2 tbsp unrefined olive oil, and 2 tbsp Parmesan cheese.

Shepherd's Pie

Ingredients for 4 servings:

1 2/3 lb (800 g) mashing potatoes
salt
1 cup (200 ml) milk
3 tbsp butter
nutmeg, freshly grated
1 2/3 lb (800 g) small mushrooms
1/2 lb (250 g) small onions
2 tbsp clarified butter
white pepper, freshly ground
2 tbsp tomato paste
2 tbsp capers
1/2 cup (100 ml) red wine
  (or substitute vegetable stock)
4 tbsp parsley, finely chopped
1 pinch each ground coriander
  and cumin
1/4 lb (125 g) Cheddar cheese
  (or substitute Emmenthal)
1–2 tbsp bread crumbs

Preparation time: 1 1/2 hrs
Calories per serving: 500
13 g protein, 19 g fat,
41 g carbohydrate

- Prepare mashed potatoes with salt, milk, 4 tsp butter and nutmeg (see page 143). Preheat the oven to 375°F (190°C). Clean and wash the mushrooms and halve the larger caps. Peel and quarter the onions.
- Heat the clarified butter and sauté the onions until translucent. Add the mushrooms and sauté. Stir in salt, pepper, tomato paste and capers and sauté them briefly. Add the red wine. Season with parsley and spices.
- Mix the Cheddar into the mushrooms and place everything in a casserole dish. Spread the mashed potatoes over top and sprinkle with bread crumbs. Bake on the middle rack for 35 minutes.

Potato Mousse with Zucchini

Ingredients for 4 servings:

1 lb (500 g) mashing potatoes
salt
1/2 cup (100 ml) milk
2 tbsp butter
nutmeg, freshly grated
2 eggs
1/2 lb (250 g) Cheddar cheese
1 lb (500 g) young zucchini
pepper, freshly ground
1/2 bunch of dill
unrefined coconut oil
  or butter for the baking dish

Preparation time: 1 1/2 hrs
Calories per serving: 290
15 g protein, 14 g fat,
26 g carbohydrate

- Prepare mashed potatoes with salt, milk, 4 tsp butter and nutmeg (see page 143).
- Separate the eggs. Blend the egg yolks, grate the cheese and add these to the purée.
- Preheat the oven to 375°F (190°C). Grease a baking dish or casserole (8 cups (2 l) capacity).
- Wash and slice the zucchini. Sprinkle salt and pepper over the zucchini. Wash and coarsely chop the dill. Beat the egg white until stiff and fold into the mashed potato.
- Arrange zucchini slices in the dish and sprinkle with dill. Add layers of potato, zucchini and dill, ending with potato. Bake on the middle rack for 30 minutes.

Tip

The shell of the nutmeg is also a spice, called mace. Mace imparts a more subtle flavor than nutmeg.

Stuffed Potato Roll

Ingredients for 4 servings:

1 1/2 lb (750 g) mashing potatoes
1 2/3 lb (800 g) fresh spinach
salt
1 egg
3/4 cup (100 g) flour
1/2 cup (70 g) Parmesan cheese,
 freshly grated
1 bunch of parsley
nutmeg, freshly grated
1/2 cup (125 g) herbed
 cream cheese
white pepper, freshly ground
unrefined coconut oil or butter
 and bread crumbs for
 the baking sheet
milk for brushing on the crust

Preparation time: 2 hrs
Calories per serving: 450
22 g protein, 19 g fat,
48 g carbohydrate

- Wash the potatoes, leave the
 skins on and boil until

cooked. Drain the potatoes,
rinse with cold water, peel
and press through a large-
meshed sieve twice, then
leave to cool completely.
- Meanwhile, wash the spinach
well. Blanch in batches in
boiling salted water, remove
with a slotted spoon and
drain.
- Loosely mix the egg, flour,
half of the cheese and 1 large
pinch of salt into the potato.
- Chop the parsley leaves and
add them to the potato
mixture. Knead by hand to a
smooth dough.
- Roll the dough into a
rectangle (8" x 12"
(20 x 30 cm)) on a plastic
cutting board or use a flat
freezer bag dusted with flour.
- Preheat the oven to 350°F
(175°C). Grease the baking
sheet and sprinkle it with
bread crumbs.

- Dry the spinach leaves and
mix them with nutmeg and
cream cheese. Add salt and
pepper to taste.
- Place the spinach in the
middle of the dough.
Using the plastic, fold the
dough over the spinach
lengthwise and place the roll
on the baking sheet.
- Brush the roll with milk and
bake for 35 minutes on the
middle rack. Melt the
remaining cheese over the
roll. Serve with Olive-
Tomato Dip (recipe
page 75).

Variation

You can shape boiled
dumplings from this potato
mixture. The dough should not
be too firm and should be
handled quickly. Shape fist-
sized dumplings from the
dough. Place them in boiling

salted water, cover and bring
back to a boil, then cook in the
hot water for 25 minutes,
uncovered. Remove dumplings
with a slotted spoon and drain
well. Serve fresh. Smaller
dumplings can be fried in
butter or unrefined coconut
oil. Serve with Parsley-Bread
Sauce or Roast Vegetable
Cream Sauce (both recipes
page 73).

Tip

To wash the sand from spinach,
swish the spinach around in a
sink filled with lukewarm water.
Lift the spinach out, drain and
clean the sink, fill it with cold
water and wash the spinach
again. Repeat washing with
cold water until all the sand is
gone.

Gnocchi with Peppers

Ingredients for 4 servings:

1 3/4 lb (875 g) mashing potatoes
salt
1/4 cup (60 g) pine nuts
 (or substitute sunflower seeds)
3 cups (400 g) millet flour
 (or substitute wheat flour)
1 each red, green and yellow peppers
1 lb (500 g) tomatoes
2 onions
2–3 cloves of garlic
2 sprigs of marjoram
2 tbsp cold-pressed,
 extra-virgin olive oil
pepper, freshly ground

Preparation time: 1 1/2 hrs
Calories per serving: 790
21 g protein, 18 g fat,
130 g carbohydrate

- Wash, salt and steam the potatoes unpeeled. Peel them while hot and press through a large-meshed sieve.
- Roast and finely grind the pine nuts. Knead the potato with 1 tsp salt, pine nuts and enough flour to form a non-sticky dough. Shape the dough into long rolls about 1" (2.5 cm) thick. Slice the rolls every 1 1/2" (3.5 cm). Flatten each piece with a fork.
- Drop batches of gnocchi into boiling salted water for 2 minutes. Remove them with a slotted spoon and rinse with cold water. Drain and set them on a cutting board.
- Skin the peppers (see recipe page 114) and cut them into strips. Wash and blanch the tomatoes, remove their skins and cut them into chunks.
- Peel and mince the onion and garlic. Remove marjoram leaves from the stems. Sauté the onion in oil with the peppers, tomatoes and garlic for 5 minutes. Season with salt, pepper and marjoram.
- Reheat the gnocchi in the pepper mix.

Stir-fried Surprise

Ingredients for 4 servings:

2 lb (1 kg) very small, firm potatoes
1 1/2 lb (750 g) spinach
salt
2 bunches of green onion
1 lb (500 g) Mozzarella
1 bunch of thyme
1 clove of garlic
2 tbsp clarified butter
1/2 cup (75 g) cashews
pepper, freshly ground
nutmeg, freshly grated

Preparation time: 35 min
Calories per serving: 550
25 g protein, 26 g fat,
46 g carbohydrate

• Wash and boil the potatoes,
  unpeeled, until cooked.
  Halve the larger potatoes.
• Wash the spinach, blanch in
  boiling salted water and drain
  well. If leaves are very large,
  coarsely chop the spinach.
• Wash the green onions and slice
  them diagonally.
• Cut the Mozzarella into small
  cubes. Wash the thyme and
  remove the leaves from the
  stalks. Peel the garlic and crush
  it with the flat side of a knife.
• Heat the clarified butter in a
  wok (or a large frying pan),
  add the potatoes and stir fry
  for about 5 minutes. Add the
  cashews and stir fry for another
  2 minutes. Add the green
  onion, spinach and crushed
  garlic and stir fry 3 minutes.
  Season with salt, pepper and
  nutmeg.
• Add the thyme and Mozzarella.
  Turn off the heat, cover the
  wok and allow the cheese to
  melt.

Tip
Cashews are a good source of
magnesium and vitamins B_1, B_2
and B_5.

Savory Potato Pudding with Creamed Spinach Sauce

Ingredients for 4 servings:

1 lb (500 g) mashing potatoes
3 eggs
1/4 cup (70 g) butter
1 cup (100 g) quick oats
1/2 lb (250 g) mild Feta
1–2 bunches of dill
1 onion
1 clove of garlic
1 lb (500 g) spinach
1/2 cup (125 ml) vegetable stock
1/2 cup (200 g) crème fraîche
 (see page 32)
salt, freshly ground white pepper
nutmeg, freshly grated
unrefined coconut oil and
 sesame seeds for the baking dish

Preparation time: 2 hrs
Calories per serving: 620
20 g protein, 41 g fat,
40 g carbohydrate

- Peel, lightly salt and steam the potatoes for 25 minutes.
- Thoroughly grease a non-stick pudding mold or cake pan (6 cup (1.5 l) capacity) and sprinkle with sesame seeds. Preheat the oven to 325°F (160°C). Fill a large, shallow baking dish with hot water and place in the oven to create steam while the pudding cooks. (Ideally the filled cake mold should sit on a rack in the water.)
- Separate the eggs. Beat the yolks with 3 tbsp butter until creamy. Fold in the oats. Press potatoes through a large-meshed sieve and allow to cool. Crumble the cheese very finely. Wash the dill, separate it from the stalks and chop finely. Mix potatoes, egg yolk, cheese and dill thoroughly and season with spices.

- Beat egg whites until stiff and fold into the mix. Place in the cake pan or mold and cover with a lid or tightly-fitted aluminum foil (shiny side out). Bake for about 55 minutes in the pan of water, on the middle rack.
- Peel and mince the onion and garlic. Wash the spinach. Sauté the onion and garlic in the remaining butter, add spinach and cook for about 5 minutes.
- Purée the spinach, adding stock and crème fraîche. Season with salt, pepper and nutmeg.
- Remove the lid from the cake pan and allow the pudding to steam off for a short time. Loosen the pudding around the sides of the pan with a knife and drop onto a serving platter. Serve with spinach sauce.

Variation

Instead of the spinach sauce, substitute a spinach-apple-vegetable blend. Peel and chop 1 onion and 1 clove of garlic. Sort 1 2/3 lb (750 g) spinach and wash thoroughly.
Wash 1 bunch of parsley and finely chop. Wash and quarter 2 apples, core them and cut them into large sticks.
Heat 2 tbsp olive oil and sauté the onion until translucent. Season with paprika, pepper and a little salt. Add the spinach and cook for 5 minutes on medium heat. Add the apple sticks and cook for another 5 minutes. Serve with sour cream.

Millet Omelet with Root Vegetables

Ingredients for 4 servings:

1 cup (150 g) millet flour
 (or substitute wholewheat flour)
1 cup (250 ml) milk
salt
1 lb (500 g) beets, chopped
1 lb (500 g) carrots
1 onion, chopped
4 tsp butter
1/2 cup (125 ml) vegetable stock
nutmeg, freshly grated
4 eggs
4 tbsp dill
2 tbsp crème fraîche (see page 32)
2 tbsp sour cream
unrefined coconut oil or butter

Preparation time: 40 min
Calories per serving: 430
16 g protein, 20 g fat,
45 g carbohydrate

- Blend all but 2 tbsp of the flour with the milk and salt, simmer over low heat until the mixture thickens, then let cool.
- Sauté the onions and beets in butter.
- Slice the carrots and add them to the beets. Add the stock and seasoning then simmer for 15 minutes or until all ingredients are soft.
- Separate the eggs and stir egg yolks into the flour mixture. Fold in the dill. Beat the egg whites until very stiff then fold into the flour mix.
- Melt the butter in a frying pan. Bake four omelets until golden on both sides. Thicken the vegetables with the remaining flour, bring to a boil, fold in the crème fraîche and cream and serve on top of the omelets.

Pea Omelet

Ingredients for 4 servings:

1 3/4 lb (800 g) fresh shelling peas (about 2/3 lb (300 g) when shelled, or substitute frozen peas if necessary)
4 eggs
2/3 cup (150 g) sour cream
seasoning salt
white pepper, freshly ground
1 bunch of fresh basil
1/2 lb (250 g) roma tomatoes
2 tbsp butter

Preparation time: 20 min
Calories per serving: 240
13 g protein, 17 g fat,
12 g carbohydrate

- Shell the peas. Beat eggs and cream together then fold in the peas. Season with seasoning salt and pepper.
- Remove stems from the basil and cut leaves into strips.

- Blanch the tomatoes and leave for a short time. Remove skins and seeds, and chop into large pieces.
- Heat half of the butter in a frying pan. Add half of the egg mixture, half of the basil and half the tomatoes. Cover and cook the omelet for about 5 minutes, remove from the pan and keep warm. Cook a second omelet with the remaining butter.
- Halve each of the omelets and serve on four plates.

Tip

Because omelets are very high in protein, an ideal complement is a high-carbohydrate food, such as potatoes. Mushrooms or grated carrots can be used instead of peas.

Oat Crêpes

Ingredients for 2 servings:

1/3 cup (40 g) rolled oats
1/4 cup (30 g) spelt flour
  or wheat flour
2 small eggs
salt
2 tsp cold-pressed,
  extra-virgin olive oil
about 1 cup (250 ml) milk
4 large handfuls of nettle tips
  (or substitute 1 1/3 lb (600 g)
  spinach)
1/2 cup (100 g) sour cream
1/3 cup (80 g) natural yogurt
2 tbsp nutritional yeast flakes
pepper, freshly ground
nutmeg, freshly grated
seasoning salt
unrefined coconut oil or melted
  clarified butter

Preparation time: 15 min
Calories per serving: 620
29 g protein, 40 g fat,
37 g carbohydrate

- Stir the oats together with the flour, eggs, a little salt and oil or butter. Add enough milk to form a thin batter. Set aside for a short time.
- Wash the nettles.
- Heat some oil in a frying pan and cook two crêpes. Keep them warm.
- Cook the nettles in a saucepan. Stir in the sour cream, yogurt and nutritional yeast and season with the spices.
- Fill the crêpes with the cream mixture then fold over and serve.

Tip

Nutritional yeasts, such as brewer's, engevita and torula, provide a rich source of proteins, vitamins and minerals.

"Kratzete" (Scratched Eggs)

Ingredients for 4 servings:

3 eggs
1 cup (250 g) unbleached
  flour
1 pinch of salt
about 1 1/4 cups (300 ml) milk
clarified butter or unrefined
  coconut oil

Preparation time: 35 min
Calories per serving: 360
14 g protein, 12 g fat,
48 g carbohydrate

- Separate the eggs. Beat the flour with the egg yolks and salt until the mixture is smooth. Add enough milk to form a thick batter then set aside.
- Preheat the oven to 225°F (100°C). Beat the egg whites until stiff and carefully fold into the batter. Heat the butter or oil in a frying pan then add the batter to the thickness of a pancake. Cover and let the batter set, flip it then cook it on the other side.
- The specialized technique for making *Kratzete* is to "scratch" or tear the egg batter using two forks. Tear it into bite-sized pieces and keep warm in the oven.
- Continue making pancakes until all the dough is used up.

Tip

Kratzete are traditionally served with asparagus in the Baden region of Germany. The dough can be made more nutritious by adding chopped herbs or finely grated vegetables. Served with a salad, they make a light, quick main course.

155

Eggs in Sorrel Sauce

Ingredients for 4 servings:

5 eggs
2 bunches of sorrel
 (or substitute a similar amount
 of fresh spinach)
1 ripe avocado
1 tsp lemon juice
1 cup (250 g) sour cream
 or thick yogurt
salt
pepper, freshly ground

Preparation time: 20 min
Calories per serving: 330
11 g protein, 32 g fat,
3 g carbohydrate

- Boil the eggs for 6 minutes,
 rinse in cold water then peel
 and allow to cool.
- Wash the sorrel. Cut half of
 it into fine strips.

- Halve the avocado, remove
 the pit and scoop out the
 flesh. Blend the avocado with
 the lemon juice and the
 remaining sorrel. Fold in the
 sour cream or yogurt and the
 sorrel strips and season with
 salt and pepper.
- Place the sorrel sauce on a
 plate. Cut the eggs in half
 and serve in the sauce.

Tip

Sorrel is very rich in vitamin C.
Use sparingly for people with
sensitive stomachs.

Sorrel has a stimulating
effect and is commonly used
for cleansing. The leaves taste
best in spring before the plant
blooms.

Pan-fried Stuffed Eggs

Ingredients for 4 servings:

6 eggs
2 lb (1 kg) fresh spinach
1 clove of garlic
1 small bunch of parsley
1 tbsp Parmesan cheese,
 freshly grated
1 tbsp herbed cream cheese
2–3 tbsp cold-pressed,
 extra-virgin olive oil
salt
pepper, freshly ground
nutmeg, freshly grated

Preparation time: 30 min
Calories per serving: 240
17 g protein, 18 g fat,
2 g carbohydrate

- Hard boil the eggs for
 7 minutes then rinse them in
 cold water. Peel them and
 cut in half lengthwise.

- Meanwhile, wash the spinach.
 Peel and mince the garlic.
 Wash and mince the parsley.
- Remove the egg yolks and
 mix them with the parsley,
 Parmesan cheese and cream
 cheese. Scoop the mixture
 into the egg halves so the
 filling bulges out slightly.
- Blanch the spinach in batches
 then drain. Heat the olive oil
 and lightly fry the egg halves
 for about 2 minutes over
 medium heat with the filling
 facing up. Then turn them
 over and fry on the other
 side. Remove the eggs from
 the heat.
- Briefly heat the chopped
 garlic with the spinach in the
 oil until the spinach
 collapses. Season with salt,
 pepper and nutmeg. Arrange
 the eggs on the spinach.
 Serve with potatoes.

Eggs in Aspic

Ingredients for 1 loaf pan
(6 cup (1.5 l) capacity):

6 eggs
3–4 tbsp agar-agar flakes
1 cup (250 ml) dry cider
 (or substitute dry white wine)
1 3/4 cups (400 ml) vegetable stock
2 tbsp soy sauce
Worcestershire sauce
3 tbsp fruit vinegar
salt
1/2 lb (250 g) cherry tomatoes
1/4 lb (125 g) spring herbs
 (e.g., dandelion, sorrel, chervil
 and chives)

Preparation time: 1 hr
Calories per serving: 130
11 g protein, 6 g fat,
3 g carbohydrate

- Hard boil the eggs for
  7 minutes, rinse in cold water
  then peel. Allow the eggs
  to cool.
- Meanwhile, soak the agar-agar
  in 1 cup (250 ml) cold water
  for 5 minutes.
- Warm the agar-agar in the water
  until completely dissolved.
- Stir the cider, stock, sauces
  and vinegar into the agar-agar
  spoonful by spoonful and
  season with salt.
- Pour this liquid into
  the loaf pan to a depth of
  1/4" (0.5 cm) and refrigerate.
- Wash the tomatoes. Rinse the
  herbs, remove leaves from the
  stems and chop finely.
- Distribute the eggs and half the
  tomatoes on the liquid in the
  pan, then sprinkle half of the
  herbs among them. Cover with
  more liquid and refrigerate.
- When the liquid has set, arrange
  the remaining tomatoes and
  herbs on top then pour the
  remaining liquid over top.
  Refrigerate overnight. The next
  day, remove the mold by placing
  the pan in warm water for a few
  minutes then turning it upside
  down on a serving platter.

Italian Frittata

Ingredients for 4 servings
(1 baking sheet):

8 eggs
3 tbsp milk
1/2 tsp salt
pepper, freshly ground
nutmeg, freshly grated
1/2 cup (125 g) parsley, chopped
unrefined coconut oil
 or butter for the baking sheet

Preparation time: 25 min
Calories per serving: 240
14 g protein, 21 g fat,
1 g carbohydrate

- Preheat the oven to 450°F (230°C). Grease a coated baking sheet and place it in the hot oven for 5 minutes.
- Beat the eggs with milk and spices. Pour this mixture onto the baking sheet and bake on the upper rack for about 10 minutes.
- Serve hot or lukewarm with bread, salad or vegetables.

Variations
Spinach frittata:
- Prepare the frittata as described above, then place 1 3/4 lb (875 g) blanched spinach, 4 skinned tomatoes cut into eighths and 1 cup of corn on the egg-milk mixture. Bake as described above.

Potato frittata:
- Slice 1 1/2 lb (750 g) cooked and peeled potatoes, 3 bunches of green onions, then add to the mixture. Top with 1/4 lb (125 g) grated hard cheese and paprika. Bake as above.

Tip
A standard baking sheet lined with greased aluminum foil can be used instead of a coated baking sheet. If you are cooking for two, use half the quantity and cook in a large frying pan.

Savory Asparagus-Spinach Pudding

Ingredients for 4 servings:

3/4 cup (150 g) millet
1 1/4 cups (300 ml) vegetable stock
1 lb (500 g) asparagus, washed
salt, freshly ground pepper
nutmeg, freshly grated
3 tbsp butter
1 lb (500 g) spinach, washed
1/2 cup (125 ml) milk
1/2 cup (125 g) cream
1 cup (250 g) quark (see page 32)
2 eggs
1 clove of garlic, crushed
unrefined coconut oil or butter

Preparation time: 2 hrs
Calories per serving: 430
18 g protein, 24 g fat,
34 g carbohydrate

- Rinse the millet in hot water, bring to a boil in the stock then simmer for 15 minutes.
- Cook the asparagus for 15 minutes in a little water, some salt, nutmeg and 1 tsp butter. Blanch the spinach in boiling water and drain.
- Thoroughly grease a lidded pudding mold. Beat together milk, cream, quark and eggs. Season this mixture with the garlic, salt, pepper and nutmeg.
- Place asparagus, spinach and millet in the mold and cover it with the milk mixture. Put the lid on the mold and set it in a pot large enough to allow water and air to circulate around the the sides. Pour water in the pot until the level comes halfway up the side of the mold.
- Steam for one hour. Let sit for 5 minutes before removing the mold.

Herb Tortilla with Pepper Sauce

Ingredients for 2 servings:

2 eggs
1/2 cup (100 g) corn flour
1/3 cup (40 g) wheat flour
6 tbsp milk
2 tbsp mixed chopped herbs
salt
2 red peppers
2 tbsp extra-virgin olive oil
1 cup (250 ml) tomato juice
8 stuffed green olives
1/4 cup (50 g) Feta

Preparation time: 30 min
Calories per serving: 260
10 g protein, 13 g fat,
27 g carbohydrate

- For the tortilla, beat the eggs with both flours, milk and herbs then lightly salt. Allow the batter to rest.
- Wash and halve the peppers and remove their interiors. Chop into small pieces.
- Sauté peppers in a little oil. When they begin to soften, add the tomato juice. Slice the olives into rings then add to the sautéed peppers. Cover, and simmer for 10 minutes.
- Crumble the Feta. Heat the remaining oil in a pan and pour in the egg batter. Bake the tortilla until golden on both sides. Cover the tortilla with the Feta and finish cooking with the lid on. Serve with the sauce.

Tip

To make a special brunch tortilla, use sprigs of fresh basil or oregano and pimento-stuffed olives. Add fresh jalapeno or chipotle peppers for extra spice.

Cheese-Spinach Pie

Ingredients for 6 servings
(1/2 baking sheet):

1 package (450 g) frozen phyllo
 pastry
1/2 cup (125 ml) butter, melted
2 lb (1 kg) spinach
pepper, freshly ground
salt
2 cloves of garlic
1 1/3 cups (300 g) dry Ricotta cheese
1 cup (250 g) Mascarpone cheese
 (or substitute cream cheese)
2 1/4 cups (500 g) quark
 (see page 32)
5 eggs
12 black olives, pits removed
3 tbsp pine nuts

Preparation time: 1 1/4 hrs
Calories per serving: 810
30 g protein, 38 g fat,
31 g carbohydrate

- Thaw the phyllo according to
  directions. Keep it covered or it
  will dry out.
- Wash, drain and blanch the
  spinach. Drain and add pepper
  and salt.
- Peel and mince the garlic.
  Press the Ricotta through a
  sieve, blend it with the
  Mascarpone, quark, olives,
  garlic, 4 eggs and 1 egg white
  (save the yolk) until creamy.
- Preheat the oven to 375°F
  (190°C). Lay the aluminum
  foil over half of a deep baking
  sheet and form a border along
  the middle. Lay parchment
  paper over the divided area.
- Place 3 sheets of phyllo pastry
  on top of one another, on the
  paper. Brush each with melted
  butter.
- Add half the spinach, pour the
  cheese mixture over it then
  cover with the remaining
  spinach. Lay the remaining
  pastry over top. Brush each
  with melted butter and the
  remaining egg yolk and sprinkle
  with pine nuts. Bake for
  35 minutes on the middle
  rack, then serve.

Herbed Quark Soufflé

Ingredients for 4 servings:

3 bunches of parsley
2 bunches of chives
4 eggs
1 1/3 cups (320 g) quark
  (see page 32)
2/3 cup (80 g) quick-cooking
  rolled oats
1 tsp lemon juice
salt
pepper, freshly ground
sesame seeds for garnish
unrefined coconut oil or butter
  for the baking dish

Preparation time: 35 min
Calories per serving: 380
25 g protein, 21 g fat,
18 g carbohydrate

- Preheat the oven to 375°F
  (190°C). Grease a baking
  dish. Wash and chop the
  herbs.
- Separate the eggs. Beat the
  egg yolks and blend well with
  quark, herbs and oats.
  Season with the lemon juice,
  salt and pepper. Beat the egg
  whites until stiff then fold
  them into the quark mixture.
- Place the mixture in the dish
  and sprinkle with sesame
  seeds. Bake on the middle
  rack for 20 minutes and
  serve immediately—
  before it collapses. Serve
  with fresh salad and
  wholewheat bread.

Tip

This low-fat meal is quick to
prepare and is easily digestible.
It is ideal for busy people
on the go.

Quark Pancakes with Diced Peppers

Ingredients for 4 servings:

1 small bell pepper
3 eggs
salt
2 1/4 cups (500 g) quark
  (see page 32)
2/3 cup (120 g) cream of wheat
1 pinch baking powder
1 1/4 cup (120 g) oat flakes
paprika
white pepper, freshly ground
6–8 tbsp milk
clarified butter for frying

Preparation time: 40 min
Calories per serving: 430
29 g protein, 12 g fat,
49 g carbohydrate

- Wash, clean and finely chop
  the pepper.
- Beat the eggs and blend with
  the salt and quark. Fold in

the cream of wheat, baking
powder, oats and pepper.
Season with paprika and
white pepper.
- Allow the batter to rest for
  30 minutes then stir in some
  milk to soften it. Heat some
  clarified butter in a large
  frying pan. Use a tablespoon
  to transfer some batter into
  the hot fat. Fry pancakes
  over medium heat until
  golden then turn over and
  cook on the other side.
  Serve hot.

Tip

The ideal complement to this
dish is a dip that is high in
vitamins, carbohydrates and
vitamins. Try Hot Pepper Dip
or Pear-Mustard Dip (both on
page 74).

Spring Vegetables with Herbed Cheese Crust

Ingredients for 4 servings:

1 bunch of parsley
1 bunch of carrots
4 green onions
1/2 cauliflower
1 fennel bulb
2 tbsp cold-pressed,
 extra-virgin olive oil
salt
pepper, freshly ground
1 pinch powdered ginger
2 eggs
1/2 cup (125 g) quark (see page 32)
1/2 cup (125 g) cream cheese
1 1/2 tsp cornstarch
1–2 tbsp sunflower seeds
unrefined coconut oil
 or butter to grease the dish

Preparation time: 1 1/4 hrs
Calories per serving: 380
15 g protein, 13 g fat,
18 g carbohydrate

- Wash and finely chop the
  parsley. Scrub and slice the
  carrots. Wash the green onions
  and slice diagonally into
  short sections.
- Wash the cauliflower and break
  it into small flowerets. Wash the
  fennel and add the bitter green
  parts to the parsley. Halve the
  bulb lengthwise then slice both
  halves lengthwise into strips.
- Preheat the oven to 375°F
  (190°C). Grease an ovenproof
  dish. Sauté the vegetables
  (except the onions) in oil for
  5 minutes. Season with salt,
  pepper and ginger.
- Add the onions then place all
  vegetables in the dish. Separate
  the eggs. Beat the quark and
  cheese until smooth. Fold in the
  egg yolks, cornstarch and herbs.
- Beat the egg whites and a pinch
  of salt until stiff then fold into
  the quark mixture.
- Pour over the vegetables and
  sprinkle with sunflower seeds.
  Bake for 20 minutes.
  Serve with potatoes.

Stuffed Mushrooms and Tomatoes

Ingredients for 4 servings:

4 medium-large tomatoes
8 large mushroom caps
1/3 lb (150 g) strong cheese
1 bunch of parsley
1 small onion
1 clove of garlic
2–3 tsp cold-pressed,
  extra-virgin olive oil
pepper, freshly ground
nutmeg, freshly grated
2 tbsp capers

Preparation time: 40 min
Calories per serving: 200
14 g protein, 12 g fat,
6 g carbohydrate

- Wash and halve the tomatoes and scoop out the insides.
- Clean mushrooms with a paper towel. Remove the caps and mince the stalks.
- Cut the cheese into small pieces. Wash and finely chop the parsley. Peel and mince the onion and garlic.
- Sauté the minced mushroom stalks, onion and garlic in 1 tsp oil for about 5 minutes. Season to taste.
- Place the tomatoes and mushroom caps on an oiled baking sheet.
- Preheat the oven to 375°F (190°C). Fold the parsley, 1/4 lb (100 g) of the cheese and the capers into the mushroom mixture. Spoon into the tomato halves and mushroom caps.
- Sprinkle with the remaining cheese and bake on the middle rack for 2 minutes.

Fried Cheese with Hot Peppers

Ingredients for 4 servings:

2 fresh or pickled red chili peppers
salt, freshly ground pepper
1 clove of garlic
3–4 sprigs of cilantro
2–3 tbsp lemon juice
3–4 tbsp cold-pressed,
  extra-virgin olive oil
2/3 lb (300 g) strong cheese
  (e.g., medium Gouda) cut into
  thick slices
1 egg
2–3 tbsp flour
1 cup (100 g) dry bread crumbs
1 lemon

Preparation time: 30 min
Calories per serving: 500
7 g protein, 10 g fat,
28 g carbohydrate

- Wash the peppers and skin them (see recipe page 114). Cut them into narrow strips, and add salt and pepper.
- Peel and thinly slice the garlic. Wash the parsley and remove the stems. Arrange pepper strips, garlic slices and parsley on a plate and sprinkle with a mixture of lemon juice and 1 tbsp oil.
- Cut the cheese into bite-sized cubes. Beat the egg. Roll the cheese pieces in flour, dip in egg and press into the bread crumbs. Fry in hot oil until crisp, without letting the pieces touch one another.
- Drain on a paper towel and serve with lemon segments.

Tip
Chili peppers contain an anti-inflammatory substance.

163

Basil "Spaetzle" with Gouda

Ingredients for 2 servings:

1 1/2 cups (220 g) finely ground
 millet flour (or substitute
 wholewheat flour)
2 eggs
salt
1 bunch of fresh basil
3 bunches (200 g) of green onions
4 tsp butter
2 tbsp pumpkin seeds
1/4 lb (125 g) mild fresh Gouda

Preparation time: 35 min
Calories per serving: 810
33 g protein, 37 g fat,
78 g carbohydrate

- Mix the flour and eggs,
 2 tbsp of water and a little
 salt to make a loose dough
 or a stiff batter.
- Rinse and finely chop the
 basil, fold into the dough
 and set the mixture aside for
 20 minutes.
- Wash and slice the green
 onions. Sauté them in half of
 the butter.
- Dry roast the pumpkin
 seeds.
- Bring salted water to a boil
 in a large saucepan. Add the
 dough bit by bit according
 to the technique described
 on page 94.
- Toss the finished spaetzle
 with butter, cheese, sautéed
 green onions and pumpkin
 seeds.

Variations

Use different types of flour,
herbs and cheeses. Try oregano,
dill or cilantro and substitute
Swiss or Parmesan cheese.
Use spelt or amaranth instead
of millet. Give the spaetzle a
festive color by adding puréed
beets, spinach or carrots.

Cheese Polenta in Tomato Sauce

Ingredients for 4 servings:

2 1/2 cups (400 g) cornmeal
2/3 cup (100 g) freshly grated
 Parmesan cheese
4 tbsp cold-pressed,
 extra-virgin olive oil
2 cups (500 ml) milk
4 cups (1 l) vegetable stock
1 2/3 cups (750 g) tomatoes
1 red pepper
1 shallot
3 sprigs of thyme
salt
pepper, freshly ground

Preparation time: 45 min
Calories per serving: 620
24 g protein, 20 g fat,
87 g carbohydrate

- To make polenta, mix the
 cornmeal and Parmesan
 cheese and heat them gently
 in a saucepan with 1 tbsp of
 oil. Add milk and stock.
 Bring them to a boil stirring
 constantly. Simmer, then
 remove from heat and set
 aside for 15 minutes.
- Skin the tomatoes (see
 page 128) and chop the
 flesh into small pieces.
- Wash and chop the pepper
 into small pieces. Peel and
 mince the shallot. Wash the
 thyme and remove the stems.
- Heat the remaining oil in a
 frying pan and sauté the
 shallot until translucent.
 Add tomatoes, pepper and
 thyme and cook for about
 5 minutes.
- Season with salt and pepper.
- Shape dumplings from the
 polenta and place them in
 the sauce.

Cheesy Cabbage Rolls

Ingredients for 4 servings:

3/4 cup (150 g) bulgur
  (or substitute brown rice)
1 cup (250 ml) tomato juice
8 large Savoy cabbage leaves
  (or substitute regular cabbage)
salt
1/3 cup (75 g) herbed cream cheese
pepper, freshly ground
4 large slices medium Gouda
  (not too thick)
unrefined coconut oil
  or butter for the foil

Preparation time: 40 min
Calories per serving: 400
16 g protein, 21 g fat,
5 g carbohydrate

- Bring the bulgur to a boil in
  the tomato juice. Leave it on
  the burner with the heat
  turned off for 10 minutes.
- Wash the cabbage leaves and
  blanch them in boiling salted
  water for 3 minutes. Dry them
  with a paper towel.
- Mix the cream cheese and
  bulgur; season with salt and
  pepper.
- Preheat the oven to 325°F
  (160°C). Lightly oil 4 large
  pieces of aluminum foil on the
  shiny side. Place 1 slice of
  cheese on each of 4 cabbage
  leaves. Lay the remaining
  4 leaves on top of the cheese,
  spread the bulgur mix on the
  second leaf and roll up tightly.
- Wrap each roll well in foil and
  place on a baking sheet (seams
  facing up). Heat the rolls on
  the middle rack for about
  20 minutes. Serve with
  potatoes, tomato sauce and a
  fresh salad.

Leek Pasta with Three-cheese Sauce

Ingredients for 4 servings:

1 tbsp cold-pressed,
 extra-virgin olive oil
salt
1/3 lb (175 g) flat noodles
2 leeks
2 cloves of garlic
2 tbsp unrefined organic sesame oil
1 tbsp sesame seeds
1/2 cup (125 ml) vegetable stock
white pepper, freshly ground
1/2 tsp ground lemon grass
 (available at an Asian grocery or
 substitute lemon juice)
1/3 lb (175 g) fresh Mozzarella
3 oz (75 g) Muenster cheese
1/4 lb (125 g) goat cheese or Feta

Preparation time: 35 min
Calories per serving: 480
25 g protein, 25 g fat,
35 g carbohydrate

- Bring salted water and olive oil
 to a boil. Cook the noodles
 according to directions then
 rinse in cold water and drain.
- Clean the leeks, slit the sides
 and wash them well under
 running water. Drain and cut
 lengthwise in strips the same
 width as the noodles.
- Peel and mince the garlic. Heat
 the sesame oil in a wok or large
 frying pan. Add the leek, garlic
 and sesame seeds and sauté for
 2–3 minutes, stirring
 constantly.
- Add the stock and season with
 salt, pepper and lemon grass.
 Add the noodles and toss.
- Preheat the oven to 375°F
 (190°C). Place the leek-noodle
 mix in ovenproof bowls
 (or small baking dishes).
- Slice the Mozzarella and
 Muenster cheeses; crumble the
 goat cheese or Feta. Distribute
 the cheeses over the leek-noodle
 mix and bake on the middle
 rack for 12 minutes or until
 the cheese has melted.

Grilled Brie Sandwiches

Ingredients for 4 servings:

1 red pepper
1/2 lb (250 g) tomatoes
1/2 banana
salt
soy sauce
1 tbsp tomato paste
1 tbsp mild mustard
1/2 lb (250 g) Brie cheese
2 eggs
8 slices wholewheat bread
6 tbsp milk
4 tbsp bread crumbs
unrefined coconut oil
  or clarified butter for frying

Preparation time: 10 min
Calories per serving: 450
22 g protein, 21 g fat,
37 g carbohydrate

• Wash the pepper and
  tomatoes, remove the seeds

and blend thoroughly with
the banana.
• Season with salt, soy sauce,
  tomato paste and mustard.
  If necessary, pass the mixture
  through a sieve.
• Beat the eggs and slice the
  Brie. Spread the Brie on
  4 slices of bread.
• Brush the edges with egg,
  place the remaining 4 slices
  on top and press down
  firmly, especially around
  the edges.
• Whisk the remaining egg
  with milk and dip the bread
  in it.
• Sprinkle the sandwiches with
  bread crumbs on both sides
  and fry them in oil on
  medium heat until golden.
  (Do not fry too fast or the
  crusts will burn before the
  cheese melts.)
• Serve with the natural
  ketchup.

Brussels Sprouts with Cheese Sauce

Ingredients for 2 servings:

1 lb (500 g) Brussels sprouts
 (choose small ones)
1 small onion
2 tbsp butter
salt
white pepper, freshly ground
nutmeg, freshly grated
1/2 lb (250 g) mild blue cheese
1/4 cup (50 ml) dry white wine
2/3 cup (150 g) sour cream
2 small bread rolls (or kaiser buns)

Preparation time: 25 min
Calories per serving: 830
15 g protein, 32 g fat,
25 g carbohydrate

• Wash the Brussels sprouts.
  Peel and mince the onion.
• Sauté onion in 1 tbsp butter
  until translucent. Add the
  Brussels sprouts and sauté

them briefly, then add
2 cups (500 ml) of water.
• Add salt, pepper and nutmeg
  and cook for 10 minutes.
  Cook the sprouts uncovered
  and allow the remaining
  liquid to evaporate.
• Remove the rind from the
  cheese. Cut into small pieces
  and melt it in the wine over
  low heat. Fold in the sour
  cream and season with a
  little salt and nutmeg.
  Keep the sauce warm.
• Cut a lid from the rolls and
  remove the soft interior.
  Break the interior into small
  pieces and sauté them in the
  remaining butter to make
  croutons.
• Pour the cheese sauce into
  the rolls. Serve with the
  Brussels sprouts sprinkled
  with the croutons.

Baked Savories

Potato Pancakes

Ingredients for 4 pancakes:

2 large potatoes
1 onion
1/2 tsp salt
1 tsp dried basil
2 eggs
1 lb (500 g) ripe tomatoes
1/2 lb (250 g) Mozzarella cheese
unrefined coconut oil

Preparation time: 30 min
Calories per serving: 200
12 g protein, 12 g fat,
11 g carbohydrate

- Grate the potatoes. Peel and mince the onion and stir it into the potato. Add salt, basil and eggs. Mix well.
- Oil the pan and cook 4 large golden pancakes.
- Preheat the broiler. Wash and slice the tomatoes. Cut the Mozzarella into pieces.
- Place the pancakes on an oiled baking sheet, arrange slices of tomato on top, add cheese then melt under the broiler.

Tip

Prepared in this way, potato pancakes are very low in fat. You can also make the potato batter from packaged potato patty mix available from health food stores or European delicatessens. Just mix the potato patty mix according to the directions and add the minced onion and the basil. Mix well and fry as above. Those who are watching their weight can serve the pancakes with a crisp raw vegetable salad.

Zucchini-Egg Roll

Ingredients for 4 servings:

1 lb (500 g) zucchini
5 eggs
1/2 cup (80 g) wholewheat flour
1/3 cup (70 g) ground hazelnuts
salt, freshly ground pepper
2 lb (1 kg) tomatoes
12 black olives, pits removed
1 bunch of cilantro
1 bunch of fresh basil
1 scant cup (200 g) crème fraîche
 (see page 32)
1 tbsp grated Parmesan cheese,
parchment paper

Preparation time: 45 min
Calories per serving: 570
20 g protein, 44 g fat,
28 g carbohydrate

- Preheat oven to 375°F (190°C). Line a baking sheet with parchment paper.
- Coarsely grate the zucchini.

Separate the eggs. Beat the whites until stiff. Mix the yolks with flour, 1/4 cup nuts, salt and pepper. Fold in 1/2 of the egg whites, add the zucchini then fold in remaining egg whites.

- Spread the mixture onto the baking sheet and bake on the middle rack for 20 minutes.
- Skin the tomatoes (see page 128) and cut into pieces. Chop the olives and mix with the tomatoes.
- Spread the remaining nuts on a paper towel. Place the cooked omelet, paper-side up on the nuts. Remove paper.
- Spread the tomato-olive mixture on the omelet. Roll up, return to baking sheet and bake for 15 minutes.
- Blend leaves with the crème fraîche and Parmesan cheese and season. Serve with the roll.

Pizza Rounds

Ingredients for 6 rounds:

4 1/4 cups (600 g) unbleached
  white flour
1 tsp dried yeast
1/2 cup (100 ml) cold-pressed,
  extra-virgin olive oil
1/2 bunch of mixed fresh herbs
2/3 cup (150 g) tomato purée
  or sauce
pepper, freshly ground
1 small green pepper
4 tomatoes
1/3 lb (150 g) Mozzarella cheese
unrefined coconut oil
  or butter for the baking sheet

Preparation time: 2 hrs
Calories per serving: 570
17 g protein, 23 g fat,
75 g carbohydrate

- Mix the flour with the yeast.
- Using a food processor or a
  hand mixer fitted with dough

hooks, mix 1 cup (250 ml)
warm water, the oil and
2 tsp salt.
- Work into a firm, non-sticky
  dough. Be careful not to
  overwork the dough.
- Allow the dough to rise for
  1 hour. Wash and mince the
  herbs. Mix the tomato purée
  with the herbs and season
  with salt and pepper.
- Wash and clean the green
  pepper and cut into narrow
  rings or strips.
- Wash the tomatoes and cut
  into 6–8 segments. Cut the
  Mozzarella into small pieces.
- Preheat the oven to 375°F
  (190°C). Grease a baking
  sheet and dust it with flour.
  Shape 6 flat rounds from the
  dough and spread with
  pepper, tomatoes and cheese.
- Bake on the middle rack for
  18 minutes, or until done.

Potato-Broccoli Pizza

Ingredients for 4 servings:

2 cups (300 g) flour
2 tbsp dried yeast
2 tbsp cold-pressed,
  extra-virgin olive oil
1 tsp salt
1/3 cup (100 g) tomato purée
salt
pepper, freshly ground
1 tbsp chopped fresh basil
1/3 lb (150 g) small, boiled
  potatoes
1/3 lb (150 g) broccoli flowerets
1/4 lb (125 g) small mushrooms
1/2 lb (250 g) Raclette cheese,
  cut into small pieces (or substitute
  any full-flavored hard cheese)
1 tbsp sunflower seeds
unrefined coconut oil for the
  baking sheet

Preparation time: 1 1/2 hrs
Calories per serving: 500
25 g protein, 20 g fat,
58 g carbohydrate

- Prepare the dough according
  to the recipe for pizza rounds
  (see left). Oil the baking
  sheet and shape the dough
  into a large, round, flat pizza.
- Preheat oven to 400°F
  (200°C).
- Mix the tomato purée with
  seasonings and basil then
  and spread on the pizza.
  Cut the potatoes in half and
  distribute on top.
- Clean the broccoli and
  mushrooms and place
  between the potatoes. Top
  with cheese and sunflower
  seeds. Bake for 20 minutes
  on the lower rack.

Variations

Try mixing the dough with
nuts and bake as bread rolls,
or shape it into pretzels and
rings, and bake with sesame
and pumpkin seeds sprinkled
on top.

Apple Pizza

Ingredients for 4 servings:

2 cups (300 g) unbleached flour
2 tbsp dried yeast
2 tbsp cold-pressed,
 extra-virgin olive oil (for dough)
salt, freshly ground pepper
1 1/3 cups (300 g) tomato purée
 or sauce
dried thyme
1 onion, sliced into rings
1–2 tbsp unbleached white flour
2 tbsp clarified butter
1/2 lb (250 g) small mushrooms
1/2 lb (250 g) apples, sliced
3 tbsp cold-pressed,
 extra-virgin olive oil (for topping)
1/2 lb (250 g) Mozzarella, grated
1/4 cup (50 g) sunflower seeds
unrefined coconut oil

Preparation time: 1 1/2 hrs
Calories per serving: 690
28 g protein, 36 g fat,
64 g carbohydrate

- Prepare dough as for pizza rounds (page 170). Oil a baking sheet and shape the dough into a flat circle.
- Preheat the oven to 375°F (190°C). Mix the tomato purée with the seasonings and thyme; then spread on the dough.
- Dust the onion rings with flour and sauté in butter until crisp. Distribute over the pizza.
- Clean the mushrooms. Distribute apples and mushrooms over the pizza. Add oil, Mozzarella and sunflower seeds.
- Bake for about 12 minutes on the lower oven rack. Reduce heat to 350°F (175°C) for 10 minutes then serve.

Vegetable Pizza

Ingredients for 4 servings:

2 cups (300 g) unbleached
 white flour
2 tbsp dried yeast
2 tbsp cold-pressed,
 extra-virgin olive oil
salt, freshly ground pepper
1 cup (300 g) tomato purée
2/3 cup (150 g) sour cream
2 tbsp chopped basil
1 red pepper
1 lb (500 g) carrots
4 tsp butter
2/3 lb (300 g) small zucchini
1 cup cooked fresh corn
 (or substitute frozen corn)
1/2 lb (250 g) Mozzarella cheese
1/3 lb (150 g) medium
 Gouda cheese
unrefined coconut oil

Preparation time: 1 1/2 hrs
Calories per serving: 810
37 g protein, 41 g fat,
70 g carbohydrate

- Prepare dough as for pizza rounds (page 170). Oil a baking sheet and shape the dough into a flat circle.
- Stir tomato purée into the sour cream and season with basil, salt and pepper. Wash the red pepper and cut into small pieces. Scrub and slice the carrots. Sauté carrots in butter, season them with salt and pepper then let simmer for about 15 minutes in 3 tbsp water.
- Wash the zucchini and slice. Preheat the oven to 375°F (190°C).
- Spread the tomato purée on the dough and add the vegetables. Cut the Mozzarella into small pieces and grate the Gouda. Scatter both cheeses over the pizza. Bake on the lower rack for 25 minutes.

Asparagus Quiche

Ingredients for 1 large flan pan:

1 lb (500 g) asparagus
salt
4 tsp butter
1/2 cup clarified butter
2 1/2 cups (350 g) unbleached flour
1 bunch of fresh basil
3 eggs
1/2 cup (100 g) cream
1/2 cup (100 ml) milk
1/4 cup (50 g) dry Ricotta cheese
 (or substitute mild Feta
 for a stronger flavor)
pepper, freshly ground
unrefined coconut butter and flour
 for the pie plate

Preparation time: 1 1/2 hrs
Calories per serving: 810
20 g protein, 51 g fat,
67 g carbohydrate

- Prepare the asparagus and cook
  for 10 minutes in 1/2 cup
  (125 ml) water with salt and
  butter.
- Bring the clarified butter and
  3/4 cup (150 ml) water to a
  boil in a covered saucepan.
  Blend 1 tsp salt with the flour
  and make a well in the center.
  Pour in the boiling water. Work
  the flour inward from the edges
  with a wooden spoon. Leave the
  kneaded dough in a plastic bag
  for 20 minutes.
- Preheat oven to 375°F
  (190°C). Grease a flan pan
  and dust with flour.
- Wash the basil and remove the
  stems. Blend eggs, cream, milk,
  cheese and basil and season
  with pepper.
- Roll out the dough and place it
  in the pan. Prick the base
  several times with a fork.
  Cut the asparagus short enough
  so it can be arranged in a star
  shape (tips to the center).
  Fill in the gaps with the
  remaining cut pieces. Pour the
  basil cream over the asparagus
  and bake on the middle rack for
  25 minutes.

Potato Quiche

Ingredients for 1 baking sheet (about 6 servings):

5 medium potatoes
1/4 cup (60 g) butter
2 small eggs
2 cups (300 g) wholewheat flour
salt
nutmeg, freshly grated
2–3 leeks
1 red pepper
1/2 cup (100 g) tomato paste
2 red apples
1 tbsp lemon juice
1/2 cup (125 g) cream
3 eggs
1 cup (150 g) grated Gouda cheese
1/2 tsp dried oregano

Preparation time: 1 1/4 hrs
Calories per serving: 570
22 g protein, 28 g fat,
55 g carbohydrate

- Boil the potatoes leaving skins on. Peel while hot then mash and allow to cool.
- Preheat the oven to 400°F (200°C). Mix the potatoes, 3 tbsp butter, eggs, flour, salt and nutmeg to form a dough. Line a baking sheet with parchment paper and roll the dough over it.
- Clean the leek and slice into thin rings. Sauté for about 5 minutes in the remaining butter. Wash the pepper and cut into thin strips.
- Cover the dough with tomato paste. Layer with leeks and pepper. Wash, core and thinly slice the apples. Sprinkle with lemon juice then add to the quiche.
- Beat the cream, eggs, cheese and oregano and pour over the top. Bake on the oven's lowest rack for about 20 minutes.

Tomato Quiche

Ingredients for 1 quiche (use an 11" (27.5 cm) flan pan, or fill a pie plate and use any extra for single-serving tarts):

1 1/3 cups (200 g) finely ground organic spelt flour
1 2/3 cups (400 g) quark (see page 32)
1/3 cup (80 g) butter
salt, freshly ground white pepper
2 eggs
2/3 cup (150 g) herbed cream cheese
nutmeg, freshly grated
1 lb (500 g) cherry tomatoes
butter or unrefined coconut butter and flour for the flan pan

Preparation time: 1 hr (including 30 minutes cooking time)
With 4 servings per quiche:
570 calories per serving
26 g protein, 33 g fat,
39 g carbohydrate

- Mix the flour, 2/3 cup quark, butter and salt into a flexible dough. Wrap in plastic and leave in a cool place for 30 minutes.
- Grease the pan and dust with flour. Preheat the oven to 375°F (190°C). Roll out the dough, place it in the pan and shape a border around the edge. Prick the base several times with a fork. Bake for about 8 minutes on the middle rack.
- Separate the eggs. Blend the yolks, cream cheese and remaining quark and season well. Beat the egg whites until stiff and fold in. Spread this mixture over the dough.
- Wash the tomatoes and halve them. Place them in the cheese mix cut-side down. Bake for 25 minutes.

Apricot Quiche

Ingredients for 1 large flan pan
(11"–12" (27.5–30 cm) in
diameter):

1 1/4 cups (200 g) spelt flour
  (or a combination of spelt and
  unbleached white flour)
2/3 cup (140 g) cold butter
1 tbsp sour cream
salt
1/4 cup (50 g) pine nuts
1 lb (500 g) apricots
2 small leeks
1/3 lb (150 g) mild blue cheese
1 egg
1/3 cup (100 g) crème fraîche
  (see page 32)
nutmeg, freshly grated
unrefined coconut oil or coconut
  butter and flour for the pan

Preparation time: 1 1/2 hrs
With 4 servings per quiche:
830 calories per serving
11 g protein, 50 g fat,
51 g carbohydrate

- Mix the flour with chunks of
  cold butter, sour cream and
  1/2 tsp salt to form a fairly
  soft dough. Leave in a cool
  place for 30 minutes.
- Preheat the oven to 375°F
  (190°C). Grease the pan and
  dust with flour.
- Dry roast the pine nuts.
  Wash the apricots, remove
  their pits and slice.
- Cut the cheese into large
  chunks and purée with egg
  and crème fraîche. Season
  with salt and nutmeg.
- Roll out the dough and place
  it in the pan. Prick the base
  several times with a fork.
  Spread the apricot pieces,
  leeks and pine nuts on the
  dough. Pour the cheese-egg
  mixture over top. Bake on
  the lower rack for about
  20 minutes or until golden.

Squash Quiche

Ingredients for 1 deep-dish
9" (22.5 cm) pie plate, or
a 10" (25 cm) flan pan:

2 cups (280 g) wholewheat flour
1/2 cup (120 g) cold butter
salt, freshly ground pepper
4 eggs
2 lb (1 kg) winter squash (such as
  acorn, butternut or hubbard)
1/3 cup (80 ml) port
  (or substitute apple juice)
1/3 cup (80 g) crème fraîche
  (see page 32)
5 tbsp capers
1/4 cup (50 g) green pumpkin
  seeds, hulled
1/3 lb (150 g) blue cheese,
  finely chopped
unrefined coconut oil or butter

Preparation time: 2 hrs
With 4 servings per quiche:
880 calories per serving
30 g protein, 59 g fat,
56 g carbohydrate

- Place flour, chunks of butter,
  2 eggs and a pinch of salt on
  a work surface. Quickly
  work the mixture into a soft
  dough. Cool for 1 hour.
- Remove skin, seeds and
  inner fibers from the squash.
  Cut into chunks and simmer
  in port for 25 minutes.
  Drain and purée.
- Fold in the crème fraîche, the
  remaining eggs and pepper.
  Chop the capers. Preheat the
  oven to 375°F (190°C).
- Grease the pan and dust it
  with flour. Roll out the
  dough, place it in a floured
  pan and make a border.
  Prick with a fork. Bake for
  5 minutes on the middle
  rack of the oven.
- Mix the squash with the
  capers and pumpkin seeds,
  spread over the dough and
  sprinkle with cheese. Bake for
  45 minutes or until cooked.

Savory Spelt Tart

Ingredients for 1 deep-dish
9" (22.5 cm) pie plate or
a 10" (25 cm) flan pan:

1 1/4 cups (200 g) organic spelt
  flour (or substitute wholewheat
  flour)
salt, freshly ground pepper
3/4 cup (160 g) sour cream
1/2 cup (100 g) cold butter
1 1/2 bunches of radishes
1/3 cup (80 g) crème fraîche
  (see page 32)
lemon juice
1/3 lb (150 g) broccoli
1 tbsp herbed cream cheese
nutmeg, freshly grated
unrefined coconut oil or butter
1 lb (500 g) lentils or soy beans
parchment paper

Preparation time: 1 3/4 hrs
With 4 servings per tart:
500 calories per serving
9 g protein, 35 g fat,
35 g carbohydrate

- Mix a dough from the flour,
  salt, 2 tbsp sour cream and
  chunks of butter. Wrap in
  plastic and leave in a cool
  place for 1 hour.
- Preheat the oven to 375°F
  (190°C). Roll out the dough,
  place on the greased pie plate
  and shape a border. Lay the
  paper over top and cover with
  lentils (lentils used as a
  baking weight only). Bake for
  20 minutes on the top rack.
  Remove the lentils and paper.
- Wash, clean and grate the
  radishes. Drain the radishes
  and mix them with the crème
  fraîche, lemon juice, salt and
  pepper. Clean the broccoli,
  peel the thicker stalks and
  finely chop. Mix the broccoli,
  sour cream, cream cheese, salt
  and spices.
- Spoon the broccoli and radish
  mixtures into alternating
  sections of the pie crust.

Vegetable Loaf

Ingredients for 1 loaf pan:

1 1/3 cup (225 g) unbleached flour
1 package dried yeast
1/2 cup (120 ml) dry white wine
1/3 cup (100 ml) unrefined
  organic safflower or sunflower oil
2 1/2 oz (75 g) Cheddar or
  aged Gouda cheese
1/2 cup (75 g) mixed nuts
3 sun-dried tomatoes
1/3 – 1/2 cup (75 g) pitted
  green olives
1/4 lb (125 g) bell peppers
5 eggs
1/2 tsp salt
unrefined coconut oil or butter
  and ground nuts for the pan

Preparation time: 3 hrs
With 10 servings per loaf:
310 calories per serving
9 g protein, 21 g fat,
20 g carbohydrate

- Mix the flour and yeast.
  Stir in the oil and wine.
  Cover the dough and allow
  to rise in a warm place.
- Grate the cheese. Coarsely
  chop the nuts, tomatoes
  and olives.
- Wash and clean out the
  pepper and chop into small
  pieces. Slowly mix the eggs
  and salt into the dough.
  Fold in the cheese, nuts,
  tomatoes, olives and the
  peppers.
- Grease a loaf pan and
  sprinkle with nuts. Place
  dough in the pan and let rise
  for another 45 minutes.
  Preheat the oven to 350°F
  (175°C). Bake on the lower
  rack for 55 minutes or until
  golden. Allow to rest for a
  few minutes. Remove from
  the pan and allow to cool on
  a rack.

Desserts to Delight

Quark Dumplings with Cherry Sauce

Ingredients for 4 servings:

2 cups (500 g) quark
  (see page 32)
3 eggs
3/4 cup (100 g) flour
1 cup (120 g) cream of wheat
salt
1/3 cup (50 g) bread crumbs
3 tbsp butter
1 1/2 cups cherries
1 1/2 tbsp cornstarch
sugar

Preparation time: 1 1/4 hrs
Calories per serving: 520
30 g protein, 14 g fat,
70 g carbohydrate

- Beat quark and eggs until creamy then add flour, cream of wheat and salt. Leave for 30 minutes. Boil a large quantity of salted water.

- Drop a teaspoon of dough in boiling water. If the dough falls apart, add more cream of wheat to the dough. Use a wet teaspoon to shape the dumplings. Let them slip gently into the water. Boil for 12 minutes or until they rise to the surface. Remove with a slotted spoon.
- Fry the bread crumbs in butter and roll the dumplings in them.
- Set aside a few good cherries. Place the remaining cherries and their juice in a pot. Purée the cornstarch with 3 tbsp of the cherry juice.
- Bring the cherries to a boil, stir in the mixed cornstarch and return to the boil. Sweeten the cherry sauce with sugar, to taste.

Apricot Dumplings with Bread Crumbs

Ingredients for 4 servings:

1 1/3 lb (600 g) mashing potatoes
2 cups (280 g) wholewheat flour
2 tsp soft butter
1 egg
salt
about 16 small apricots
3 tbsp butter
3/4 cup (100 g) dry bread crumbs
2 tbsp raw sugar
cinnamon

Preparation time: 1 1/4 hrs
(including 40 minutes
working time)
Calories per serving: 620
17 g protein, 17 g fat,
98 g carbohydrate

- Leave potatoes unpeeled and steam them until soft. Peel them and press through a sieve while still hot. Cool.

- Mix the potatoes, flour, butter, egg and a pinch of salt into a firm dough. Shape the dough into a long roll and cut it into 16 pieces.
- Wash and pit the apricots. Working with damp hands, flatten the pieces of dough and wrap each one around an apricot, then roll it into a smooth dumpling.
- Bring a large pot of salted water to a boil, cook the dumplings in it for about 10 minutes on low heat, or until they all float to the surface.
- Remove with a slotted spoon and rinse briefly under cold, running water. Melt the butter in a frying pan, fry the bread crumbs until golden. Mix with sugar and cinnamon. Roll the dumplings in the breadcrumb mix and serve.

Black & White Pudding

Ingredients for 4 servings:

1/4 lb (125 g) milk chocolate
1/2 cup (100 g) butter
2 1/2 tbsp cocoa powder
4 eggs
3 tbsp sugar
1/2 cup (60 g) unbleached flour
1/2 cup (50 g) bread crumbs
3/4 cup (75 g) ground hazelnuts
1 1/2 cups (200 g) pitted cherries

Preparation time: 1 1/4 hrs
(includes 20 minutes
working time)
Calories per serving: 670
13 g protein, 46 g fat,
47 g carbohydrate

- Melt the chocolate in the top
  of a double boiler. Beat the
  melted chocolate with butter
  and cocoa powder until
  foamy.

- Separate the eggs. Beat the
  yolks into the chocolate
  mixture. Beat the egg whites
  until stiff while gradually
  adding the sugar. Fold the
  flour, bread crumbs and nuts
  into the chocolate.
- Fold in cherries and egg
  whites.
- Sprinkle a cake mold
  (6 cup (1.5 l) capacity) with
  the remaining cocoa powder.
  Fill with the batter, cover
  with a lid of aluminum foil
  and place in the top of the
  double boiler. If the double
  boiler is too small, make
  your own steamer
  (see page 159).
- Steam for about 50 minutes,
  then remove the foil and let
  it rest for a short time.
  Remove the pudding to
  dessert bowls and serve with
  cream.

Millet Pudding with Blueberries

Ingredients for 4 servings:

1 cup (200 g) millet
1 3/4 cups (400 g) kefir
1 vanilla bean
1 pinch salt
3 eggs
1/3 cup (70 g) honey
1/2 lb (250 g) blueberries
unrefined coconut oil and millet
  for the cake pan

For the sauce:

1 cup (250 g) quark (see page 32)
1/2 cup (100 g) kefir
2 tbsp honey
4 tbsp blueberry juice or crushed
  berries

Preparation time: 1 hr 40 min
Calories per serving: 520
23 g protein, 13 g fat,
68 g carbohydrate

- Bring the millet to a boil
  with the kefir, vanilla bean
  and salt. Simmer for about
  15 minutes then let cool.
- Separate the eggs. Cream the
  yolks with the honey then
  carefully fold them into the
  millet. Wash the berries and
  mix into the millet.
- Prepare a steamer, as on page
  159. Grease a lidded tube
  pan or pudding mold and
  sprinkle with millet. Pour in
  the mixture, cover and place
  in the steamer, allowing the
  water to rise up 1/3 of its
  height. Bring the water to a
  boil and steam the pudding
  for 50 minutes.
- Allow the pudding to cool
  then remove it from the
  mold. For the sauce, beat the
  quark with kefir and honey
  until creamy and dilute with
  the blueberry juice. Serve the
  sauce with the pudding.

Rice Pudding with Raspberry Sauce

Ingredients for 4 servings:

2 cups (500 ml) milk
1 cup (200 g) short-grain rice
salt
lemon zest
1 package vanilla sugar (or substitute
 1 tsp homemade vanilla sugar)
1/4 cup (60 g) raisins
1/4 cup (40 g) dried papaya
 or apricots
3 eggs
3 tbsp butter
3 tbsp sugar
2 tbsp chopped pistachios
unrefined coconut oil
 and grated coconut for the mold

For the sauce:
2/3 lb (325 g) raspberries
1 ripe banana

Preparation time: 2 hrs
Calories per serving: 600
16 g protein, 25 g fat,
80 g carbohydrate

- Add rice, salt, lemon peel and vanilla sugar to the milk and bring to a boil. Simmer over low heat for 35 minutes, then allow to cool slightly.
- Wash the raisins. Cut the papaya into pieces. Separate the eggs. Cream the butter with 2 tbsp sugar, then fold in the yolks, cooked rice, raisins, papaya and pistachios.
- Grease a pudding mold and sprinkle with grated coconut. Prepare a steamer (see page 159) and bring to a boil.
- Beat the egg whites until stiff while adding the remaining sugar. Fold into the rice. Place the mixture in the mold and cover. Steam for 1 hour.
- Remove the mold, uncover and allow to vent steam for a few minutes. Loosen the edges carefully and allow the pudding to drop onto a serving dish.
- For the sauce, blend raspberries with a little water and mashed banana.

Fruit-filled Buns

Ingredients for 4 servings:

16 prunes
2 cups (300 g) flour
4 tbsp dried yeast
2 cups yogurt
2 tbsp sugar
1 pinch salt
1 egg
1/4 cup (60 g) butter
icing sugar for dusting

Preparation time: 1 1/2 hrs
Calories per serving: 570
13 g protein, 17 g fat,
88 g carbohydrate

- If the prunes are too dry, soak
  them in warm water until they
  soften. Combine the flour and
  yeast. Warm the yogurt slightly,
  blend with the sugar, salt and
  egg then fold into the flour
  mixture. Knead the dough until
  it is no longer sticky (add flour
  if necessary—1 tbsp at a time).
  Shape the dough into a roll and
  separate into 16 equal parts.
- Melt the butter in a cake pan
  (about 6" x 8" (15 x 20 cm)).
  Using floured hands, flatten a
  section of dough, place a prune
  in the center and fold over.
  Shape the dough like a
  dumpling. Roll on all sides in
  the melted butter and place in
  the pan. Proceed to work all the
  dough this way, placing the
  dough balls snugly side by side
  in the pan.
- Preheat the oven to 325°F
  (160°C). Meanwhile, let the
  buns rise in a warm place for
  15 minutes. Bake on the middle
  rack for 25 minutes or until
  golden. Remove the buns while
  still hot and dust with icing
  sugar.

Orange-Date Soufflé

Ingredients for 4 servings:

3 oranges
1/2 lb (250 g) fresh dates
2 eggs
1 3/4 cups (400 g) quark
  (see page 32)
4 tsp maple syrup
1/3 cup (50 g) unbleached flour
2 tbsp cream of wheat
1/4 cup (40 g) ground almonds
icing sugar for dusting
unrefined coconut oil
  or butter for the pie plate

Preparation time: 1 hr
Calories per serving: 480
23 g protein, 11 g fat,
62 g carbohydrate

- Grease a large flat pie plate
  (9" (22.5 cm) deep-dish,
  or flan pan) and preheat the
  oven to 325°F (160°C).

- Peel the oranges with a sharp
  knife, removing the white
  pith, and separate the
  segments. Save the juice.
  Halve the dates and pit
  them, if necessary. Remove
  the skins. Separate the eggs.
  Mix the quark, maple syrup,
  egg yolks, orange juice, flour,
  cream of wheat and grated
  almonds.
- Pour this mixture into a
  greased pie plate. Arrange the
  orange segments and date
  halves in a star shape.
- Bake for about 40 minutes
  on the middle rack. Dust
  immediately with icing sugar
  and serve before it collapses.

Tip

One fresh, medium orange
provides more than twice the
daily needs of vitamin C.

Baked Rhubarb Pudding

Ingredients for 4 servings:

1 cup (200 g) quinoa
3 cups (750 ml) milk
1 vanilla bean
3 eggs
3/4–1 cup (200 g) honey
1 1/3 lb (600 g) rhubarb stalks
2/3 cup (150 g) cream
cinnamon
unrefined coconut oil
  or butter to grease the dish

Preparation time: 1 hr
Calories per serving: 640
18 g protein, 26 g fat,
89 g carbohydrate

- Bring the quinoa and vanilla
  bean to a boil in the milk
  and simmer for 10 minutes.
  Preheat the oven to 325°F
  (160°C). Grease a large
  baking dish.

- Separate the eggs. Beat the
  yolks with 1/2 cup (150 g)
  honey until very foamy then
  mix with the quinoa.
- Wash the rhubarb and cut
  into short sections. Beat
  egg whites until stiff, fold
  into the quinoa mix and
  spread the mixture in the
  dish. Distribute half of the
  rhubarb pieces in the
  quinoa mixture.
- Bake for 30 minutes on the
  middle rack. Meanwhile,
  cook the remaining rhubarb
  in a little water until soft.
  Add the rest of the honey
  and blend together. Whip the
  cream until stiff, fold it into
  the rhubarb purée, season
  with cinnamon and add to
  the mix.

Baked Strawberry Pudding

Ingredients for 2 servings:

3 cups (750 ml) milk
1 3" (7.5 cm) cinnamon stick
1 1/4 cups (200 g) cream of wheat
5 tbsp honey
4 eggs
1 lb (500 g) strawberries
unrefined coconut oil or butter for
 the baking dish

Preparation time: 45 min
Calories per serving: 980
39 g protein, 29 g fat,
140 g carbohydrate

- Bring the milk and the
  cinnamon stick to a boil, add
  the cream of wheat and cook
  for 5 minutes or until thick.
  Stir frequently.
- Stir in 3 tbsp honey and
  allow to cool a little.
  Separate the eggs and stir in
  the egg yolks. Beat the egg
  whites until stiff then fold
  into the cream of wheat
  mixture.
- Preheat the oven to 375°F
  (190°C). Grease a flat
  baking dish (about 7" x 11"
  (17.5 x 27.5 cm)). Spread
  half of the cream of wheat
  evenly in the pan. Clean the
  strawberries, distribute half
  of them over top then cover
  evenly with the remaining
  cream of wheat.
- Bake for 15–18 minutes on
  the middle rack. Purée the
  remaining strawberries and
  season with the rest of the
  honey. Serve together.

Tip

This dish makes a good food
for weaning babies. The
combination of milk and wheat
with the vitamin-rich sauce also
makes this ideal for the elderly.

Baked Fruit Salad

Ingredients for 4 servings:

12 wholewheat zwiebacks or
 standard zwieback crackers
2 eggs
2 cups (500 ml) milk
2 bananas
1 cup (250 g) quark
3/4 cup (100 g) pitted cherries
4 mandarin oranges (or substitute
 1 small can of mandarins)
2 kiwis
1 tbsp sugar
unrefined coconut oil or butter for
 the dish

Preparation time: 1 hr
Calories per serving: 430
11 g protein, 9 g fat,
49 g carbohydrate

- Grease a small casserole or
  deep baking dish. Preheat the
  oven to 400°F (200°C).
  Place a layer of zwiebacks in
  the bottom. Separate the
  eggs. Blend the milk with
  bananas, egg yolks and
  quark.
- Peel and separate the
  mandarins into segments.
  Peel and slice the kiwis.
- Distribute part of the fruit
  over the zwieback then pour
  a little banana milk over top.
  Place alternating layers of
  zwieback, fruit and banana
  milk in the dish.
- Bake for 25 minutes on the
  middle rack.
- Meanwhile, beat the egg
  whites with the sugar until
  stiff. Spoon the egg whites
  onto the gratin and bake for
  another 8 minutes.

Fruit Clafouti

Ingredients for 4 servings:

3 eggs
3 tbsp sugar
1/4 cup (50 g) millet flour
  (or substitute wholewheat flour)
1/4 cup (50 g) unbleached flour
1/2 cup (125 ml) milk
2/3 cup (150 g) quark which has
  been drained in a sieve
1/2 lb (250 g) berries of your
  choice, use frozen if necessary
3 nectarines or peaches
salt
icing sugar for dusting
1 cup (200 g) cream
3 tbsp egg liqueur or to taste
1 tbsp sugar
unrefined coconut oil
  or butter for the dish

Preparation time: 1 hr
Calories per serving: 520
15 g protein, 24 g fat,
53 g carbohydrate

- Grease a large baking dish or lasagna pan. Preheat oven to 325°F (160°C).
- Separate the eggs. Mix the egg yolks with sugar, flour, milk and quark.
- Wash the berries. Wash and halve the nectarines, remove pits and cut the fruit into narrow segments.
- Add a pinch of salt to the egg whites and beat them until stiff. Fold the whites into the egg yolk mixture.
- Place the batter in the baking dish and lay the fruit on top. Bake for about 40 minutes on the middle rack. Dust with icing sugar after baking. Whip the cream until stiff, fold in the egg liqueur, add sugar to taste and serve with the clafouti.

Cherry Trifle

Ingredients for 4 servings:

1 large jar of naturally preserved
  sour cherries
4 tsp kirsch, or to taste
5 slices of day-old bread
4 eggs
1/3 cup (80 g) sugar, or to taste
1 tbsp cocoa powder
2 tbsp slivered almonds
unrefined coconut oil
  or butter for the baking dish

Preparation time: 1 1/4 hrs
Calories per serving: 450
13 g protein, 11 g fat,
74 g carbohydrate

- Drain the cherries and save the juice. Marinate the fruit in the kirsch for about 15 minutes.
- If the bread is still moist, toast it. Break up the bread and dampen it with cherry juice. Grease a flat baking dish and preheat the oven to 325°F (160°C).
- Separate the eggs, beat the yolks with sugar and cocoa until creamy. Beat the whites until stiff.
- Fold the egg yolk mixture and cherries into the bread mixture. Spread in the dish and sprinkle with slivered almonds. Bake for about 40 minutes on the middle rack.

Tip

This recipe puts old bread to good use. It is low in fat, high in carbohydrates and the fruit provides additional vitamins.

French Provincial Melon-Rice Pudding

Ingredients for 4 servings:

1 cup (200 g) short-grain rice
2 cups (500 ml) milk
1 tsp dried lavender blossom (or substitute 1/2 vanilla pod, grated)
1/3 cup (80 g) honey
1 small honeydew melon
1 cantaloupe

Preparation time: 45 min
Calories per serving: 520
12 g protein, 8 g fat,
100 g carbohydrate

- Bring the rice to a boil in the milk, add lavender then simmer over low heat for 30 minutes, stirring often.
- Fold in the honey. Remove from the heat. Cover the rice with a tea towel and let cool.

- Halve the melons, remove seeds and rind and save the juice. Cut the fruit into pieces. Add the melon juice and melon pieces to the rice and serve.

Variation

Instead of melon you can use a compote of plums, cherries or berries soaked in sugar. Whenever possible, use a natural, unrefined sweetener like evaporated sugar cane juice—it will provide healthy minerals to your dish. If you prefer a thinner pudding, add more milk.

Tip

This cool dish is particularly welcome in the summer. It is high in potassium which promotes healthy tissues.

Quark-Fruit Dessert

Ingredients for 4 servings:

2 cups (500 g) quark
  (see page 32)
2/3 cup (150 g) natural yogurt
1 1/3 lb (600 g) mixed berries
3 tbsp maple syrup
1 tsp lemon juice
1/2 cup (125 g) cream
1 1/2 packages (200 g) ladyfinger cookies (about 40 cookies)

Preparation time: 30 min
Calories per serving: 500
24 g protein, 15 g fat,
67 g carbohydrate

- Blend quark and yogurt together. Wash, sort and drain the berries. Blend half the berries with maple syrup and lemon juice.
- Fold the berry mix into the quark.

- Beat the cream until stiff and fold it into the mix. Place alternating layers of the cream mix and ladyfingers in a large dish. End with a layer of cream mix and refrigerate for at least 1 hour.
- Distribute the remaining berries on the top.

Variation

In England, this dish is called trifle. Instead of ladyfingers try using leftover cake, wholewheat bread crumbs or zwiebacks.

Whenever possible, use fresh, local berries but if they are not available, use frozen berries. You can also substitute the berries with whatever fruit is in season.

Chilled Fruited Zucchini Soup

Ingredients for 4 servings:

2/3 lb (300 g) zucchini
2/3 lb (300 g) apricots
2 cups (500 ml) apple juice
1 small cinnamon stick
1–2 tbsp honey
1/3 lb (150 g) raspberries
lemon balm to taste

Preparation time: 30 min
Calories per serving: 120
3 g protein, 6 g fat,
27 g carbohydrate

- Wash the zucchini and apricots. Peel and slice the zucchini. Pit the apricots, and quarter them. Bring the zucchini, apricots and honey to a boil in apple juice. Cover and simmer over low heat for 15 minutes or until cooked.

- Allow the liquid to cool a little then purée it with an electric hand mixer and refrigerate. Before serving, add the raspberries, pour into a deep bowl and garnish with lemon balm to taste.

Variation

Any mild vegetable such as carrots, pumpkin, peppers and ripe tomatoes is suitable for this recipe.

Tip

This combination of a fruit and vegetable makes for a particularly refreshing dessert that is high in vitamins and minerals. Zucchini is an excellent source of vitamin C and apricots provide dietary fiber and potassium.

Chilled Cherry Sauce with Quark Dumplings

Ingredients for 4 servings:

1 1/3 cup (300 g) dry quark,
  drained in a sieve
2 tbsp grated blanched almonds
1/3 cup (80 g) double cream
2 tbsp sugar
1 pinch of grated lemon peel
2/3 lb (300 g) sour cherries
2/3 lb (300 g) sweet cherries
2 cups (500 ml) peach juice
2 tbsp tapioca
1 pinch grated vanilla bean

Preparation time: 45 min
Calories per serving: 360
14 g protein, 14 g fat,
37 g carbohydrate

- Blend the quark, almonds, double cream, sugar and lemon peel until creamy then refrigerate.
- Pit the cherries. Bring the peach juice and tapioca to a boil. After 5 minutes add the sour cherries. Boil for another 5 minutes. Mix in the sweet cherries and grated vanilla then refrigerate the liquid.
- Make about 24 balls from the quark mixture. Use a teaspoon or shape them with damp hands. Pour the chilled sauce into bowls and distribute the "dumplings" on top.

Tip

The chilled sauce (without dumplings) is excellent for replacing fluids and minerals lost in hot weather.

Drinks for Fitness and Energy

Exotic Punch

Ingredients for 1 large glass:

1 tsp tropical dried fruit mix from
  the health food store
1 tsp pine nuts
1 cup (250 ml) multivitamin juice
  (e.g., a fruit-based liquid
  multivitamin diluted to 1 cup)
2 tbsp thick apple juice or natural
  apple sauce

Preparation time: 15 min
Calories per glass: 170
1 g protein, 4 g fat,
33 g carbohydrate

• Coarsely chop the dried fruit
  and pine nuts separately.
  Slowly warm the fruit with
  the juice over low heat and
  let soak for 5 minutes.
• Add the pine nuts to the
  punch and season with
  apple juice.

Kiwi Sour

Ingredients for 1 glass:

1 kiwi
1 tbsp fruit vinegar
1 tsp liquid sugar
  (or substitute maple syrup)
mineral water

Preparation time: 5 min
Calories per glass: 55
0.5 g protein, 0 g fat,
12 g carbohydrate

• Peel the kiwi and coarsely
  chop. Purée the kiwi with the
  fruit vinegar and the
  sweetener.
• Add the fruit purée to a glass
  and top up with mineral
  water.

Lavender Infusion

Ingredients for 2 glasses:

1 tsp dried lavender blossoms
1/2 tsp anise seeds
1 tbsp honey
juice of 1 orange

Preparation time: 10 min
Calories per glass: 52
0.4 g protein, 0 g fat,
12 g carbohydrate

• Bring the lavender blossoms
  and anise seeds to a boil in
  1 cup (250 ml) water. Set
  aside for 5 minutes. Dissolve
  the honey in the hot liquid.
• Pour the infusion through a
  sieve and allow to cool. Add
  the orange juice and serve.

Rhubarb Cooler

Ingredients for 4 glasses:

2/3 lb (300 g) rhubarb stalks
1 3" (7.5 cm) cinnamon stick
2 tsp dried mallow blossoms
4 tbsp acacia honey
mineral water

Preparation time: 30 min
Calories per glass: 57
0.4 g protein, 0 g fat,
14 g carbohydrate

• Wash the rhubarb and cut
  into pieces. Boil together
  with the cinnamon for
  20 minutes in 2 cups
  (500 ml) water.
• Add the mallow blossoms
  for the last 5 minutes.
  Pass through a sieve.
  Add the honey and allow to
  cool. Top up the glass with
  mineral water.

Strawberry-Orange Shake

Ingredients for 2 glasses:

1 large orange
1/4 lb (125 g) strawberries
1 cup (250 g) kefir
1 tbsp natural maple syrup
 (or substitute honey)
2 orange slices and 2 small
 strawberries for garnishing

Preparation time: 15 min
Calories per glass: 150
5 g protein, 5 g fat,
16 g carbohydrate

- Peel the orange and separate the segments.
- Wash and halve the strawberries. Purée with the kefir and maple syrup in a blender.

- Place 1 orange slice and 1 strawberry on each of 2 cocktail sticks. Pour the shake into the glasses and place a cocktail stick on the edge of each glass.

Variation

Substitute fresh, locally grown fruit at their peak season to ensure that you get full nutrient value from your produce.

Try using peaches with blueberries, or bananas with blackberries, or a touch of coconut with pineapple and orange.

Tip

Kefir is made from fermented milk or soy milk. It is a good food for lactose-intolerant people and promotes the growth of friendly bacteria in the intestines.

Yogurt Shake

Ingredients for 1 large glass:

1/4 lb (125 g) gooseberries
 (or substitute any other berries)
1/4 cup (100 g) natural yogurt
1/4 cup (100 ml) pineapple juice
1 tbsp nutritional yeast
a few drops of lemon juice

Preparation time: 10 min
Calories per glass: 200
9 g protein, 4 g fat,
30 g carbohydrate

- Wash and coarsely chop the gooseberries.
- Purée gooseberries, yogurt, pineapple juice and yeast in a blender or food processor. Season with lemon juice to taste.

Raspberry-Buttermilk Shake

Ingredients for 2 large glasses:

1/2 lb (250 g) raspberries
1 3/4 cups (400 g) buttermilk
1 tbsp natural maple syrup
 or honey

Preparation time: 5 min
Calories per glass: 120
8 g protein, 1 g fat,
15 g carbohydrate

- Remove the raspberry stems. Purée the raspberries with a little buttermilk and maple syrup.
- Add the remaining buttermilk and blend together.

Blueberry-Whey Shake

Ingredients for 1 glass:

1/2 tsp sesame seeds
1/4 lb (125 g) blueberries
2/3 cup (150 g) whey
 (or substitute buttermilk)
1 tsp thick pear juice
a few drops of lemon juice

Preparation time: 10 min
Calories per glass: 150
3 g protein, 2 g fat,
18 g carbohydrate

• Dry roast the sesame seeds
 until golden.
• Wash and sort the
 blueberries. Blend them with
 the whey and pear juice until
 foamy.
• Flavor the shake with lemon
 juice and serve sprinkled
 with sesame seeds.

Apple-Date Drink

Ingredients for 2 glasses:

4 fresh dates
1 apple
1/2 tsp lemon juice
2/3 cup (150 ml) milk
2 tbsp sour cream or extra-thick
 yogurt
1 pinch ground cinnamon

Preparation time: 10 min
Calories per glass: 200
5 g protein, 4 g fat,
38 g carbohydrate

• Pit and quarter the dates.
 Wash, peel and quarter the
 apple. Remove the core,
 coarsely chop the quarters
 and sprinkle with lemon
 juice.
• Purée the dates, apple pieces,
 milk and sour cream
 together. Pour into glasses
 and dust with cinnamon.

Carrot-Almond Milk

Ingredients for 2 glasses:

1/4 cup (100 g) carrots
1 tbsp ground almonds
1 tsp honey
1 cup (250 ml) milk
parsley for garnish

Preparation time: 10 min
Calories per glass: 500
5 g protein, 6 g fat,
11 g carbohydrate

• Wash and peel and coarsely
 chop the carrots.
• Dry roast the almonds until
 lightly browned. Remove
 them from the pan.
• Purée carrots, almonds,
 honey and milk in a blender.
 Serve with a little parsley on
 the edge of the glass.

Tip

It is well known that the
carotenoids in carrots must
combine with fat in order to be
absorbed. But should carrots be
eaten raw or cooked? If you
consider only the beta-carotene
content, then the carrots
should be cooked for
assimilation by the body.
However, the fiber content and
the quality of accessory
nutrients are reduced during
the cooking process. Decide for
yourself, and alternate between
the two, according to your
personal health priorities.

Kefir-Sprout Cocktail

Ingredients for 1 glass:

1/2 container alfalfa sprouts
1 bunch of dill
2/3 cup (150 g) kefir
1 tbsp cream
1 tsp nutritional yeast
a few drops of lemon juice
seasoning salt
1 pinch pepper, freshly ground
mineral water

Preparation time: 15 min
Calories per glass: 160
10 g protein, 9 g fat,
10 g carbohydrate

• Chop the sprouts and
  separate the dill tips from
  the stalks.
• Purée the sprouts, dill, kefir,
  cream and yeast. Season with
  lemon juice, salt and pepper.
  Top up with mineral water.

Tomato-Buttermilk Cocktail

Ingredients for 2 tall glasses:

1 1/4 cups (300 ml) tomato juice
1 cup (250 ml) buttermilk
1 tbsp millet flakes or to taste
1 tsp cold-pressed,
  extra-virgin olive oil
1 pinch basil in oil
seasoning salt, pepper
2 celery stalks, washed

Preparation time: 5 min
Calories per glass: 98
6 g protein, 3 g fat,
13 g carbohydrate

• Chill the ingredients
  (except the celery) then
  purée together. Place a
  celery stalk in each glass.
• Pour the cocktail into
  glasses. Serve immediately—
  before the flakes sink to the
  bottom.

Creamed Carrot Shake

Ingredients for 4 glasses:

1 lb (500 g) carrots
1 large apple
1 lb (500 g) creamed cottage
  cheese
1 1/4 cups (300 ml) milk
1–2 tbsp lemon juice
1 heaping tbsp sunflower seeds
salt
sugar
mineral water (optional)

Preparation time: 15 min
Calories per glass: 180
8 g protein, 8 g fat,
19 g carbohydrate

• Wash and peel the carrots
  and apple. Core the apple
  and cut it in half. Cut one
  half of the apple into
  4 segments, sprinkle them
  with lemon juice and set
  aside. Coarsely chop the
  other half apple and the
  carrot.
• Purée all the ingredients
  (except the apple segments)
  until smooth and creamy.
  Season with lemon juice, salt
  and sugar to taste. Add
  mineral water if the drink is
  too thick. Hook the apple
  segments onto the rims of
  the glasses and serve.

Tip

Because of its high sugar
content, carrot is a versatile
vegetable to use in desserts and
drinks.

Carrots are one of the richest
sources of vitamin A, which is
important for healthy eyes and
bones. Carrots are also a good
source of vitamin C, potassium
and dietary fiber.

Tomato Cocktail

Ingredients for 4 glasses:

2 large fleshy tomatoes
10 black olives
1/2 bunch of fresh basil
1 1/3 cups (330 ml) tomato juice
seasoning salt
pepper, freshly ground
mineral water
4 small cherry tomatoes and
  4 stuffed green olives for
  the garnish

Preparation time: 15 min
Calories per glass: 260
2 g protein, 3 g fat,
7 g carbohydrate

- Blanch the tomatoes then
  immediately plunge them
  into cold water. Let them
  cool and remove the skins
  and seeds with a sharp knife.

- Pit the olives. Wash the basil
  and remove the stems. Purée
  tomatoes, olives, basil and
  tomato juice in a blender.
  Season with salt and pepper.

- Pour the mixture into four
  glasses and top up with
  mineral water. Put 1 cherry
  tomato and 1 green olive on
  each cocktail stick or
  toothpick and lay across the
  top of each glass.

Tip

Drink freshly prepared fruit
juices, cocktails and shakes as
soon as possible. The longer
they are exposed to air and
light, the more nutrients will
be lost.

Tomatoes are rich in vitamin
C, good sources of vitamin E,
folate and dietary fiber, and
provide some vitamin A and
potassium.

Sorrel Cocktail

Ingredients for 4 glasses:

1 lemon
1 bunch of sorrel
1 tbsp clover honey
2 cups (500 ml) buttermilk
mineral water for topping up

Preparation time: 10 min
Calories per glass: 67
5 g protein, 0.8 g fat,
9 g carbohydrate

- Juice the lemons and grate
  the peel. Wash the sorrel, set
  4 good leaves aside and
  coarsely chop the rest.
- Purée the chopped sorrel
  leaves with the honey. Slowly
  add the buttermilk, then the
  lemon juice and peel.
- Pour the drink into four tall
  glasses, top up with mineral
  water and garnish each glass
  with a sorrel leaf.

Sour Pepper

Ingredients for 2 glasses:

1 large yellow pepper
1 tbsp pine nuts
3 1/2 tbsp mild sauerkraut
1 3/4 cups (400 ml) sauerkraut
  juice
1 dash Tabasco sauce

Preparation time: 20 min
Calories per glass: 86
5 g protein, 4 g fat,
9 g carbohydrate

- Wash and quarter the pepper,
  remove the seeds and insides.
  Dry roast the pine nuts.
- Purée all the ingredients
  thoroughly in a blender.
  Season with Tabasco sauce
  and serve.

193

Better Boxed Lunches

Cheese Terrine

Ingredients for 1 loaf pan
(8 servings):

1 cucumber, seeded and cut into
  narrow strips
salt, freshly ground black pepper
2 tbsp agar-agar flakes
1/2 cup (125 ml) milk
2/3 cup (150 g) butter
2 cups (500 g) quark
  (see page 32)
1/2 lb (250 g) blue cheese,
  cut into small pieces
1 bunch of parsley, washed
3/4 cup (120 g) green olives,
  pitted
1 clove of garlic, minced
8 thin slices unleavened
  pumpernickel bread
1/3 cup (50 g) chopped chives

Preparation time: 30 minutes
(+6 hours refrigeration time)
Calories per serving: 160
19 g protein, 6 g fat,
7 g carbohydrate

- Line the pan with plastic
  wrap. Salt the cucumber
  lightly and let it drain.
- Stir the agar-agar in milk,
  dissolve it on low heat for
  2 minutes then cool slightly.
  Stir in 1/4 cup (50 g) of
  butter. Stir in the quark
  and cheese by the spoonful.
  Purée the mixture and season
  with salt and pepper.
- Remove thick parsley stems.
  Purée the remaining butter,
  olives and parsley. Spread
  garlic on the pumpernickel.
- Press alternating layers of
  the bread, half of the cheese
  mixture and cucumber into
  the pan. Begin and end with
  bread slices. Save the
  remaining cheese mixture.
- Press down firmly and
  refrigerate for 6 hours.
  Remove from the pan, top
  with the remaining cheese
  and sprinkle with chives.

Stuffed Pepper Slices

Ingredients for 2 servings:

1 red pepper
1 egg
1 cup (200 g) quark
1 tsp soft butter
a few stalks each parsley and dill
1/2 bunch of chives
salt
pepper, freshly ground

Preparation time: 2 1/2 hrs
(including 30 min working time)
Calories per serving: 160
19 g protein, 6 g fat,
7 g carbohydrate

- Wash the pepper, cut out the
  stalk area and widen the
  opening so that an egg will
  fit in. Remove the seeds and
  interior walls without
  damaging the pepper. Hard
  boil the egg, rinse in cold
  water, peel and let cool.

- Squeeze the quark in a
  cheesecloth and drain as
  much water as possible.
  Mix the quark with the
  butter. Wash and chop the
  herbs, fold them into the
  quark and add salt and
  pepper.
- Fill half of the pepper with
  the mixture, leaving a hollow
  in the middle. Place the egg
  in the middle then add the
  remaining mixture.
- Refrigerate the stuffed
  pepper for at least 2 hours.
  Cut it into slices using a
  sharp wet knife and serve.

Tip

Peppers are a rich source of
vitamin C. One red pepper
provides twice as much
vitamin C as a green pepper.

195

Mild Winter Salad

Ingredients for 2 servings:

1 small Chinese cabbage
2 oranges
2 tbsp raisins
1 kiwi
1 tsp unrefined, organic
 pumpkin seed oil
1 tbsp sour cream or thick yogurt
salt
pepper, freshly ground
1 bunch of chives
1 tbsp unshelled pumpkin seeds

Preparation time: 30 min
Calories per serving: 380
13 g protein, 12 g fat,
53 g carbohydrate

- Wash the cabbage and chop it into strips. Juice 1 orange and soak the raisins in the juice. Peel the second orange, removing the white pith, separate it into segments then cut it into slices. Peel and slice the kiwi. Mix the cabbage with the orange and kiwi slices.
- Drain the raisins and save the juice. Whisk the orange juice with the oil and sour cream. Season with salt and pepper. Wash and chop the chives then mix them into the dressing.
- Toss the dressing with the cabbage. Dry roast the pumpkin seeds. Sprinkle raisins and pumpkin seeds over the salad.

Tip

Add 3/4 cup (100 g) cooked buckwheat or rice to make this salad a main course. It can be made even tastier and higher in vitamins by using a mixture of Chinese cabbage and sauerkraut.

Crunchy Potato Salad

Ingredients for 2 servings:

1/2 lb (250 g) potatoes
salt
several leaves Romaine lettuce
1/2 small kohlrabi
1/2 bunch of chives
1/3 cup (75 g) sour cream
1–2 tsp hot mustard
1/3 cup (75 ml) vegetable stock
pepper, freshly ground
1 pinch grated horseradish

Preparation time: 1 hr
Calories per serving: 240
9 g protein, 2 g fat,
43 g carbohydrate

- Wash the potatoes and steam them until cooked through. Rinse in cold water, peel and let them cool. Slice thinly.
- Wash the lettuce and tear it into bite-sized pieces.

Clean and coarsely grate the kohlrabi. Wash and finely chop the chives.

- Mix a dressing from the sour cream, mustard, stock, salt and pepper. Fold in the potato slices, add the chives, lettuce and grated kohlrabi. Season the salad with horseradish.

Tip

To keep the salad fresh longer, add a little more stock and vinegar.

Variation

Mix a dressing from 3 tbsp Feta cheese, 1/2 cup (125 ml) vegetable stock, mild mustard, salt, pepper and herbes de Provence. Replace the kohlrabi with fennel.

Layered Salad

Ingredients for 4 servings:

1/2 lb (250 g) ravioli with
  vegetable stuffing
salt
4 eggs
3 bunches of parsley
1 onion
1 cup (250 ml) vegetable stock
1/2 cup (50 g) bread crumbs
3 tbsp cream mixed with
  horseradish (to taste)
1 cup (250 ml) light cream
white pepper, freshly ground
1 1/2 lb (750 g) tomatoes

Preparation time: 30 min
Calories per serving: 400
15 g protein, 24 g fat,
30 g carbohydrate

- Cook the ravioli until *al dente*
  in plenty of salted water.
  Rinse in cold water and let
  cool. Hard boil the eggs,

rinse them in cold water, peel
and allow them to cool.
Wash and finely chop the
parsley. Peel and mince the
onion.
- Mix the parsley, onion,
  stock, bread crumbs, creamed
  horseradish and light cream.
  Season with salt and pepper.
- Wash the tomatoes and cut
  out the stalk. Slice the eggs
  and tomatoes. Arrange
  alternating layers of ravioli,
  tomatoes, parsley cream
  mixture and sliced eggs in a
  bowl. Let the salad sit for at
  least 1 hour before serving.

Tip
The creamy dressing keeps all
the layers in this salad moist.

Cheesy Stuffed Tomatoes

Ingredients for 4 servings:

8 Roma tomatoes
1/2 bunch of fresh basil
1/4 lb (125 g) fresh Mozzarella
2 tbsp Ricotta cheese
salt
pepper, freshly ground
4–6 green olives, pitted

Preparation time: 15 min
Calories per serving: 120
9 g protein, 7 g fat,
6 g carbohydrate

- Wash the tomatoes and cut
  the tops off to make lids.
  Spoon out the interior and
  use elsewhere.
- Wash the basil, remove the
  stems and coarsely chop the
  leaves.
- Purée the Mozzarella while
  adding Ricotta and basil.

- Chop or thinly slice the
  olives. Fold them into the
  cheese mixture and season.
  Press the filling into the
  tomatoes and replace the
  lids.

Variation
Roast 2 tbsp chopped almonds
and let cool. Mix them with
1/4 lb (125 g) finely grated
carrots, 1 minced clove of
garlic, 10 chopped black olives,
1 cup (150 g) cooked
couscous, juice of 1/2 lemon,
1–2 tbsp unrefined sesame oil,
salt, pepper and a little cumin.
Fill the tomatoes.

Tip
Green and black olives are the
same fruit; the green ones are
picked underripe and they
contain more juice than black
olives.

Spring Rolls

Ingredients for 4 servings:

1/2 lb (250 g) carrots
4 green onions
1/2 red pepper
1/4 lb (125 g) unsalted peanuts
2 tbsp unrefined sesame oil
2 tbsp rice wine
1/2 tsp ground lemon grass
  or 1 tsp lemon juice
1 pinch powdered ginger
soy sauce
8 sheets rice paper (or substitute
  thin homemade pancakes)
unrefined coconut oil or clarified
  butter for deep frying

Preparation time: 45 minutes
Calories per serving: 150
4 g protein, 11 g fat,
7 g carbohydrate

- Scrub the carrots and cut
  them into matchsticks. Wash
  and slice the green onions.

- Wash and julienne the
  pepper. Chop the peanuts.
- Sauté the vegetables and
  peanuts in oil for 5 minutes.
  Season with rice wine, lemon
  grass, ginger and soy sauce.
- Soak the rice paper in cold
  water. Lay each sheet on a
  paper towel and blot it dry
  with a second paper towel.
  Place the filling on the rice
  paper then roll it up while
  folding in the ends.
- Heat about 3/4" (2 cm) of
  oil in a frying pan and fry
  the rolls until golden.

Variation

To make thin homemade
pancakes, mix 1 cup (120 g)
unbleached white flour, 2 eggs,
1 cup (250 ml) milk and salt.
Add more milk to form a thin
batter. Melt butter in a frying
pan and cook 6–8 crêpes.

Sprout Pockets

Ingredients for 8 pockets:

1/3–1/2 cup (100 g) butter
2 1/3 cups–2 1/2 cups (340 g)
  wholewheat flour
salt
1 tsp honey
2/3 cup (150 g) Ricotta or mild
  Feta cheese
1/2 cup (100 g) quark (see page 32)
2/3 cup (150 g) herbed cream
  cheese
2 eggs
2/3 lb (300 g) mung bean sprouts
2 tbsp sunflower seeds
coconut oil or butter

Preparation time: 1 hr
Calories per pocket: 380
15 g protein, 24 g fat,
29 g carbohydrate

- Bring 2/3 cup of water to a
  boil. Add the butter, honey,
  flour and a pinch of salt and

mix into a dough. Form a
smooth ball, wrap in plastic
and let cool slightly.
- Preheat the oven to 375°F
  (190°C). Grease a baking
  sheet and dust it with flour.
  Crumble the Feta, blend it
  with the quark, cream cheese
  and 1 egg. Separate the other
  egg. Reserve the egg yolk.
  Stir the egg white into the
  cheese.
- Wash the sprouts, drain and
  fold them into the cheese.
  Divide the dough into
  8 square pieces and place
  1/8 of the filling on each
  piece. Fold the dough over.
  Place "pockets" on the
  baking sheet with the seams
  down.
- Brush egg yolk on the
  pockets; sprinkle with
  sunflower seeds. Bake for
  25 minutes on the middle
  rack.

Muesli Bars

Ingredients for 15 slices:

1 lb (500 g) carrots
1/2 lb (250 g) dried apples
peel and juice of 1 orange
1/4 lb (125 g) buckwheat
2 tbsp sesame seeds
2 tbsp millet
1 cup (100 g) six-grain cereal
2 tbsp honey
1 tbsp raw sugar
1/3 cup (75 g) raisins
1/2 lb (250 g) unsweetened
 shredded coconut

Preparation time: 1 hr
(+overnight freezing time)
Calories per slice: 120
2 g protein, 2 g fat,
25 g carbohydrate

• Wash, peel and coarsely grate
 the carrots. Chop the apples
 into small pieces.
• Place the carrots, apples,

orange juice and orange peel
in a saucepan. Bring them to
a boil over medium heat,
cook covered for 20 minutes.
• Meanwhile, gently dry roast
 the buckwheat, sesame seeds,
 millet and cereal.
• Fold the cereal mixture into
 the carrot paste with the
 honey and sugar and bring
 back to a boil.
• Line a 9" x 12"
 (22.5 x 30 cm) cake pan or
 baking dish with parchment
 or wax paper. Sprinkle 1/2 of
 the coconut into the pan.
 Spread the muesli mixture
 on the coconut, sprinkle with
 raisins, and cover with the
 remaining coconut and
 another layer of paper.
• Press down firmly and
 evenly. Freeze overnight.
 Cut into bars, wrap in waxed
 paper and refrigerate.

Muesli-Apple Buns

Ingredients for 10 buns:

2 cups (275 g) unbleached flour
2 tbsp dried yeast
sugar
1/4 cup (50 ml) lukewarm milk
1 small tart apple
1 tbsp lemon juice
1/2–2/3 cup (125 g) quark
 (see page 32)
3 tbsp butter
1 egg
1 tsp salt
1/2 cup (75 g) unsweetened
 dry fruit muesli mix
unrefined coconut oil or butter
 and flour for the baking sheet
2–3 tbsp milk to brush on top

Preparation time: 2 hrs
Calories per bun: 200
6 g protein, 7 g fat,
28 g carbohydrate

• Mix flour, yeast, sugar and
 milk into a dough. Let rise
 in a warm place for
 20 minutes.
• Wash, peel and core the
 apple; grate it coarsely and
 sprinkle with lemon juice.
• Add quark, butter, egg, salt,
 muesli and apple to the
 dough and knead well. Set it
 aside for 20 minutes.
• Grease the baking sheet and
 dust it with flour. Shape
 10 buns, place them on the
 baking sheet and let rise for
 15 minutes. Preheat the oven
 to 375°F (190°C). Place an
 ovenproof dish filled with
 water in the oven.
• Cut an X into the top of the
 buns. Mix the milk with
 1 tbsp of water and brush
 on the buns. Bake for
 45 minutes on the middle
 rack, brushing twice with the
 milk mixture during baking.

Apple-Avocado Muesli

Ingredients for 4 servings:

1 avocado
2 tbsp lemon juice
1/4 cup (60 g) clover honey
1/4 cup (40 g) non-instant rolled oats
4 sour apples
1/4 cup (40 g) raisins
2/3 cup (150 g) natural yogurt
1/2 cup (125 ml) whipping cream

Preparation time: 25 min
Calories per serving: 430
5 g protein, 25 g fat,
45 g carbohydrate

- Scoop the avocado flesh from its peel. Purée it thoroughly with the lemon juice and honey.
- Lightly dry roast the rolled oats. Wash and core the apples; grate medium fine.
- Mix the grated apple, cooled rolled oats, raisins and yogurt with the avocado mixture. Whip the cream until stiff and fold it in carefully.

Variation

Add nuts and seeds to this dish for extra texture, protein and healthy fats. Try hazelnut, almond, walnut, flax seed and sunflower seed.

Tip

The glucose in fruit and grains provides quick energy but, because digestion is slowed down by the presence of grain, the energy lasts longer. Vegetable protein makes the dish more filling. This recipe is ideal for breakfast, brunch or as a fitness snack.

Couscous-Berry Mix

Ingredients for 4 servings:

1/2 lemon
1/2–2/3 cup (125 g) couscous (or substitute rolled oats)
1/2 cup (125 ml) natural, tropical fruit juice or nectar
1 heaping tbsp sesame seeds
2/3 cup (150 g) each red currants and gooseberries or other berries
meringue (from a bakery) or shredded coconut for garnish

Preparation time: 35 min
Calories per serving: 180
6 g protein, 2 g fat,
35 g carbohydrate

- Juice the lemon. Pour the tropical nectar and lemon juice over the couscous and soak for 30 minutes.
- Meanwhile, dry roast the sesame seeds and let them cool.
- Wash the berries and remove any stems.
- Crumble the meringue (if using coconut, dry roast it first) and fold it into the couscous with the sesame seeds. Add the berries.

Variation

Tropical

Use 2 kiwis and 1 star fruit instead of the berries.
If desired, substitute lime for the lemon.

Orange

Omit the lemon juice and use orange juice instead of the tropical nectar. Use 2 peeled and segmented oranges instead of the berries.
Add 1 red-skinned apple cut into matchsticks and 1 tbsp of liquid honey.

Rice Pudding with Fruit Sauce

Ingredients for 2 servings:

1/2 cup (100 g) short-grain white
rice (adjust cooking time if
substituting brown rice)
1 cup (250 ml) milk
1/2 tsp lemon peel, grated
1 pinch salt
1 package vanilla sugar (substitute
2 tsp homemade vanilla sugar)
1 1/2 lb (750 g) sweet cherries
honey to taste
3 peaches
1 tbsp chopped almonds
1 tbsp chopped pistachios

Preparation time: 50 min
Calories per serving: 600
14 g protein, 12 g fat,
110 g carbohydrate

• Mix rice, peel, salt, sugar and
milk. Boil, then simmer for
30 minutes. Stir well.

• Wash and pit the cherries
and purée them to a medium
consistency with an electric
hand blender. Sweeten the
sauce with a little honey.
• Pour boiling water over the
peaches and remove the
skins. Remove the pits and
cut into sections. Mix the
peaches into the cherry sauce
and set aside in a cool place.
• When the rice is cooked, mix
in the almonds and
pistachios. Rinse a small
pudding mold in cold water
and press the rice into it;
cool before removing. Top
with the sauce.

Tip

Substitute leftover cooked rice
to save cooking time. Combine
milk, peel, salt and sugar, then
boil. Add cooked rice and
simmer slowly for 15 minutes.

Fruit Salad with Crispy Quinoa

Ingredients for 2 servings:

1/3 cup (80 g) quinoa (see tip)
1 tsp unrefined coconut oil
2 tsp maple syrup or honey
1 cup (250 ml) buttermilk
4 apricots
1 lb (500 g) mixed berries

Preparation time: 30 min
Calories per serving: 430
12 g protein, 4 g fat,
57 g carbohydrate

• Heat the quinoa with the oil
in a covered frying pan on
low heat until it "pops."
• After 1–2 minutes, slowly
add 1 tsp syrup and stir
briefly. Pour the quinoa-
syrup mixture onto a cold
baking sheet and spread it
out to cool.

• Mix the buttermilk with the
remaining maple syrup and
pour it into a bowl.
• Wash the fruit. Halve the
apricots and remove the pits.
Slice the halves into strips.
Clean the berries. Add the
fruit to the buttermilk.
Sprinkle the cooled quinoa
over top.

Tip

Instead of quinoa, amaranth
may be popped in the frying
pan (you could even use
popcorn). An even faster
version can be made with rolled
oats or multigrain cereal.
If you only want the salad as a
dessert, omit the quinoa and
other cereals.

Cooking at the Table

Vegetable Fondue

Ingredients for 8 servings:

For the plum dip:
1/2 cup (100 g) prunes
1/2 cup (125 ml) beer
salt
pepper, freshly ground
2 tbsp mild mustard
2 tbsp natural ketchup
1–2 tbsp Worcestershire sauce

For the batter:
2 cups (280 g) flour
1 cup (250 ml) beer
4 eggs
1 pinch salt
1/4 cup (50 g) rolled oats

For the fondue:
1/2 lb (250 g) cherry tomatoes
1/2 lb (250 g) zucchini
1/2 lb (250 g) small mushrooms
1/2 lb (250 g) broccoli flowerets
1 bunch of sage
1 tbsp lemon juice
unrefined coconut oil

Preparation time: 1 hr
Calories per serving: 260
10 g protein, 4 g fat,
42 g carbohydrate

- Bring the prunes to a boil in the beer, cool slightly and purée them thoroughly with a food processor or electric hand blender. Add spices and dilute with water if necessary. Season the sauce well and pour in a bowl.
- Make a batter with the flour by gradually adding 1/3 cup (100 ml) beer, the eggs, salt and rolled oats. Set aside for 15 minutes then add the rest of the beer. The batter should be thick and not too runny.

- Meanwhile, wash the vegetables and the sage and dry them well. Remove the stalk from the tomatoes. Clean and thickly slice the zucchini. Clean the mushrooms with a dry towel. Halve the larger mushrooms and immediately sprinkle them with lemon juice. Remove sage leaves from the stems. Arrange the vegetables decoratively on 1 or 2 plates.
- Pour the batter into small bowls. Half fill the fondue pot with oil. Heat the oil to about 350°F (190°C) on the stove. (When a wooden stick is held in the fat, small bubbles should appear.) Keep the fondue pot warm on a hot plate (or use an electric fondue pot).

- Dip vegetables into the batter one at a time, and cook them in the oil.

Tip
Take care to maintain the correct oil temperature. If the oil cools, the batter will take too long to cook, and will remain soggy. If the oil is too hot, the batter will burn on the outside and the vegetables will be undercooked.

Variation
You can cook many different vegetables in a fondue. Use cauliflower flowerets or thinly sliced carrot, eggplant, squash and sweet potato.

Cheese Fondue

Ingredients for 4 servings:

1/2 lb (250 g) medium Gouda
1 cup (200 g) buttermilk
1 lb (500 g) broccoli
1 bunch of carrots
1/2 cup (125 ml) vegetable stock
1/2 cup (200 g) cherry tomatoes
1/2 lb (250 g) gnocchi
  (ready-made)
1 baguette
2/3 cup (150 g) herbed cream
  cheese
2–3 tsp cornstarch
1 pinch powdered saffron
nutmeg, freshly grated
pepper, freshly ground

Preparation time: 45 min
Calories per serving: 604
26 g protein, 28 g fat,
24 g carbohydrate

- Cut the Gouda into small
  pieces. Soak it in buttermilk.

- Wash the vegetables. Cut the
  broccoli into flowerets. Peel
  the carrots and cut them
  into bite-sized pieces then
  simmer in the stock for
  6–8 minutes. They should
  still be somewhat crisp. Drain.
- Wash the cherry tomatoes
  and arrange all the vegetables
  on a plate.
- Prepare the gnocchi according
  to the directions then drain
  and place them in a bowl.
- Cut the baguette into bite-
  sized pieces.
- Pour the buttermilk-cheese
  mixture into an ovenproof
  dish and slowly warm it,
  stirring constantly. When the
  Gouda has melted, add the
  cream cheese. Blend the
  cornstarch and saffron in a
  little water and add it to the
  fondue, stirring constantly.
  Simmer gently for
  2 minutes, stirring all the

time then season with
nutmeg and pepper. Place on
a hot plate. Serve with
Parsley-Avocado Dip
(following recipe).

Variation

The original cheese fondue
recipe from Switzerland is
much heavier than our light
version. Rub a ceramic baking
dish with a clove of garlic.
Heat 1 tbsp of butter, add
3/4 lb (375 g) of grated
Emmenthal and 2 1/3 cups
(500 g) of cream, stirring
continuously. Whisk together
4 egg yolks and a little salt and
add the cheese with 1 shot of
kirsch. Bring the mixture to a
boil and simmer for 5 minutes
or until the cheese has
completely melted.

Parsley-Avocado Dip

Ingredients for 4 servings:

2 bunches of parsley
1 avocado
1/2 lemon
salt
pepper, freshly ground

Preparation time: 20 min
Calories per serving: 140
2 g protein, 12 g fat,
1 g carbohydrate

- Wash the parsley and remove
  thick stems.
- Halve the avocado, remove
  the pit and scoop out the
  flesh with a spoon. Juice the
  lemon, add it to the avocado
  and the other ingredients.
  Purée and season to taste.

Chinese Fondue

Ingredients for 4 servings:

3/4 cup (125 g) quark
1/4 cup (50 g) each hazelnuts
  and walnuts
1 cup (250 ml) vegetable stock
1/2 cup (80 g) cream of wheat
1 egg
2 tbsp chopped chives
salt
1/2 lb (250 g) broccoli flowerets
1/2 lb (250 g) carrots
1/2 lb (250 g) mushrooms
1/2 lb (250 g) small zucchini
6 cups (1.5 l) vegetable gravy
  or vegetable stock
soy sauce

Preparation time: 1 hr
Calories per serving: 310
16 g protein, 18 g fat,
24 g carbohydrate

- Drain the quark in a sieve.
  Grind the nuts well. Bring
  1 cup of the stock to a boil,
  add the cream of wheat and
  leave it on the burner for a
  few minutes with the heat
  turned off.
- Cool the cream of wheat to
  lukewarm, mix in the nuts,
  quark, egg, chives and salt.
- Shape small dumplings,
  using damp hands. Set them
  aside (do not cover).
- Clean the vegetables. Cut the
  carrots into bite-sized pieces
  and slice the zucchini.
- Bring the stock to a boil and
  season with the soy sauce.
- Cook the carrots in the gravy
  for 10 minutes (they should
  still be crisp). Blanch the
  broccoli for 5 minutes and
  the zucchini and mushrooms
  each for 3 minutes.

- Drain the vegetables and
  arrange them on a plate.
  Check the stock again as it
  will become more
  concentrated during cooking;
  it should not be too salty.
- Skewer the vegetables and
  dumplings and cook them in
  the stock. Try to use the
  small wire strainers available
  from oriental cooking-supply
  outlets.
- Serve with Avocado-Basil
  Dip (recipe page 74) or
  Peanut Sauce (right). You
  can even drink the stock at
  the end!

Variation

The Chinese often use an
electric rice cooker as the
fondue pot. Savory soup stock
is simmered in the rice cooker,
and dumplings, vegetables
and marinated tofu are dipped
into it.

Peanut Sauce

Ingredients for 4 servings:

1/2 lb (250 g) onions
1 tbsp unrefined, organic
  sesame oil
3/4 cup (100 g) unsalted peanuts
1/2 cup (125 ml) vegetable stock
2 tbsp cream
Worcestershire sauce
pepper, freshly ground

Preparation time: 20 min
Calories per serving: 180
7 g protein, 14 g fat,
7 g carbohydrate

- Peel the onions and mince
  half of them. Sauté them in
  the hot oil with the nuts.
- Cook the rest of the onion
  in the stock.
- Purée everything in a blender.
  Fold in the cream and season
  it with Worcestershire sauce
  and pepper.

Children's Raclette

Ingredients for 6 servings:

1 lb (500 g) small potatoes
salt
2 cups (500 g) cooked spinach
  bow noodles
3 oz (80 g) fresh Gouda
3 oz (80 g) Raclette cheese (from a
  specialty cheese shop), rind removed
1/2 cup (100 g) solid cream cheese
  or butter cheese
1/4 lb (125 g) Mozzarella
1 yellow pepper
1 tbsp cold-pressed, extra-virgin olive oil
2–3 green onions
2 tomatoes
1/4 lb (125 g) mushrooms
juice of 1 lemon
1 red apple
1 green pear
2 oranges
sesame seeds, sunflower seeds and
  green pumpkin seeds for sprinkling

Preparation time: 50 min
Calories per serving: 520
25 g protein, 19 g fat,
63 g carbohydrate

Diners create their own dishes
using the tabletop raclette and
choosing from an array of
ingredients.
- Cook potatoes in a little salted
  water, drain and keep warm.
- Keep noodles warm. Thinly slice
  the harder cheeses and cut the
  soft cheese into chunks. Arrange
  all cheeses on one plate.
- Clean and chop the pepper, sauté
  in olive oil for a few minutes
  then place in a bowl. Clean and
  slice the green onions, sauté
  them briefly in oil and add to
  the peppers. Skin the tomatoes
  and cut into pieces. Clean the
  mushrooms, slice them then
  sprinkle with lemon juice.
- Wash and core the apple and
  pear, slice them thinly and
  sprinkle with lemon juice. Peel
  the oranges, separate into pieces
  and cut each piece into three.
- Arrange the separate ingredients
  on the table and proceed with the
  raclette.

Summer Raclette

Ingredients for 4 servings:

1/2 cup (100 g) coarse cornmeal
1 1/4 cups (300 ml) vegetable
  stock
1/2 bunch of mixed herbs, minced
1 onion, peeled and chopped
1 clove of garlic, minced
1 1/2 tbsp butter
1/2 lb (250 g) mixed mushrooms
1 lb (500 g) spinach, blanched
1/2 lb (250 g) carrots, thinly sliced
salt, pepper, freshly ground
1 small eggplant, sliced
1 tbsp cold-pressed,
  extra-virgin olive oil
nutmeg, freshly grated
1/2 cup (100 g) sour cream
1 3/4 lb (875 g) Raclette cheese
  (from a specialty cheese shop)

Preparation time: 50 min
Calories per serving: 1,000
67 g protein, 70 g fat,
27 g carbohydrate

- Boil the cornmeal in the stock then simmer for 10 minutes, stirring continuously.
- Mix the herbs with the cornmeal and spread in a rectangular baking dish. Let cool, remove from the pan and cut into squares.
- Sauté the onion and garlic in 1 tbsp butter. Slice the mushrooms and sauté with half of the onions. Season the spinach with the rest of the onions, salt, pepper and nutmeg. Sauté carrots in the remaining butter and season with a little salt.
- Preheat the broiler to 375°F (190°C). Lay the eggplant slices on a baking sheet.
- Sprinkle the oil, salt and pepper over the eggplant. Broil until golden, turning once.

- Beat the sour cream until smooth. Slice the cheese. Arrange the separate ingredients on the table and proceed with the raclette.

Radish Salad

Ingredients for 4 servings:

3 bunches of radishes
3 tbsp sour cream
2 tbsp white wine vinegar
salt
pepper, freshly ground
1 bunch of parsley

Preparation time: 10 min
Calories per serving: 22
1 g protein, 0.8 g fat,
2 g carbohydrate

- Wash and thinly slice the radishes.
- Beat the cream with vinegar until smooth then season with salt and pepper. Blend

the cream and vinegar with the radishes.
- Wash and mince the parsley and mix into the salad.

Tip

The following are excellent accompaniments to raclette: Tzatsiki (page 75), Salsa Verde (page 77) and Olive Spread (page 218). Delicately Marinated Vegetables (page 55) can be prepared ahead of time as an alternative to the salad. The cheese may be varied in summer: grated Parmesan cheese combined with Mozzarella will impart an Italian flavor.

Cheese-Potato Kabobs

Ingredients for 4 servings:

48 very small new potatoes
salt
1 lb (500 g) small zucchini
1 lb (500 g) Gouda
2 tbsp cold-pressed,
 extra-virgin olive oil

Preparation time: 1 hr
Calories per serving: 620
33 g protein, 34 g fat,
48 g carbohydrate

- Wash the potatoes then boil
  in a little salted water. Cool.
- Cut the zucchini into
  medium-thick slices. Cut the
  cheese into bite-sized pieces.
  Lightly oil the zucchini and
  potatoes; salt the zucchini.
  Slide all pieces onto a skewer.
- Cook on a table-top grill,
  turning constantly until the
  cheese begins to melt.

Hearty Eggplant Slices

Ingredients for 2 servings:

1 eggplant
2 tbsp natural ketchup
1 tbsp dried basil
1/2 tsp salt
1 tbsp cold-pressed,
 extra-virgin olive oil
pepper, freshly ground

Preparation time: 20 min
Calories per serving: 90
2 g protein, 4 g fat,
10 g carbohydrate

- Wash and thickly slice the
  eggplant.
- Mix the ketchup with the
  other ingredients. Soak the
  slices for 10 minutes.
- Cook slices on the table-top
  grill for 4 minutes per side,
  or cook them in aluminum
  foil for 12 minutes.

Tomato-Tofu Kabobs

Ingredients for 4 servings:

1 lb (500 g) tofu
4 tbsp soy sauce
4 tbsp cold-pressed,
 extra-virgin olive oil
2 tbsp natural ketchup
4 sprigs of basil
1 lb (500 g) cherry tomatoes
16 green olives, pitted

Preparation time: 1 1/2 hrs
Calories per serving: 210
10 g protein, 15 g fat,
10 g carbohydrate

- Cut the tofu into bite-sized
  cubes. Purée the soy sauce
  with oil, ketchup and
  coarsely chopped basil leaves.
- Marinate the tofu in this
  mixture for 1 hour.
- Meanwhile, wash the
  tomatoes and remove the
  stems. Halve the olives.

Skewer the tofu, alternating
with the tomatoes and olives.
Cook them on a table-top
grill just long enough for the
tofu to turn golden.

Tip

Tofu is made of soy bean curd.
It is nutritious, economical and
absorbs other flavors well.
Tofu was developed in China
over 2,000 years ago and is an
important source of protein
throughout Asia. The soy bean
is one of the few complete
protein foods.

Barbecued Corn

Ingredients for 2 servings:

2 cobs of corn
salt
1 tbsp cold-pressed,
 extra-virgin olive oil
1 tbsp mixed herbs,
 finely chopped

Preparation time: 30 min
Calories per serving: 93
0.2 g protein, 4 g fat,
2 g carbohydrate

- Boil the corn in salted water
  for 10 minutes then drain.
- Mix the oil with the herbs
  and drizzle it over the corn.
  Cook the corn on the table-
  top grill, turning often until
  the corn is crisp and golden.
  Drizzle with oil again during
  cooking.

Bannock

Ingredients for 2 servings
(8–10 small cakes):

1/4 cup (50 g) sunflower seeds
1 medium onion
3 tbsp unrefined coconut oil
 or clarified butter
1 tsp (1/2 package) dried yeast
1 1/4 cup (150 g) wholewheat
 flour
3/4 cup (100 g) spelt flour
 (or substitute unbleached flour)
1 tsp salt

Preparation time: 1 1/2 hrs
Calories per serving: 690
22 g protein, 27 g fat,
90 g carbohydrate

- Lightly dry roast the
  sunflower seeds. Peel and
  mince the onion. Sauté the
  onion in butter or oil until
  brown, then mix with
  sunflower seeds and let cool.

- Dissolve the yeast in 3 tbsp
  of lukewarm water, then
  slowly stir it into a mix of
  both types of flour, salt and
  the onion mixture. At the
  same time, add 1 cup
  (200 ml) lukewarm water to
  produce a soft, flexible
  dough. Knead and let the
  dough rise for 1 hour.
- Shape 8–10 thin, flat
  bannock cakes (about
  1/4" or 0.5 cm thick) from
  the dough and cook them on
  the table-top grill for about
  10 minutes. Turn the cakes
  over and cook them for
  5 minutes.
- Bannock tastes good plain,
  with butter or with a slice of
  cheese melted on top.

Variation

Bannock is a traditional staple
of the North American native
peoples. It is also delicious
when cooked with fresh fruit
such as peaches, blueberries,
blackberries and apples.
Mix the fruit into the batter
or press the fruit onto the
bannock as it cooks. You can
also serve it with preserves.

Tip

Bannock can be prepared on a
charcoal barbecue in the
summer, or on a simple
campfire grill. When bannock
is cooked on an outdoor
barbecue, place it on a piece of
lightly oiled aluminum foil.
All of our grill recipes can be
similarly adapted. The corn
cobs can be skewered on long,
sharp sticks.

Stuffed Zucchini and Peppers

Ingredients for 4 servings:

For the zucchini:
2 medium zucchini
1/4 cup (50 g) mild Camembert,
 grated
1/2 cup (75 g) cooked rice
1 tbsp chives, chopped
1 tbsp cold-pressed,
 extra-virgin olive oil

For the peppers:
10 small pointed mild yellow peppers
 (or substitute green peppers)
1 lb (500 g) leaf spinach
salt, freshly ground pepper
1 onion
3 cloves of garlic
1 tsp cold-pressed,
 extra-virgin olive oil
1/2 cup (50 g) bread crumbs
1/2 cup (100 g) garlic cream cheese
2 tbsp pistachios, chopped

Preparation time: 1 1/2 hrs
Calories per serving: 440
22 g protein, 21 g fat,
40 g carbohydrate

- Wash the zucchini, remove the
  ends and cut in half across the
  middle. Scoop out the interior.
- Mix the Camembert, rice and
  chives and press them into the
  zucchini.
- Oil the zucchini, wrap in
  aluminum foil and seal the
  ends.
- Cut the tops from the peppers
  and wash them. Wash the
  spinach, blanch it in salted
  water, drain well and coarsely
  chop. Peel and mince the onion
  and garlic.
- Heat the oil, sauté the onion
  and garlic until translucent, add
  the spinach and sauté briefly.
  Add salt and pepper then cool.
- Mix the bread crumbs with
  cream cheese, spinach and
  pistachios. Stuff the mixture
  into the peppers.
- Cook the vegetables on the
  table-top grill for 15 minutes,
  turning them several times.

Garlicky Carrots

Ingredients for 4 servings:

8 young carrots
3 tbsp butter
1 clove of garlic
salt

Preparation time: 40 min
Calories per serving: 120
2 g protein, 9 g fat,
8 g carbohydrate

- Scrub the carrots. Mix the butter, chopped garlic and salt. Spread the mixture on the carrots.
- Wrap the carrots individually in aluminum foil with the shiny side facing inward. Cook on the table-top grill for 20–30 minutes.

Kohlrabi with Bay Leaves

Ingredients for 4 servings:

8 small kohlrabi with leaves
8 bay leaves
2 tbsp cold-pressed, extra-virgin olive oil
salt
pepper, freshly ground

Preparation time: 1 hr
Calories per serving: 100
5 g protein, 4 g fat,
10 g carbohydrate

- Break off the kohlrabi leaves, remove the stalks and wash. Peel the bulbs.
- Stick the bay leaves into the kohlrabi, rub them with oil, salt and pepper. Wrap in the kohlrabi leaves and then in foil.
- Cook for 30 minutes on the table-top grill.

Baked Potatoes

Ingredients for 4 servings:

4 large, firm potatoes
1 tbsp butter
salt
2 green onions
2 cooking apples
2 tsp lemon juice
1 tbsp cold-pressed, extra-virgin olive oil
2 tbsp sour cream
3 tbsp blue cheese, finely chopped

Preparation time: 1 1/2 hrs
Calories per serving: 190
2 g protein, 7 g fat,
20 g carbohydrate

- Preheat the oven to 400°F (200°C). Wash the potatoes, cut a flat lid from each one and hollow out. Leave a wall of flesh attached to the skin. Spread butter and salt on the insides.
- Clean the onions and chop them into thin rings. Wash, peel and core the apples, cut them into thin sticks and sprinkle with lemon juice.
- Heat the oil in a frying pan. Sauté the onions. Remove from heat and blend the onions, apple and sour cream. Salt them lightly then stuff them into the potatoes. Sprinkle with the cheese. Place the potato lids on top.
- Wrap the potatoes in aluminum foil (shiny side inward) and cook for 70 minutes on the middle rack of the oven.

Tip
The cooking quality of potatoes depends on the amount of starch they contain. Potatoes that are low in starch, such as new potatoes, tend to be dry when baked.

Preserving

Mustard Fruit

Ingredients for 1 gal (5 l):

2 cups (500 ml) white wine
2 cups (500 ml) white
  wine vinegar
1 lb (500 g) sugar
4–5 1/2 lb (2–2.5 kg) unblemished
  organic fruit
1/4 cup (50 g) mustard seeds
3 bay leaves
10 each allspice seeds and
  peppercorns
5 cloves
3 juniper berries
4 thin slices fresh ginger
1 star anise
2 tbsp fruit brandy (at least
  45% alcohol by volume)

Preparation time: 2 hrs
Calories: 3,800
20 g protein, 11 g fat,
860 g carbohydrate

- Heat the wine with vinegar and sugar in a saucepan.
- Clean the fruit and cut into chunks as desired. Pierce citrus fruit to release the juice but do not peel them.
- Simmer in the wine-vinegar liquid. Kumquats, lemons, halved apples, pears need 8 minutes, whole peaches and apricots 4 minutes. Grapes, plums, halved peaches and apricots, apple and pear pieces need about 2 minutes. Melons are preserved raw.
- Drain the simmered fruit and place it in hot, sterilized jars. Boil the liquid with the spices for 10 minutes, then pour enough into the jar to cover the fruit.
- Pour the brandy into the glass lid and ignite. When the flame burns out, close the lid tightly. Open after 1 month.

Berries in Spicy Syrup

Ingredients for 13 cups (3 l):

1 cup (250 g) apple butter
2 cups (500 ml) fruit vinegar
1 lb (500 g) raw sugar or
  evaporated sugar cane juice
2 tsp cinnamon
scrapings from the inside
  of a vanilla bean
1 tsp mustard powder
1 pinch each powdered nutmeg,
  cloves, allspice and pepper
3 1/2–4 1/2 lb (1.5–2 kg) mixed
  berries and cherries

Preparation time: 1 1/2 hrs
Calories: 3,300
18 g protein, 9 g fat,
800 g carbohydrate

- Slowly heat the apple butter, vinegar, sugar and spices and cook to a syrup.

- Sort and wash the berries and cherries. Drain well and dry them thoroughly by spreading them out on paper towels.
- Wash the jars, place them in boiling water for 10 minutes and drain.
- Layer the dry fruit in the jars. Pour the boiling syrup over the fruit mixture and seal the jars. Leave them in a cool place for at least 1 week. The fruit can be kept for about 2 months. The berries are a good accompaniment for roasted and grilled vegetables.

Tip

Imagine the joys of picking a warm, sun-kissed berry fresh off the bush. A visit to your local berry grower makes a fun day trip, especially for the kids.

Cucumber Relish

Ingredients for about 1 cup (250 ml):

2 cucumbers
1 shallot
2–3 stalks of dill
1 1/2 tbsp salt
1/2 cup (100 g) mustard seeds
white pepper, freshly ground
1 pinch powdered ginger
1/2 cup (125 ml) fruit vinegar

Preparation time: 9 hrs
(including 30 min working time)
Calories: 290
13 g protein, 8 g fat,
30 g carbohydrate

- Wash and purée the cucumbers. Peel and mince the shallot. Wash the dill and chop it medium-fine.
- Mix the cucumber, shallot, dill and salt and leave them overnight in a sieve to drain. Mix the paste with mustard seeds, pepper, powdered ginger and fruit vinegar.
- Wash a jar, boil it in water for 10 minutes, drain and fill it with the Cucumber Relish. It will keep for 1 month.

Tip
Salt, vinegar and mustard act as natural preservatives and mustard oil has antibacterial properties. This relish is a refreshing addition to simple potato dishes and barbecued recipes.

Did you ever wonder where the phrase, "cool as a cucumber" comes from? The inside of a cucumber can be up to 70°F (20°C) cooler than the outside.

Mushroom Flavoring Sauce

Ingredients for about 1 cup (250 ml):

2 lb (1 kg) mushrooms
1/2 cup (100 g) salt
1 bay leaf
1 tbsp vinegar
4 each cloves, allspice seeds and peppercorns

Preparation time: 2 1/2 hrs
(+1 week for marinating)
Calories: 140
26 g protein, 3 g fat,
7 g carbohydrate

- Wipe the mushrooms dry and cut off the stems. Chop or grind them to a mealy consistency.
- Mix the mushrooms with salt and leave them covered in a cool place for 1 week.
- Simmer the mixture with the bay leaf, vinegar, cloves, allspice and peppercorns.
- Press the sauce through a cheesecloth. Wash a bottle, boil it in water for 10 minutes then drain. Bring the mushroom sauce to a boil again and pour into the bottle and seal well. Unopened, this sauce keeps for several years.

Tip
This sauce is similar to soy sauce. During the week the mushroom juice undergoes a fermentation process: this gives it color and flavor. The mushrooms should not be eaten after fermentation. The sauce is safe because boiling destroys any bacteria.

Tomato Ketchup

Ingredients for about 8–9 cups (2 l):

1 large onion
2 lb (500 g) carrots
1 red pepper
4 1/2 lb (2 kg) tomatoes
2 cloves of garlic
2 tsp salt
4 peppercorns
1 tsp mustard seeds
2 cloves
1 bay leaf
juice of 1 lemon
1 tbsp soy sauce
1 tbsp Worcestershire sauce
1–2 tbsp raw sugar or regular sugar

Preparation time: 1 hr
Calories: 690
32 g protein, 7 g fat,
140 g carbohydrate

- Peel and coarsely chop the onion. Scrub and slice the carrots. Wash, halve, clean and chop the peppers. Blanch the tomatoes, wait for a minute then remove their skins. Cut out the stalk area and set aside the flesh. Place the seeds and juice of the tomatoes in a saucepan.
- Peel and mince the garlic. Add the other vegetables, the garlic and spices to the tomato juice and seeds and bring to a boil, stirring constantly.
- Simmer for 40 minutes until cooked, stirring occasionally. Press the vegetables through a sieve.
- Purée the tomato and fold it into the strained vegetables. Season the mixture with lemon juice, soy and Worcestershire sauces and sugar. Wash jars, place them in boiling water for 10 minutes then drain. Fill the jars with the ketchup. This ketchup keeps, refrigerated, for about 2 weeks.

Tip
The sweeter and riper the tomatoes, the better the ketchup.

Mixed Pickles

Ingredients for two 4 cup (1 l) jars:

1/2 lb (250 g) very small pickling
  cucumbers (no larger than gherkins
  if possible)
1 large carrot
1/2 cauliflower
salt
4 small shallots
1 yellow and 1 red pepper
1 bunch of dill
2 cups (450 ml) herb vinegar
1 heaping tsp each peppercorns
  and mustard seeds

Preparation time: 45 min
Calories per jar: 140
9 g protein, 2 g fat,
17 g carbohydrate

- Wash the cucumbers. Wash,
  peel and thickly slice the
  carrots. Separate the cauliflower
  into small flowerets.
- Briefly blanch the carrot slices
  and cauliflower pieces in
  boiling salted water. Peel the
  shallots.
- Wash the peppers and cut them
  into chunks, removing the stalk,
  seeds and interior. Wash the dill
  and separate the leaves from the
  stalks.
- Wash the jars, place them in
  boiling water for 10 minutes
  then drain. Layer the vegetables
  and dill in the sterilized jars.
  Boil the vinegar in 2 cups
  (450 ml) water, 2 tbsp salt and
  the spices. Immediately pour
  the boiling liquid over the
  vegetables and seal the jars.
- When kept in a cool place
  mixed pickles will last for
  2–3 months. Opened jars
  should be used in 4–5 days.

Tip
Mixed pickles are an ideal side
dish for cheese recipes,
particularly Raclette.

Apricot Chutney

Ingredients for 4 jars:

1 lb (500 g) apricots, pitted
1/2 lb (250 g) onions
1/2 lb (250 g) rhubarb
1 piece fresh ginger (walnut-sized)
1 lime
1/3 cup (75 g) yellow raisins
1 1/4 cups (300 ml) fruit vinegar
1 cup (200 g) raw sugar
1 tsp mustard seeds
1 pinch cayenne pepper
1 package or vial of saffron
1/3–1/2 cup (75–100 g) pecans
 or walnuts

Preparation time: 1 1/2 hrs
Calories per jar: 500
6 g protein, 13 g fat,
87 g carbohydrate

- Wash and coarsely chop the
  pitted apricots. Peel and
  thinly slice the onions.
  Wash the rhubarb, remove

the stringy outer fibers and
slice. Peel and mince the
ginger. Grate the lime peel
and juice the lime.
- Place all ingredients except
  the nuts in a saucepan and
  cook the chutney to a soft
  pulp over low heat for
  1 hour.
- Coarsely chop the nuts and
  add them to the finished
  chutney. Wash the jars, place
  them in boiling water for
  10 minutes then drain. Fill
  the sterilized jars and seal.
  The chutney develops its full
  flavor after about 1 month.
  Unopened, it will keep for
  9 months to 1 year.

Plum-Mango Chutney

Ingredients for 600 ml:

1 mango
2/3 lb (300 g) yellow plums
1 bunch of green onions
3/4 cup (150 g) raw sugar
3/4 cup (150 ml) white wine
 vinegar
1/4 cup (50 g) raisins
2 tbsp unhulled sesame seeds

Preparation time: 1 hr
Calories: 1,300
9 g protein, 12 g fat,
260 g carbohydrate

- Peel the mango and cut the
  flesh into small pieces.
- Wash, pit and quarter the
  plums. Wash the green
  onions and slice into rings.
- Mix fruit with raw sugar,
  vinegar, raisins and sesame
  seeds.

- Bring to a boil in a large
  saucepan. Boil vigorously,
  uncovered, for 20 minutes,
  stirring occasionally. Wash
  jars, boil them in water for
  10 minutes, then drain. Pour
  the chutney while still hot
  into the sterilized jars.
  It will keep for 6 months.

Tip

Chutney can be made from a
vegetable base. A sweet and
sour combination is
particularly appealing:
e.g., pineapple with leek,
blackberries with peppers and
apricots with tomatoes.

Olive Spread

Ingredients for 2 lb (1 kg):

3 1/2 cups (500 g) black olives
1 cup (150 g) almonds
1–2 tsp hot mustard
1 cup (200 g) capers
1/2 cup (100 ml) cold-pressed,
  extra-virgin olive oil
salt
pepper, freshly ground
1 1/2 tbsp cognac, or to taste

Preparation time: 45 min
(+3–4 days refrigeration)
Calories: 3,600
40 g protein, 360 g fat,
39 g carbohydrate

- Pit and purée the olives.
  Pour boiling water over the
  almonds and set them aside
  for 2–3 minutes. Remove
  the skins and thoroughly
  grind the nuts.

- Mix the puréed olives with
  the almonds and the
  mustard. Drain and mince
  the capers. Stir the capers
  into the olive mixture while
  slowly adding the oil. Blend
  the mixture well.
- Season with the salt, pepper
  and cognac.
- Fill into well-sealing,
  sterilized jars (jars boiled in
  water for 10 minutes) and
  refrigerate for 3–4 days.
  Keeps for about 8 weeks.

Tip

Olive spread may be simply
served on a fresh baguette, as a
raw vegetable dip or as part of
a buffet.

In addition to tasting great,
this spread provides a rich
source of healthy fats. Select
firm, blemish-free olives as
they begin to spoil once they
are damaged or bruised.

Pesto

Ingredients for 1 cup (250 g):

2 bunches of fresh basil
1 stalk marjoram
1 clove of garlic
3/4 cup (120 g) pine nuts
1/4 cup (50 ml) cold-pressed,
  extra-virgin olive oil
2 tbsp lemon juice
3/4 cup (100 g) Parmesan cheese,
  freshly grated
salt

Preparation time: 30 min
Calories: 1,600
52 g protein, 150 g fat,
28 g carbohydrate

- Wash the basil and marjoram
  and remove stems. Peel and
  coarsely chop the garlic.
- Purée the herbs, garlic and
  pine nuts to a paste while
  adding the oil and lemon
  juice.

- Fold in the cheese and, if
  necessary, add salt. Pesto will
  keep for about 6 weeks.

Tip

Mixing herbs with nuts and oil
keeps them fresh longer.
Basil, parsley and cilantro are
particularly well suited for
pesto. The blend may be added
to fresh pasta as a sauce or
used as a seasoning in cooking.
A very simple method of
keeping herbs fresh, apart from
freezing, is to salt them.
Chopped herbs are packed in a
jar between layers of salt and
stored in a cool place.

Plum Vinegar

Ingredients for 1 cup (250 ml):

1/2 lb (250 g) plums
1 1/4 cups (300 ml) fruit vinegar
1 star anise
1 small cinnamon stick

Preparation time: 15 min
(+14 days storage)
Calories: 200
2 g protein, 0 g fat,
34 g carbohydrate

• Wash the plums and pierce
  them all over. Place them in
  a prepared jar and add the
  vinegar.
• Add the star anise and
  cinnamon and leave them in
  a sunny place for 14 days.
• Filter the vinegar and pour it
  into a clean bottle. Stored in
  a cool place, this vinegar will
  keep for about 6 months.

Variations

Orange Vinegar

Peel an orange in a spiral.
Pour 1 1/4 cups (300 ml)
fruit vinegar over the peel and
leave it in a sunny place for
14 days. Filter the vinegar,
pour into clean bottles then
store in a cool place.

Strawberry Vinegar

Clean 1/2 lb (250 g)
strawberries. Pour 1/4 cup
(50 ml) strawberry syrup (or
use strained natural strawberry
jam) and 1 1/4 cups (300 ml)
fruit vinegar over them. Leave
in a sunny place for about
14 days. Filter the vinegar then
store in a cool place. This
vinegar will be all the more
flavorful if you can make it
with wild strawberries.

Garlic Oil

Ingredients for 2 cups (500 ml):

4–5 cloves of garlic
4 sprigs of basil
2 cups (500 ml) cold-pressed,
 organic oil

Preparation time: 10 min
Calories: 4,500
1 g protein, 500 g fat,
7 g carbohydrate

• Peel the garlic, wash the
  basil, dry it thoroughly and
  remove the stems.
• Place the garlic and basil in a
  clean bottle. Add the oil and
  serve.

Tip

This oil should be used only
for decorative purposes if it is
not refrigerated. Do *not* store
garlic in oil as this can produce
dangerous bacteria. Only add
garlic to the oil immediately
before serving.

Use the oil only in salad
dressings or drizzle it over
fresh pasta. Choose a delicate
oil such as walnut oil, flax oil,
pumpkin seed oil or a high-
quality olive oil for best
results.

Variation

Sage-Nut Oil

Wash 2 sprigs of sage and dry
thoroughly. Place in a bottle.
Coarsely chop 1/4 cup (50 g)
fresh hazelnuts and add to the
bottle. Add 2 cups (500 ml)
unrefined, organic almond,
pistachio or pumpkin seed oil.
Serve immediately.

Zucchini-Almond Spread

Ingredients for about 1 cup (250 g):

1/4 lb (125 g) zucchini
1/4 cup (50 g) almonds
1 apple
a few drops lemon juice
1/2 cup (100 g) crème fraîche
 (see page 32)
1 tbsp thick apple juice
 or natural apple sauce
salt
1/2 tsp grated lemon peel

Preparation time: 15 min
Calories: 760
13 g protein, 68 g fat,
24 g carbohydrate

- Wash and coarsely chop the zucchini.
- Pour boiling water over the almonds and allow them to soak for 2–3 minutes. Remove the skins. Grind the almonds thoroughly.
- Wash, peel and core the apple. Purée the apple, lemon juice, zucchini, crème fraîche and thick apple juice. Add the almonds and blend until creamy.
- Season with salt and lemon peel. This spread keeps for about a week when sealed and kept in a cool place.

Variation
Chocolate spread
To make this sweet, nutritious spread for bread, roast 1/2 cup (100 g) hazelnuts in a pan for 10 minutes. Rub the skins off with a paper towel. Grind the nuts thoroughly with 1/2 cup (50 g) blanched almonds. Add 1 tbsp cocoa powder, 5 tbsp maple syrup, 1 pinch each of cinnamon and cardamom. Process until creamy. Keeps for 1 week when stored in a cool place.

Tip
Both spreads taste great on wholewheat bread.

Onion Spread

Ingredients for 1 1/3 cup (300 g):

1 1/3 lb (600 g) small onions
4 tbsp cold-pressed,
  extra-virgin olive oil
2 tbsp tomato paste
3 tbsp port
1/3 cup (75 ml) vegetable stock
salt, pepper, freshly ground
soy sauce
Worcestershire sauce

Preparation time: 45 min
Calories: 550
9 g protein, 34 g fat,
43 g carbohydrate

- Peel and quarter the onions, leaving only the very smallest ones whole.
- Sauté the onions in oil, stirring until they begin to separate. Add the tomato paste, port and stock and season with salt and pepper.
- Simmer uncovered over low heat until the onions are soft and the liquid has steamed off. (If necessary, add water during simmering.)
- Cool the onions and then purée the mixture. Season with soy sauce and a shot of Worcestershire sauce.

Tip
You will find this spread soothing when you are suffering from an infection, particularly when the breathing passage is affected. It tastes good as a thin spread on toast served with bouillon, as a dip for dumplings and pancake dishes or as a garnish for cheese and eggs.

Peanut Butter

Ingredients for 1 1/3 cup (300 g):

1/2 lb (250 g) unsalted peanuts
1/3 cup (75 g) sour cream
salt

Preparation time: 30 min
Calories: 1,600
68 g protein, 140 g fat,
36 g carbohydrate

- Shell the peanuts and rub off the fine inner skins. Roast the peanuts in a frying pan over medium heat or until they become fragrant.
- Remove them from the pan and let them cool.
- Grind peanuts into a paste while adding the sour cream. Season with a little salt.
- Seal and refrigerate. This peanut butter keeps for 2 weeks.

Tip
Coarsely chopped peanuts may also be added to make the peanut butter crunchy.

Shell your own peanuts for the best possible taste. Once shelled, dry roast them in a pan. Let them cool then grind them. The more you grind, the more oil will come out of the peanuts. Avoid stale-tasting peanuts as they will not contain enough oil to bind the peanut butter. When you're making your own peanut butter, you might as well have the best!

Variation
Hot Peanut Sauce
Make the peanut butter as described above but add 1/2 tsp jalapeno pepper and 1 pinch of sambal with the sour cream. Wait 8 hours for the flavor to fully develop.

Apricot-Tomato Jam

Ingredients for about 6 cups
(1.4 kg):

1 lb (500 g) apricots
3 1/2 cups (750 g) sugar
1 1/3 lb (650 g) vine tomatoes
1/2 vanilla bean
1 star anise
3 tbsp walnuts

Preparation time: 1 hr
Calories: 2,600
15 g protein, 21 g fat,
450 g carbohydrate

- Wash and pit the apricots.
  Leave them overnight in the
  sugar to allow the sugar to
  penetrate the fruit.
- Blanch the tomatoes and
  remove the skins. Cut out
  the seeds and the stalk.
- Add the tomatoes to the
  apricots then purée to a
  medium consistency.

- Scrape out the inside of the
  vanilla bean. Wrap the vanilla
  bean and star anise in a bit
  of cheesecloth and place
  them in the fruit purée.
- Bring the purée to a boil and
  allow to boil vigorously for
  2 minutes. Coarsely chop the
  walnuts and add them to the
  fruit and the vanilla
  scrapings. Boil again for
  1 minute.
- Remove the spice bag and, if
  necessary, skim off any foam.
  Pour the hot jam into
  sterilized jars (jars boiled in
  water for 10 minutes), seal
  them and allow to cool
  upside down for about
  2 minutes.

Uncooked Berry Jam

Ingredients for about 2 3/4 cups
(650 ml):

1 lb (500 g) red currants
1/2 lb (250 g) strawberries
1 cup (250 g) berry sugar

Preparation time: 35 min
Calories: 980
2 g protein, 2 g fat,
140 g carbohydrate

- Wash the red currants, drain
  and remove stems. Press
  through a large-mesh sieve.
- Wash and clean the
  strawberries. Cut the largest
  strawberries into pieces.
- Blend or process the red
  currant purée together with
  the strawberries and sugar.
- Blend at the highest speed
  until the mixture begins to
  gel.

- Wash jars, place them in
  boiling water for 10 minutes
  and drain. Fill the jars and
  refrigerate. Uncooked berry
  jam keeps for 4–6 weeks.

Variation

Unfortunately this jam will not
keep for very long. In winter it
can be prepared from frozen
fruit. The jam should always
contain red currants so it will
gel. Pears or figs may be used
instead of strawberries.

Tip

Strawberries ripen very little
after they have been picked, so
look for ones that are ripe and
unhulled. Hull strawberries
only after you wash them or
they will absorb water.

Cherry-Pineapple Sauce

Ingredients for 6 cups (1.5 l):

1 1/2 cups pineapple pieces
(if using canned pineapple,
drain the water first)
2 lb (1 kg) sour cherries
3/4 cup (50 g) grated coconut
1 package vanilla sugar
(or substitute 2 tsp homemade
vanilla sugar)
2 1/2 cups (500 g) berry sugar

Preparation time: 9 hrs
(+12 hrs for sugaring)
Calories per cup: 1,600
11 g protein, 19 g fat,
470 g carbohydrate

- Drain the pineapple and save
  the juice. Wash the cherries
  and boil them in a covered
  saucepan with the pineapple
  juice for 10 minutes or until
  the cherries burst.

- Push the sauce through a
  large-mesh sieve to remove
  the pits.
- Mix the cherry purée with
  the pineapple pieces, grated
  coconut and sugars and leave
  overnight. The next day
  bring the mixture to a boil,
  stirring continuously. Allow
  to boil vigorously for
  4 minutes, then pour
  immediately into sterilized
  jars (jars placed in boiling
  water for 10 minutes) and
  seal.
- The sauce will keep for at
  least 3 months if stored in a
  cool place.

Tip
This sauce goes particularly
well with vanilla or chocolate
pudding and ice cream.

Carrot-Rhubarb Sauce

Ingredients for about 3 1/4 cups
(750 ml):

1 lb (500 g) young carrots
1 lb (500 g) rhubarb stalks
1 small piece fresh ginger
2 1/2 cups (500 g) raw sugar
1/2 cup (125 ml) orange juice

Preparation time: 2 hrs
Calories: 2,300
10 g protein, 2 g fat,
550 g carbohydrate

- Wash, peel and finely grate
  the carrots. Wash, peel and
  thinly slice the rhubarb. Peel
  and finely chop the ginger.
- Place all ingredients in a
  saucepan with 1/2 cup
  (125 ml) water and the
  sugar then bring to a boil.
  Cover then simmer for about
  1 hour over low heat.

- Add the orange juice and
  bring to a boil again.
- Meanwhile, wash the jars,
  place them in boiling water
  for 10 minutes then drain.
- Purée the sauce while it is
  still hot. Immediately pour
  the sauce into the sterilized
  jars and seal tightly.
- The sauce will keep for at
  least 3 months if stored in a
  cool place.

Tip
This sauce goes well with
yogurt, ice cream or pancakes.

Fruit sauces are more of a
convenience food than they are
a health food. Our sauces allow
you to have an instant dessert
on hand. Simply fold the sauce
into quark (see page 32) or
baking cheese, and add whipped
cream.

The Building Blocks of Nutrition: Proteins, Carbohydrates and Fats

Knowing More About a Healthy Diet

Today, it is possible to maintain a healthy, balanced diet through all four seasons. In spite of this, we are still a long way from eating as carefully as we should. The *1992 German Report on Nutrition* acknowledged that 20% of the population is very obese, almost one quarter has high cholesterol levels, and about 30% suffers from high blood pressure. At the same time, research indicated that only one-fifth of the population had a fundamental understanding of nutrition. This group was actually much healthier than the rest of the population. In other words, those who are informed are living healthier lives.

How Much Energy Does a Person Need?

- Our body gets its energy by "burning" the nutritional building blocks—fats, proteins and carbohydrates together with inhaled oxygen. This energy is measured in calories. Everyone has their own unique energy requirements based on their basal metabolic rate, activity-induced metabolic rate and growth requirements.
- Basal metabolic rate is the necessary amount of energy needed to sustain

vital functions. In addition to the basal metabolic rate, the performance-induced metabolic rate, varies according to workload and activity. Because of increased automation in the workplace, our average daily energy requirements have dropped considerably, decreasing by 500 calories between 1950 and 1970. No wonder older people have a particularly difficult battle against weight gain. Their dietary habits still reflect higher energy requirements. Anyone filling up with more calories than needed will store this energy as fat.

- The bathroom scale will always deliver the final verdict on whether or not we are eating according to our needs. On the other hand, an ideal weight does not necessarily reflect a healthy diet. Not only is number of calories important but so too is the quality of the food.

Protein: Cell Matter

- One gram of protein contains 4.1 calories. The body can transform it into energy but it is primarily used for building new cell matter, enzymes and hormones. Protein consists of amino acids—8 of which are essential and need to be obtained from food. The rest can be produced by the body itself.
- Protein is found in animal products like meat, fish and dairy or in plant foods like grains, potatoes, nuts and pulses. The more closely a protein comes to fulfilling our body's requirements, the higher is its "nutritive value."
- No one food on its own can ever reach full nutritive value of 100. For example, eggs have a value of 94, milk 86, beef 76, potatoes 67 and beans 58. This value increases only by combining foods, e.g., potato and egg combined have a value of 136.
- Optimal value is achieved by combining bread with cheese, potato gratin with milk, potatoes with quark, kidney beans with corn tortilla, pasta with pesto and sunflower seeds in bread. Between 12% and 15% of the energy in our diet

should come from protein. This even applies to people doing heavy physical work. All too often, protein requirements are overestimated—most people consume too much. Protein deficiency is virtually unknown in our western society.

Carbohydrates Are Loaded

Our primary source of energy should come from carbohydrates. The body uses carbohydrates efficiently, delivering quick energy on demand. Their caloric content is the same as protein: 4.1 calories per gram.

The main sources of this nutritional building block—grains, vegetables, potatoes and fruit—contain large quantities of vitamins, minerals and fiber. These are the foods with the highest nutritional density, the most valuable nutrients per calorie. Between 55%–60%

of our calories should come in the form of carbohydrates.

Unfortunately, we tend to eat too few of the right carbohydrates. About half our carbohydrate intake (too much) comes from non-nutritious snack products such as candies, pop and desserts. The refined sugar in these snack foods has no nutritive value and provides quick energy that does not last long. Choose foods containing unrefined, natural sugars. These sugars contain many minerals and provide sustained energy through the day as they take longer to digest.

Fiber: Nothing Moves Without It

Fiber is plant material that is not digested by the body. Therefore it has no caloric value. It does, however, have many health benefits. By filling the stomach and extending digestion time, fiber prolongs our feeling of fullness. Fiber binds to cholesterol and helps to eliminate it from the body, thus lowering the level of cholesterol. Fiber regulates bowel function, allowing continuous, quick elimination of waste products which keeps our body healthy and fit, and keeps our tissues firm and elastic.

So eat a lot of whole grains, pulses, fruit (especially berries, apples, pears and bananas) and vegetables like cabbage,

potatoes and root vegetables. These foods rate highest in fiber, particularly when eaten raw and with the skins left on. Adults should eat approximately 30 g of fiber daily. The following foods contain 10 g of fiber, or 1/3 of our daily requirement:
- 7 oz (200 g) whole rye bread (3–4 slices)
- 2 lb (1 kg) potatoes
- 1.1 lb (550 g) apples
- 0.9 lb (450 g) strawberries
- 5 oz (150 g) rolled oats
- 3.5 oz (100 g) spelt
- 1 lb (500 g) cabbage

The Body Needs Good Fat

The body needs fat for many good reasons. There are good fats and bad fats.

Saturated fats, which are commonly found in animals, are hard at room temperature. They are required to provide energy. If the body does not use them for energy, it will store these fatty acids for future use. And, even though they are heat stable and suitable for frying, saturated fats have little nutritional value.

Unsaturated fats are of two varieties—monounsaturated and polyunsaturated. Olive and avocado oils contain oleic acid which is monounsaturated. These oils are stable at room temperature and can be used for baking and cooking, but not for frying, as they are

Energy Requirements
According to DGE* Recommendation
(calories/day)

Age in Years	Males	Females
3–4	1,300	1,300
4–7	1,800	1,800
7–10	2,000	2,000
10–13	2,250	2,150
13–15	2,500	2,300
15–19	3,000	2,400
19–25	2,600	2,200
25–51	2,400	2,000
51–65	2,200	1,800
65 and older	1,900	1,700

*German Society for Nutrition

heat stable only up to 222°F (106°C). Polyunsaturated fatty acids come from oil-bearing seeds and their oils are liquid even when refrigerated; they spoil quickly at room temperature or when exposed to oxygen. The oils from seeds often contain significant amounts of essential fatty acids, alpha-linolenic (omega-3) and linoleic (omega-6) fatty acids. These are the healthy fats and they are found in especially good proportions in flax, sunflower and pumpkin seeds, also in walnuts, hazelnuts and pistachios. The oils from these seeds and nuts must be cold pressed and unrefined; they cannot be subjected to any heat and should therefore be used in cold dishes and salads.

Most oils sold in supermarkets, unfortunately, are subjected to high heat in a stabilizing process called hydrogenation. This process turns healthy oils into unhealthy fats by structurally changing the fatty acids into a *trans* form, which the body cannot metabolize properly. Trans-fatty acids are found in margarine, vegetable shortening and refined oils.

North Americans consume large and ever increasing amounts of hydrogenated fats with trans-fatty acids despite scientific evidence that has established their carcinogenity. By blocking the normal fat metabolism, trans-fatty acids are also responsible for raising the blood level of cholesterol and increasing the risk of

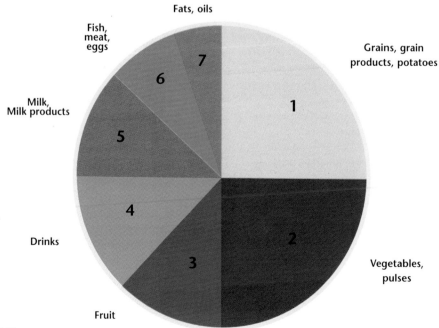

Fats, oils

Fish, meat, eggs

Milk, Milk products

Drinks

Fruit

Grains, grain products, potatoes

Vegetables, pulses

1 · 2 · 3 · 4 · 5 · 6 · 7

cardiovascular disease. Trans-fatty acids and hydrogenated fatty acids are hidden in baked goods, chocolate bars, salad dressings as well as in fried and fast foods.

The recommendation that North Americans should decrease their overall fat consumption from 40% to 25–30% will not have the desired effect on people's health unless the consumption of trans-fatty acids in refined oils, margarine and vegetable shortening is drastically reduced or eliminated, while the consumption of healthy, unrefined oils containing omega-3 and omega-6 is increased.

The essential fatty acids, omega-3 and omega-6, are the precursors of substances known as prostaglandins. They have a very positive effect on normal functioning of the brain, the skin, the nervous system and the sexual organs. They keep the blood level of cholesterol normal, prevent cardiovascular disease and certain cancers, and protect against arteriosclerosis. A low-fat diet cannot be advocated, as it will result in essential fatty acid deficiencies.

Finally, a good word needs to be said for butter. The much-maligned butter has turned out to be one of the healthiest fats for human consumption. It consists of saturated, mono and polyunsaturated fatty acids and is easily metabolized (it bypasses the liver) without any negative effect on human health. Best of all, butter, like other natural fats and unrefined oils, enhances the flavor of any dish.

The pie chart (left), developed by the DGE, shows the recommended daily intake of major food groups: foods from groups 1 and 2 should equal 1/2 of your daily food intake. Group 5 equals 1/4 l of milk and 3 slices of calcium-rich cheese. Group 6 allows 200 g meat products 2–3 times a week and fish twice a week. Substitute vegetarian protein where possible.

Healing Plants

Secondary Plant Nutrients	You'll find it in...	What they do
Carotenoids	Yellow fruit, particularly apricots; kale, carrots, squash, spinach, tomatoes, lettuce, broccoli and Brussels sprouts.	Strengthen the immune system, protect the skin and cell membranes from smog, ozone and stress. They are effective against tumors.
Bioflavonoids	The skin of red-purple-blue fruit and vegetables, especially cherries, berries, plums, apples, red cabbage and eggplant.	Strengthen the immune system, have anti-inflammatory properties and support the effectiveness of vitamin C. Because they inhibit blood clotting, they can prevent a heart attack.
Glucosinates	All cabbage varieties; kohlrabi, cress, radish, mustard and canola.	Protect us from infections. They are important in preventing cancer and in helping lower cholesterol levels.
Sulfides	Garlic, onion, leek and chives.	Lower cholesterol levels and at the same time inhibit blood clotting. They are ideal for preventing heart attacks and arteriosclerosis. They improve the immune response, support digestion and kill bacteria. They also protect against urinary tract infections. As with all bio-active nutrients, they protect cells from cancer.
Protease inhibitors	All protein-rich plants: pulses, particularly soybeans and mung beans; peas and peanuts, potatoes and grains like wheat, rice, corn and barley.	Protect against cancer by trapping free radicals. They also balance blood glucose levels, inhibit inflammations and regulate blood pressure.
Saponins	Pulses, especially chickpeas and soybeans.	Lower cholesterol levels by blocking cholesterol and stimulating bile production in the digestive system. They also prevent colon cancer and fungus infections of the intestines.
Polyphenols	All plants, particularly in tea and coffee, yam, nuts, berries, apple and cabbage	Combat urinary tract infections, they guard against harmful environmental effects and prevent the development of cancer.

Vitamins: Absolutely Essential

They spark our metabolism, initiating and maintaining vital responses in our body. Nothing in the body works without them. Vitamins belong to the "essentials" group, meaning they are nutrients that our body cannot produce and so they must be absorbed from food. All, that is, except for vitamin D which is produced under the skin as a result of exposure to the sun. Vitamin deficiencies which can lead to serious diseases are a rarity in our society. However, don't skip this section just because you don't have any symptoms of vitamin deficiency—there is a wide gap between deficiency and optimum health. Between the two are varying degrees of health. Research shows that young women are the group most frequently affected by an inadequate vitamin supply.

Vitamin	Sources	Daily Requirements	Vitamin "Robbers"
A and its precursor (beta-carotene)	Yellow and green vegetables, cheese, eggs, apricots, persimmons	83 g carrot, 110 g spinach, 285 g broccoli (Daily requirement: 0.9 mg)	Light and air
B_1	Whole grains, sprouts, pulses, sunflower seeds	235 g rolled oats, 130 g rye sprouts, 145 g peanuts (Daily requirement: 1.2–1.4 mg)	Heat
B_2	Dairy products, eggs, yeast, sprouts	190 g rye sprouts, 80 g corn flakes, 60 g yeast flakes (Daily requirement: 1.5–1.7 mg)	Light and heat
B_3 (Niacin)	Whole grains, pulses, mushrooms, potatoes	15 g raw peanuts, 250 g dried cooked peas, 100 g bran (Daily requirement: 0.15–0.3 mg)	Stable vitamin
B_5 (Pantothenic Acid)	Yeast, egg yolks, whole grains, melons, broccoli, mushrooms	300 g mushrooms, 175 g mung beans (Daily requirement: 6 mg)	Heat and acid
B_6	Whole grains, wheat germ, soy, bananas, cabbages, leeks, peppers	100 g rye sprouts, 45 g wheat germ, 1 large banana (Daily requirement: 0.003 mg)	Light and heat
B_{12}	Milk, soured milk products, eggs, cheese, lactic acid-fermented vegetables	500 g low-fat yogurt, 175 g Brie (50% fat), 300 g quark (Daily requirement: 0.003 mg)	Light and air
Biotin	Dried yeast, egg yolks, sprouts, soy, carrots, peas	1–2 eggs, 100 g brewer's yeast, 300 g rolled oats, 175 g hazelnut (Daily requirement: 0.03–0.1 mg)	Stable vitamin
Folic Acid	Vegetables (red beets, spinach, fennel, asparagus), baker's yeast, orange juice	150 g raw soy sprouts, 50 g wheat germ, 350 g cooked broccoli (Daily requirement: 0.15–0.3 mg)	Heat and light
C	Vegetables (cabbages, spinach, peppers, broccoli), fruit (citrus, berries)	70 g broccoli, 80 g fennel, 55 g raw pepper, 200 g orange (Daily requirement: 75 mg)	Heat, light and air
E	Vegetable fats and oils, grains, nuts, pulses	120 g peanut oil, 45 g hazelnut oil, 25 g sunflower seed oil (Daily requirement: 12 g)	Light and air

Mineral

Mineral	Sources	Daily Requirements	Mineral "Robbers"
Calcium (Ca)	Dairy products, hard cheeses, kale	1 l milk, 1 kg natural yogurt, 100 g farmer's cheese, 675 g broccoli (Daily requirement: 1,200–1,500 mg)	Oxalate (from spinach and rhubarb), phytine (from wholegrain cereals) and iron bind calcium.
Iron (Fe)	Whole grains, pulses, vegetables, apricots	240 g spelt, 115 g millet, 220 g rolled oats, 285 g fresh spinach (Daily requirement: 10–15 mg)	Calcium, oxalate, phytine and the fluoride in black tea bind iron.
Magnesium (Mg)	Potatoes, whole grains, pulses, vegetables, bananas	265 g oats, 190 g brown rice, 170 g kidney beans, 235 g bananas (Daily requirement: 300–400 mg)	Washing foods rinses the magnesium out; iron and phytine bind it.
Potassium (K)	Potatoes, vegetables, fruit, pulses, whole grains	455 g potatoes, 500 g cauliflower, 525 g bananas, 245 g lentils (Daily requirement: 2,000 mg)	Boiling in plentiful water and washing will rinse iron from foods.
Zinc (Zn)	Whole grains, dairy products	75 g rolled rye, 250 g farmer's cheese (Daily requirement: 15 mg)	Phytine (wholegrain cereals) and calcium bind zinc.

Minerals: Solid Components and Activators

These are essential to our bones, blood, cell function, hair, teeth and nails. Although critically important, our mineral supply is threatened by too much processed food, "junk food," and artificial additives. Only the most necessary minerals are listed below. We get more than enough sodium and chloride from table salt. Cheese and processed foods supply us with plenty of phosphorus though we would do better with less of it. Fluoride and iodine come to us through our drinking water. You probably have an adequate supply of these nutrients in your diet already, without even thinking about it.

Effects on the Body	When Do We Need More?	Signs of Deficiency
Important in cell regeneration, skin protection and immune system strengthening	When taking oral contraceptives, antibiotics or laxatives	Symptoms of night blindness. In extreme cases, growth disruptions and scaly wrinkled skin
Important in carbohydrate metabolism and for nerves and heart	With frequent consumption of sugar, white flour, alcohol, oral contraceptives or antibiotics	Circulation problems, feelings of general ill-health, nausea, depression
Involved in metabolism, important for growth, skin, hair and nerves	With smoking, taking oral contraceptives, antibiotics and sulfa drugs	Loss of weight, vitality and regeneration ability. In extreme cases, cracks appear in the corners of the mouth
Involved in the metabolism of all nutritional components, important for skin and hair	With severe diarrhea and regular intake of alcohol	Feelings of despondency to the point of depression. Also nausea, dizziness, diarrhea, vomiting and raw skin
Involved throughout the body in energy production	Under stress, after illness, during pregnancy	Bad skin, dull hair
Important in protein metabolism, physical growth, skin, hair and nerves	When smoking, drinking alcohol, taking medications or when pregnant	Poor skin. Feelings of weakness (poor blood), simultaneous nervousness to the point of sleeplessness
Involved in cell construction and ensures fresh blood	During illnesses and recovery, when smoking, taking oral contraceptives, antibiotics and during pregnancy	Fatigue and listlessness, prone to sickness
Important in cell metabolism, blood cell renewal, good for nerves, skin and hair	After eating raw protein (e.g., in a dessert)	Hair loss, skin changes, feelings of exhaustion
Essential in building new cells (blood formation)	When smoking, drinking and taking medications; requirements are doubled during pregnancy	Feelings of weakness, proneness to infections and sensitive, dry mucous membranes
Involved in interior cell protection, immune system strengthening and tissues	When taking oral contraceptives, antibiotics, diabetic or high blood pressure medications	Growth disruption due to insufficient oxygen because of blood deficiency
Involved in cell wall protection and the removal of toxins from the liver	In situations of stress, recovery from illness, taking oral contraceptives, antibiotics or laxatives	In extreme cases, loss of muscle tone. Also increased proneness to bladder infections, blood deficiency and general proneness to infections
Important in ensuring strong bones and teeth and for facilitating all muscle movements	During pregnancy and nursing, using salicylic acid (aspirin)	Frequent muscle cramps, slow onset of osteoporosis
Involved in blood clotting and the cell oxygen balance	During pregnancy, kidney problems, high blood pressure	Fatigue, headaches, cold hands and feet
Important component of bone structure and maintains correct pressure between cells	During growth periods, pregnancy and nursing and for osteoporosis	Muscle cramps and shaking hands
Important in ensuring correct internal cell pressure, metabolic reactions (such as protein construction and energy reserves in muscles)	With stress, infectious diseases, after operations	Onset of heart problems and tingling in hands and feet
Important for immune system and growth and is part of many enzymes	During pregnancy and nursing, using oral contraceptives and regular alcohol intake	Problems with entire metabolism, feelings of listlessness and weakness, slow-healing wounds

Your Individual Goal	What Helps	Where to Find it
Strong hair and nails	The minerals fluoride, zinc and calcium strengthen hair structure; sufficient protein ensures shine and growth; biotin prevents hair loss and silica prevents split ends.	Millet provides silica, fluoride and protein. When combined with dairy products, eggs, rolled oats and wheat fiber, they build up the hair's inner structure.
Beautiful, clear skin 	Vitamins—and almost all of them! Pantothenic acid, biotin and vitamins B_2 and B_{12} support cell growth and therefore ensure skin regeneration. B_6 is effective against greasy skin, B_2 helps with redness and over-sensitivity, beta-carotene protects cells and vitamin C ensures healthy tissues.	Citrus fruit, kiwis and berries are full of vitamin C. Carrots, cabbages and spinach provide vitamin A; whole grains, rolled oats, all types of sprouts and mushrooms provide vitamin B. Avocados and peanuts are particularly nutritious; eat these only in moderation, because they are high in fat!
Healthy teeth and gums	When combined, calcium, vitamin D and fluoride harden tooth enamel. If one of these substances is deficient, teeth will suffer. Gum tissue is strengthened by vitamin C and pantothenic acid. Chewing helps gums by massaging the tissues and stimulating saliva.	Dairy products provide calcium, millet provides fluoride. Vitamin D comes from egg yolks, butter and mushrooms but is activated only by sunlight on the skin. Eat citrus fruit and berries for vitamin C. In addition, plenty of whole grains will strengthen teeth.
Healthy tissues 	Potassium and salt regulate the body's water balance which is most essential for healthy tissues. At the same time, good fluid intake and active digestion ensure continuous cleansing of the body.	Most fruits provide sufficient potassium. Dried fruits are also effective. Asparagus, artichokes, potatoes, brewer's yeast, garlic, nuts and sage are other good sources of potassium.
More muscle	Anyone building muscle needs extra calories to meet training requirements. Extra protein, as well as plenty of iron, zinc, vitamin B_{12} and folic acid are necessary for cell structure; vitamins B_2 and B_6 are needed for the increased protein metabolism.	Nutritious protein combinations (225) are relatively low in calories but valuable nonetheless. They provide the necessary B vitamins, iron and zinc. Nuts and hard cheese (in moderation) help the development of muscles.
Strengthen the body's own immune system	The antioxidants, vitamin C, beta-carotene and vitamin E protect cells against damage. All secondary plant nutrients enhance this defense and help prevent cancer.	All substances that enhance our immune system are sensitive to heat and air. However, their effectiveness is improved by fermentation. Plenty of raw vegetables, fruit, uncooked cereal, sprouts, sour dairy products, sauerkraut and other lactic acid fermented vegetables have a positive effect.
Memory power/ nerves of steel	Iron, folic acid and vitamin B_{12} sustain red blood cells and therefore improve the supply of oxygen to the body and the brain. Easily digestible, carbohydrate-rich foods with plentiful B vitamins have a positive effect on nerves and mood.	A high cereal intake accomplishes three things at once: it supplies plenty of carbohydrates, B vitamins and it promotes easy digestion. Citrus fruit, peppers, broccoli and sauerkraut are also recommended.
Vitality and energy	Iron, vitamin B_{12} and folic acid ensure that blood binds oxygen well. Protein boosts the metabolism with its "dynamic effect." Sufficient iodine ensures healthy functioning of the thyroid. The antioxidants beta-carotene, vitamins C and E keep cells healthy.	Vegetables, particularly cabbages, pulses, mushrooms and herbs provide antioxidants, folic acid and iron. Millet, amaranth and quinoa provide plenty of protein and minerals. Eggs and dairy products provide B_{12} and usable protein.

Applicable Recipes	Additional Tips
Alfalfa Appetizer (44), Cheese Carpaccio (49), Eggplant Rolls With Creamed Millet (50), Corn Salad With Red Lentils and Egg (58), Quinoa With Radishes (61), Mild Lentil Soup (83), Creamed Millet Soup with Peppers (87), Millet Dumplings with Peppers (106), Couscous-Berry Mix (200)	Hair care recipe: mix about 3/4 cup (100 g) neutral henna powder (from the health food store) with 1 egg yolk and 3 tbsp olive oil. Apply to hair, cover with a towel and leave for 1 hour. Wash hair.
Alfalfa Appetizer (44), Artichoke-Orange Cocktail (45), Mushroom Carpaccio (49), Wild Herb Salad with Nettle Gouda (55), Orange-Endive Flower (59), Cheese in Carrot-Watercress Salad (62), Roasted Pepper and Avocado Salad (64), Mild Sprout Salad (65), Avocado-Basil Dip (74), Cream of Radish Soup (91), Carrot Star (103), Quinoa Ring with Wild Herb Sauce (110), Giant Stuffed Mushrooms (137), Herbed Quark Soufflé (161)	Apply a nourishing mask of 3 tbsp yeast flakes (from the health food store), 1 tbsp grated almonds and 1 tbsp wheatgerm oil. Leave on for 15 minutes. Remove with a tissue and wait at least 1 hour before washing with lukewarm water.
Alfalfa Appetizer (44), Pepper Boats (48), Cheese Carpaccio (49), Wild Herb Salad (55), Cheese in Carrot-Watercress Salad (62), Creamed Millet Soup with Peppers (87), Cheesy Rice Fritters (101), Millet Pudding with Chive Sauce (107), Fresh Spring Vegetables with Cheese (120), Eggs in Sorrel Sauce (156), Spring Vegetables with Herbed Cheese Crust (162), Basil "Spaetzle" with Gouda (164), Cheesy Stuffed Tomatoes (97), Apple-Avocado Muesli (200)	If you have an unpleasant feeling on your teeth after eating rhubarb, spinach or other foods containing oxalates slowly drink a glass of milk to reseal your tooth surfaces.
Asparagus with Creamed Quark (41), Marinated Zucchini (41), Artichokes with Tomato Sauce (42), Eggplant Rolls with Creamed Millet (50), Delicately Marinated Vegetables (55), Fruity Radicchio Salad (58), Sweet and Sour Zucchini Salad (63), Mild Sprout Salad (65), Exotic Carrot Soup (86), Saffron-Orange Risotto (98), Stuffed Coconut-Rice Ring (99)	A day of eating rice is a good diuretic treatment. Boil 1 1/2 cups (300 g) brown rice in 3 cups (600 g) water. Eat a bit at a time throughout the day; add fruit and vegetables, but no salt. Drink plenty of herb tea or water only — do not consume any other liquids.
Asparagus with Creamed Quark (41), Baked Vegetables with Amaranth Butter (42), Colorful Vegetables with Egg Dip (48), Mushroom Carpaccio (49), Corn Salad with Red Lentils and Egg (58), Carrot-Watercress Salad (62), Fruity-Spicy Adzuki Bean Soup (81), Mild Lentil Soup (83), Savoy Cabbage with Roast Chickpeas (85), Cream of Pea Soup with Croutons (87), Amaranth-Mushroom Fry (111), Quinoa "Tortilla" (111)	Don't waste money on protein drinks. Once a day drink the following: Blend 1 cup (200 ml) buttermilk with 1/2 orange, 1–2 tbsp wheatgerm, 1 tbsp ground millet, 2–3 peeled almonds and sweeten with honey or fruit sugar.
Artichoke-Orange Cocktail (45), Colorful Vegetables with Egg Dip (48), Pepper Boats (48), Cheese Carpaccio (49), Wild Herb Salad with Nettle Gouda (55), Fruity Radicchio Salad (58), Corn Salad with Red Lentils and Egg (58), Orange-Endive Flower (59), Roasted Pepper and Avocado Salad (64), Mild Sprout Salad (65), Exotic Carrot Soup (86), Cream of Radish Soup (91)	Starting your day with muesli gives you an advantage. Fresh rolled grains mixed with fruit juice (freshly squeezed is best) or buttermilk, plenty of fruit and a little honey can guarantee 1/4 of the day's calorie requirements in the form of raw food.
Baked Vegetables with Amaranth Batter (p. 42), Beet Rounds with Dip (43), Eggplant Rolls with Creamed Millet (p. 50), Bruschetta (52), Couscous Mix (57), Wild Rice-Pineapple Salad (56), Bulgur Salad (56), Quinoa with Radishes (61), Creamy Nut Dip (77), Salsa Verde (77), Creamy Corn and Tomato Soup (82), Creamed Millet Soup with Red Peppers (87)	Mix a "nerve tonic" from 1 cup (200 g) whey, 3 soaked dried apricots, 1 orange, 1 tbsp each of nutritional yeast and ground millet and 1 tbsp wheatgerm.
Asparagus with Creamed Quark (41), Alfalfa Appetizer (44), Colorful Vegetables with Egg Dip (48), Cheese Carpaccio (49), Wild Rice-Pineapple Salad (56), Spicy Bean Salad (66), Borscht (81), Savoy Cabbage with Roast Chickpeas (85), Spelt Patties with Cheese Sauce (104), Amaranth Mushroom Fry (111), Quinoa "Tortilla" (111), Fresh Spring Vegetables with Cheese (120), Herbed Asparagus Quiche (122), Garden Vegetables au Gratin (125), Oyster Mushroom Schnitzel with Herb Sauce (136), Apple-Date Drink (191), Carrot-Almond Milk (191)	

Index

Index of Special Characteristics

Recipe Names Alphabetically Sorted

Cover Photo:
Potato Goulash (page 145)

Published originally under the title
Kochvergnügen vegetarisch
©1996 Gräfe und Unzer Verlag GmbH,
München.
English translation ©1998 *alive* books

Canadian Cataloguing in Publication Data
Von Cramm, Dagmar
The vegetarian gourmet

Includes index.
ISBN 0-920470-80-7

1. Vegetarian cookery. I. Title.
TX837.V65 1998   641.5'636
C98-910332-3

A special thank you to the following companies for supplying equipment:

Rösle Metallwarenfabrik
GmbH & Co KG
Marktoberndorf
(pages 13, 14–15 all equipment except pressure cooker and wok, 28, 168, 212)

Fissler GmbH
Idar-Oberstein
(page 15, pressure cooker)

Schulte-Ufer, Sundern
(page 15, wok)

Sigg Haushaltsgeräte AG
Frauenfeld (Schweiz)
(Pages 202–203, 205, 206–207, 208–209, 210–211)

Eschenfelder, Hauenstein
(page 30)

Important Note:
It is best to buy natural essential oils intended for cooking in a health food store, from companies like Primavera Life or La balance. They should be exclusively from certified organic growers, and must be produced without chemicals. It is extremely important that they be 100% pure essential oils.

Project Team:
Dagmar von Cramm, Ursula Block, Barbara Bonisolli, Hans-Albrecht Gerlach

Ursula Block is a qualified dietitian and ecotrophologist (FH). As Dagmar von Cramm's assistant, she spends most of her time in the test kitchen.

Barbara Bonisolli started taking pictures professionally in 1989. By 1993, she had developed a love of photographing not only gourmet food but also the details that make for beautiful presentation. Barbara Bonisolli creates the attractive ambiance that marks all of her photos. Her numerous clients include magazine and cookbook publishers and advertising agencies.

Hans-Albrecht Gerlach works closely with Barbara Bonisolli. He styled all of the food for *The Vegetarian Gourmet.*

Test Kitchen:
Barbara Hagmann, Traute Hatterscheid, Astrid Keese, Christa Konrad-Seiter, Marianne Obermayer

Translation:
Marga & Thomas Hannon

Localization:
Hélène Meurer, Christel Gursche

Editorial Team:
Paul Razzell, Julie Cheng

Typography, Design and Production:
Corina Messerschmidt, Kevin Mok, Ingo Neufeld, June Vance

Original Design:
BuchHaus Robert Gigler GmbH

All Recipe Photos:
Barbara Bonisolli, Fotodesign

Other Photos:
Silvestris/Lenz Leonard
(pages 5 and 11)
Thomas Stankiewicz (page 21)
Das Fotoarchiv (page 32)
Christophe Schneider (page 227)
Silvestris/Siegfried Kerscher
(page 231)

Reproductions:
Fotolitho Longo, Copydot

Printing and binding:
Friesens